Lēoþ

SIX OLD ENGLISH POEMS

LEOÐ

SIX OLD ENGLISH POEMS

−A HANDBOOK−

by

Bernard James Muir
Department of English
University of Melbourne
Australia

GORDON AND BREACH

New York   Philadelphia   London   Paris   Montreux   Tokyo   Melbourne

© 1989 by OPA (Amsterdam) B.V. All rights reserved. Published under license by Gordon and Breach Science Publishers S.A.

Gordon and Breach Science Publishers

Post Office Box 786
Cooper Station
New York, New York 10276
United States of America

5301 Tacony Street
Box 330
Philadelphia, Pennsylvania 19137
United States of America

58, rue Lhomond
75005 Paris
France

3-14-9, Okubo
Shinjuku-ku, Tokyo 169
Japan

Post Office Box 197
London WC2E 9PX
United Kingdom

Post Office Box 161
1820 Montreux 2
Switzerland

Private Bag 8
Camberwell, Victoria 3124
Australia

This book was set by the author using *DITROFF*, the *UNIX* text-processing system, and printed with an Apple LaserWriter™ at the University of Melbourne, Victoria.

Library of Congress Cataloging-in-Publication Data

Muír, Bernard James.
  Leod: six Old English poems

  Includes bibliographical references.
  Contents: Widsith — Deor — Waldere — The Finnsburh fragment — The battle of Brunanburh — The battle of Maldon.
  1. English poetry—Old English, ca. 450–1100.
2. English language—Old English, ca. 450–1100–Versification. 3. Beowulf. I. Title.
PR1505.M76   1989   829'.1   89-16959
ISBN 2-88124-357-6

No part of this book may be reproduced by any means, electronic or mechanical, including photocopying and recording, or by any information storage or retrieval system, without permission in writing from the publishers. Printed in the United States of America.

Leoð wæs asungen / gleomannes gyd.

(*Beowulf*, 1159b-60a)

CONTENTS

Preface ix

Acknowledgements x

Plates xi

Introduction xiii

Abbreviations xvii

Bibliography xix

WIDSITH 1

DEOR 25

WALDERE 39

THE FINNSBURH FRAGMENT 53

THE BATTLE OF BRUNANBURH 65

THE BATTLE OF MALDON 81

Glossary 111

Glossary of Proper Names 153

PREFACE

This edition has developed from the teaching of these six texts in conjunction with *Beowulf* over the past six years to students with at least one year of introductory training in Old English language and literature, and is offered with such an audience in mind. It is hoped, however, that even a specialist will find it helpful, and this is primarily why it has been set up as a 'Handbook', with detailed Bibliography and technical Introductions to each text. Teachers of undergraduates can determine for themselves how much of this information is necessary for their classes. It brings together six poems which have much in common thematically, linguistically, and historically among themselves and with the only surviving secular epic poem from the Anglo-Saxon period, and which have not been available in a single scholarly edition for a number of years.

Over the years my students have caught minor oversights — especially in the Glossary — and these have been corrected, but I am sure a few remain hidden from me; anyone who has compiled a glossary will be sympathetic to my situation — Samuel Johnson, as many know, defined a lexicographer as "A writer of dictionaries; a harmless drudge, that busies himself in tracing the original, and detailing the signification of words."

ACKNOWLEDGEMENTS

I should like to thank the following libraries for granting permission for the printing of the plates in this edition: the Library of the Dean and Chapter, Exeter Cathedral; the Bodleian Library, Oxford; the Master and Fellows of Corpus Christi College, Cambridge; and Det Kongelige Bibliotek, Copenhagen.

I am grateful to the Committee on Research and Graduate Studies of the University of Melbourne for its generous support of this project.

I should like also to thank Professor George Russell of the University of Melbourne for reading the typescript and for being so helpful in his criticism of it, and Joy Symons for her assistance in compiling the Glossary. Dr. Patrick Conner of the University of West Virginia made a number of helpful suggestions concerning the Bibliography. Dr. Judith Garde and Elizabeth King made a final check of the typescript and brought a number of errors to my attention, for which the edition is better than it would otherwise have been. And finally, I must thank Ross Millward of the University's Computing Services, who has shown great interest in this project and helped to develop a new program for the editing of medieval manuscripts.

This book is dedicated to Professor Emeritus Laurence K. Shook C.S.B. of the Pontifical Institute of Mediaeval Studies who always supported me in my undertakings while I was at the University of Toronto.

PLATES

1 *Widsith* 1-13; Exeter, Library of the Dean and Chapter, MS 3501, f. 84^v [p. 7]

2 *Deor* 1-22; Exeter, Library of the Dean and Chapter, MS 3501, f. 100^r [p. 24]

3 *Deor* 22-42; Exeter, Library of the Dean and Chapter, MS 3501, f. 100^v [p. 28]

4 *Waldere* 17-32; Copenhagen, Royal Library, Ny Kgl. S. MS 167b, f. 1^v [p. 38]

5 *The Battle of Brunanburh* 1-12; Cambridge, Corpus Christi College MS 173, f. 26^r [p. 64]

6 *The Battle of Brunanburh* 13-57; Cambridge, Corpus Christi College MS 173, f. 26^v [p. 68]

7 *The Battle of Brunanburh* 58-73; Cambridge, Corpus Christi College MS 173, f. 27^r [p. 69]

8 *The Battle of Maldon* 1-26; Oxford, Bodleian Library, MS Rawlinson B.203, p. 7 [p. 85]

9 Casley's script in Oxford, Bodleian Library, MS Top. Northants c.23, f. 7^r [p. 86]

INTRODUCTION

I have set out this critical edition in a format I refer to as a handbook; such a volume should, I think, deal with texts comprehensively, systematically, and as objectively as possible. Thus the Introductions to the poems have identical format and contain the same kinds of information, gathered in two sections under the headings **Manuscript** and **Text**. Each poetic text is followed by a Commentary that draws upon the works cited in the Bibliography. As is the case with any new edition, I am indebted to those who have gone before me; this is the case especially with *Widsith*, where the research of Chambers (1912), Malone (1962) and others led to the identification of the numerous individuals and tribes whose names appear in that poem, though it is true that Hill (1984) has brought to our attention that it is probably time for a major reconsideration of many of these names; (see 1.18 note). Throughout the edition, I have attempted to present a survey of critical opinion rather than impose my own interpretations upon the reader (realizing, of course, that any decision by an editor involves some degree of bias); in the Glossary, I have tried not to provide secondary meanings which are derived solely from context without regard for etymology.[1]

I have not repeated all the information readily available in earlier critical editions of individual poems; Scragg's edition of *Maldon* (1981), for example, will not be eclipsed by this one. This edition, however, serves a need not addressed by others in that it brings these six texts together, and tries to illustrate their kinship with *Beowulf*.

---

[1] Fred Robinson has illustrated recently the subjectivity involved in translating any compound Anglo-Saxon word into modern English (1985, 14-18); choosing one translation over another (which anyone attempting a coherent rendering must ultimately do) necessarily prejudices subsequent readings of the text. Thus it is better to give a literal translation of the component parts in the Glossary as the first offering, and to advise the reader to determine the most suitable meaning for himself from the context in which the word appears.

Reference to critical literature from the Bibliography cited throughout the edition is by author's surname, followed by the year of publication and page number(s) in brackets. Internal cross-references among the poems are by text number (1 to 6), fullstop, and line number(s), so that 3.4 refers to *Waldere,* line 4; cross-references within a text being commented upon are by line number only.

The work of Bruce Mitchell and others on both syntax and punctuation has illustrated how inappropriate modern punctuation can be for medieval texts,[2] often depriving a passage of desirable ambiguity, or causing it to say something an editor wants it to say at the expense of other possible meanings. Yet this nagging problem cannot be resolved easily. I have endeavoured to make the punctuation as light as possible without making the text totally obscure to those still striving for expertise in the field. In general, punctuation has not been added where there is a clear linguistic marker that a new clause is beginning (for example, after a conjunction, or with a relative pronoun). Fullstops occur at the end of complete sense units; that is, if a single action is being described, the sentence will continue until the description is complete, however long it may be. Intermediate stages in the advance of the narrative within these units is marked by the semicolon, colon or dash. As a result of this, the poems are divided into verse paragraphs of varying length.[3]

Letters and words supplied in the texts by the editor are enclosed in crotchets; letters substituted to improve a reading are not marked, but notice of such emendations is given in the critical apparatus at the foot of each page. In only one instance (4.24) have words been deleted from the text; these are enclosed in pointed brackets. Three asterisks are used to mark places where there has been obvious loss of text, and a series of fullstops within crotchets indicate places where the manuscript is illegible and the reading cannot be ascertained. For the most part, I am not concerned in this edition with

---

[2] Bruce Mitchell, "The Dangers of Disguise: Old English Texts in Modern Punctuation," *RES* NS 31 (1980), 385-413; M.B. Parkes, "Punctuation, or Pause and Effect," in J.J. Murphy ed. *Medieval Eloquence* (Berkeley: Univ. of California Press, 1978), 127-44; and Norman Blake, *The English Language in Medieval Literature* (London: Methuen, 1977), Chpt. 3, 'The Editorial Process.'

[3] On three occasions in *Maldon* I have forsaken this practice, since it seemed to me that the poet had deliberately used the staccato effect of the lines *Se flod ut gewat* (72a) and *Wæl feol on eorþan* (126b and 303b) to punctuate the narrative; the fact that the second of these is repeated seems to confirm this observation.

regurgitating information detailing how the present text was arrived at over the years; what is presented here, with a few modifications, is what is generally regarded today as the received texts of these poems. Unless they are subject to heavy emendation in the future, their texts are unlikely to undergo much change; what will evolve is critical reaction to them, and this is what is primarily recorded in this edition. Where the text is restored or emended, the editor who first suggested the reading (where this is known) is acknowledged in crotchets at the beginning of the Commentary for the line concerned; full bibliographical details for these editions are given in Sections A and B of the Bibliography.

The texts of all quotations of Anglo-Saxon poetry cited in the Commentaries are taken from *The Anglo-Saxon Poetic Records*, except in the case of *Beowulf*, where Klaeber's edition has been used.

As is the case with all modern editions, the letter 'w' replaces runic *wynn*. Since they present no unusual problem, all abbreviations have been expanded silently; accent marks in the manuscripts have not been reproduced. Vowel length is indicated in the Glossaries, but not in the edited texts of the poems.

ABBREVIATIONS

AIUON	Annali, Istituto Universitario Orientale di Napoli
AN&Q	American Notes and Queries
ASE	Anglo-Saxon England
BBCS	Bulletin of the Board of Celtic Studies
BGdSL	Beiträge zur Geschichte der deutschen Sprache und Literatur
EHR	English Historical Review
ELN	English Language Notes
ES	English Studies
ESC	English Studies in Canada
HUSL	Hebrew University Studies in Literature
IF	Indogermanische Forschungen
JEGP	Journal of English and Germanic Philology
JMH	Journal of Medieval History
MÆ	Medium Ævum
MLR	Modern Language Review
MP	Modern Philology
N&Q	Notes and Queries
Neophil	Neophilologus
NM	Neuphilologische Mitteilungen
PMLA	Publications of the Modern Language Association of America
PQ	Philological Quarterly
RES	Review of English Studies
SBVS	Saga-Book of the Viking Society for Northern Research
SP	Studies in Philology

Spec	Speculum
TRHS	Transactions of the Royal Historical Society
UES	UNISA English Studies
YES	Yearbook of English Studies
ZfdA	Zeitschrift für deutsches Altertum und deutsche Literatur

BIBLIOGRAPHY

The following Bibliography is select before 1972 and attempts to be comprehensive from 1973 onwards; for a comprehensive treatment of earlier critical writing see *A Bibliography of Publications on Old English Literature to the end of 1972*, eds. Stanley B. Greenfield and Fred C. Robinson (Toronto: Univ. of Toronto Press, 1980). Another useful reference text is *Old English Literature: A Select Bibliography*, Toronto Medieval Bibliographies, ed. Fred C. Robinson (Toronto: Univ. of Toronto Press, 1970), which offers brief critical summaries of the works cited.

A   MAJOR EDITIONS, FACSIMILES AND TRANSCRIPTS

Campbell, Alistair, ed. *The Battle of Brunanburh*. London: Heinemann, 1938.

Chambers, Raymond W., Max Förster, and Robin Flower. *The Exeter Book of Old English Poetry*. London: Percy Lund, Humphries and Co., 1933. [Facsimile]

Chambers, Raymond W. *Widsith: A Study in Old English Heroic Legend*. Cambridge, 1912.

Dickins, Bruce. *Runic and Heroic Poems of the Old Teutonic Peoples*. Cambridge: Cambridge UP, 1915. [Texts with Translations]

Dobbie, Elliott van K., ed. *The Anglo-Saxon Minor Poems*. Anglo-Saxon Poetic Records VI. New York: Columbia UP, 1942.

Flower, Robin, and H. Smith. *The Parker Chronicle and Laws* (CCCC MS. 173). E.E.T.S. OS 208 London: OUP, 1941.

Fry, Donald K., ed. *Finnsburh Fragment and Episode*. London: Methuen, 1974.

Gordon, Eric V., ed. *The Battle of Maldon*. London 1937; rpt. with a supplement by Donald G. Scragg. Manchester: 1976.

Hickes, George. *Linguarum Veterum Septentrionalium Thesaurus, grammatico-criticus et archaeologicus.* Oxford: 1703-05; rpt. Hildesheim: Olms, 1970.
Hill, Joyce, ed. *Old English Minor Heroic Poems.* Durham and St. Andrews Medieval Texts 4. Durham: Univ. of Durham, 1983.
Klaeber, Friedrich, ed. *Beowulf and the Fight at Finnsburg.* 3rd ed. Boston: D.C. Heath, 1950.
Krapp, George. P., and Elliott van K. Dobbie, eds. *The Exeter Book.* Anglo-Saxon Poetic Records III. New York: Columbia UP, 1936.
Malone, Kemp, ed. *Widsith.* 2nd ed. Copenhagen: Rosenkilde and Bagger, 1962.
_____, ed. *Deor.* 2nd ed. Exeter: Univ. of Exeter Press, 1977.
Norman, Fred, ed. *Waldere.* 2nd ed. London: Methuen, 1949.
Plummer, Charles, ed. *Two of the Saxon Chronicles Parallel, with Supplementary Extracts from the Others. A Revised Text on the Basis of an Edition by John Earle.* 2 vols. rev. D. Whitelock. London: OUP, 1952.
Scragg, Donald G., ed. *The Battle of Maldon.* Manchester: Manchester UP, 1981.
Taylor, Simon, ed. *The Anglo-Saxon Chronicle: A Collaborative Edition.* Vol. 4. (MS. B) Cambridge: Cambridge UP, 1983.
Thorpe, Benjamin, ed. and trans. *Codex Exoniensis: A Collection of Anglo-Saxon Poetry from a Manuscript in the Library of the Dean and Chapter of Exeter, with an English Translation, Notes, and Indexes.* London, 1842.
Tolkien, John R.R. *Finn and Hengest: The Fragment and the Episode.* Ed. Alan Bliss. London: George Allen and Unwin, 1982.
Zettersten, Arne, ed. *Waldere.* Manchester: Manchester UP, 1979. [Edition with Facsimile]
BL Add. MS. 9067: a transcript of the *Exeter Book* made by R. Chambers in 1831, subsequently collated with the manuscript by Sir Frederic Madden in 1831-32.

B OTHER WORKS USED IN ESTABLISHING THE TEXT

Bugge, Sophus. "Spredte iagttagelser vedkommen de oldengelske digte om Beowulf og Waldere." *Tidskrift for Philologi og Pædagogik,* 8 (1868-69), 72-78 and 305-07.

Conybeare, John J. *Illustrations of Anglo-Saxon Poetry.* Ed. W.D. Conybeare. London, 1826.
Ettmüller, Ludwig. *Engla and Seaxna Scopas and Boceras.* Quedlinberg and Leipzig, 1850.
Grein, Christian W.M., ed. *Bibliothek der angelsächsischen Poesie.* Erster Band. Göttingen, 1857.
_____. *Beovulf nebst den Fragmenten Finnsburg und Valdere.* Cassel, 1867.
Grimm, Jacob. *Geschichte der deutschen Sprache.* Leipzig, 1868.
Holthausen, Ferdinand. *Die altenglischen Waldere-Bruchstücke.* Göteborgs Högskolas Arsskrift, 5. Gothenburg, 1899.
_____. "Zur altenglishen Literatur." *Anglia,* Beiblatt 21 (1910), 12-14.
Kemble, John M. *The Anglo-Saxon Poems of Beowulf, the Traveller's Song and the Battle of Finnes-Burh.* London, 1833; 2nd ed. 1835.
Müllenhoff, Karl and F. Dietrich. "Waldere." *ZfdA,* 12 (1860), 264-273.
Rieger, Max. *Alt- und angelsächsisches Lesebuch.* Giessen, 1861.
Schwab, Ute, ed. *Waldere: Testo e Commento.* Messina, 1967.
Stephens, George, ed. *Two Leaves of King Waldere's Lay.* Copenhagen and London, 1860.
Wülker, Richard P., ed. *Beowulf: Text nach der Handschrift.* Kassel, 1879.

C A SELECTION OF TRANSLATIONS

Bradley, S.A.J. *Anglo-Saxon Poetry.* London: Dent, 1982.
Crossley-Holland, Kevin. *The Anglo-Saxon World.* Bury St. Edmunds, Suffolk: St. Edmundsbury Press, 1982.
Garmonsway, G.N. *The Anglo-Saxon Chronicle.* Letchworth, Herts.: Aldine Press (for Dent), 1953. rev. 1954.
Gordon, Robert K. *Anglo-Saxon Poetry.* London: 1926; rev. ed. London: Dent, 1954.
Kennedy, Charles, W. *An Anthology of Old English Poetry.* New York: OUP, 1960. [Translated into alliterative verse]

D CRITICAL LITERATURE

Addison, James C., Jr. "Aural Interlace in 'The Battle of Brunanburh.'" *Language and Style*, 15 (1982), 267-76.
Allen, Michael J.B., and Daniel G. Calder, trans. *Sources and Analogues for Old English Poetry: The Major Latin Texts in Translation*. Cambridge: D.S. Brewer, 1976.
Amos, Ashley C. *Linguistic Means of Determining the Dates of Old English Literary Texts*. Cambridge, Mass.: The Medieval Academy of America, 1980.
Anderson, Earl R. "Flyting in *The Battle of Maldon*." *NM*, 71 (1970), 197-202.
———. "The Sun in *The Battle of Brunanburh*, 12b-17a." *N&Q*, 20 (1973), 362-63.
———. "Formulaic Typescene Survival: Finn, Ingeld, and the *Nibelungenlied*." *ES*, 61 (1980), 293-301.
———. *Cynewulf: Structure, Style, and Theme in His Poetry*. Rutherford, Madison and Teaneck, N.J.: Fairleigh Dickinson Univ. Press, 1983.
———. "*The Battle of Maldon*: A Reappraisal of Possible Sources, Date, and Theme." In *Modes of Interpretation in Old English Literature*. Eds. P.R. Brown, G.R. Crampton and F.C. Robinson. Toronto: Univ. of Toronto Press, 1986, pp. 247-272.
Anderson, James E. "*Deor, Wulf and Eadwacer*, and *The Soul's Address*: How and Where the Old English Exeter Book Riddles Begin." In *The Old English Elegies: New Essays in Criticism and Research*. Ed. M. Green. Rutherford, Madison and Teaneck, N.J.: Fairleigh Dickinson Univ. Press, 1983, pp. 204-30.
———. *Two Literary Riddles in the Exeter Book*. Norman: Univ. of Oklahoma Press, 1986.
Banerjee, Jacqueline. "*Deor*: The Refrain." *The Explicator*, 42 No. 4 (1984), 4-6.
Bauschotz, Paul C. "*The Well and the Tree: World and Time in Early Germanic Culture*. Amherst: Univ. of Massachusetts Press, 1982.
Beck, Heinrich. "Zur literaturgeschichtlichen Stellung des althochdeutschen Ludwigsliedes und einiger verwandter Zeitgedichte." *ZfdA*, 103 (1974), 37-51.
Berkhout, C.T. "*Feld Dennade* — Again." *ELN*, 11 (1974), 161-62.

Bessinger, J.B., Jr. "*Maldon* and the *Olafsdrapa*: An Historical Caveat." In *Studies in Old English Literature in Honour of Arthur G. Brodeur*. Ed. S.B. Greenfield. Eugene, Oregon: Univ. of Oregon Books, 1963, pp. 23-35.

Blake, Norman F. "The Flyting in *The Battle of Maldon*." *ELN*, 13 (1976), 242-45.

———. "The Genesis of *The Battle of Maldon*." *ASE*, 7 (1978), 119-29.

Bliss, Alan. "Single Half-Lines in Old English Poetry." *N&Q*, 18 (1971), 442-49.

———. "The Aviones and *Widsith* 26a." *ASE*, 14 (1985), 97-106.

———, and Allen J. Frantzen. "The Integrity of *Resignation*." *RES*, NS 27 (1976), 385-402.

Bloomfield, Morton W. "The Form of *Deor*." *PMLA*, 79 (1964), 534-41.

———. "*Deor* Revisited." In *Modes of Interpretation in Old English Literature*. Eds. P.R. Brown, G.R. Crampton and F.C. Robinson. Toronto: Univ. of Toronto Press, 1986, pp. 273-82.

Bolton, W.F. "'Variation' in *The Battle of Brunanburh*." *RES*, 19 (1968), 363-72.

———. "Boethius, Alfred, and *Deor* Again." *MP*, 69 (1972), 222-27.

Boren, James L. "The Design of the Old English *Deor*." In *Anglo-Saxon Poetry: Essays in Appreciation*. Eds. L.E. Nicholson and D.W. Frese. Notre Dame: Univ. of Notre Dame Press, 1975, pp. 264-76.

Brown, George Hardin. "An Iconographic Exploration of 'The Wanderer', lines 81b-82a." *Viator*, 9 (1978), 31-38, ill.

Brown, Phyllis R., Georgia R. Crampton and Fred C. Robinson, eds. *Modes of Interpretation in Old English Literature: Essays in Honour of Stanley B. Greenfield*. Toronto: Univ. of Toronto Press, 1986.

Busse, W.G. and R. Holtei. "*The Battle of Maldon*: A Historical, Heroic and Political Poem." *Neophil.*, 65 (1981), 614-21.

Bzdyl, Donald G. "Prayer in Old English Narratives." *MÆ*, 51 No. 2 (1982), 135-51.

Cable, Thomas. "Metrical Style as Evidence for the Date of *Beowulf*." In *The Dating of Beowulf*. Ed. Colin Chase. Toronto: Univ. of Toronto Press, 1981, pp. 77-82.

Campbell, Alistair. "The Old English Epic Style." In *English and Medieval Studies presented to J.R.R. Tolkien*. Eds. N. Davis and C.L. Wrenn. London: George Allen and Unwin, 1962, pp. 13-26.

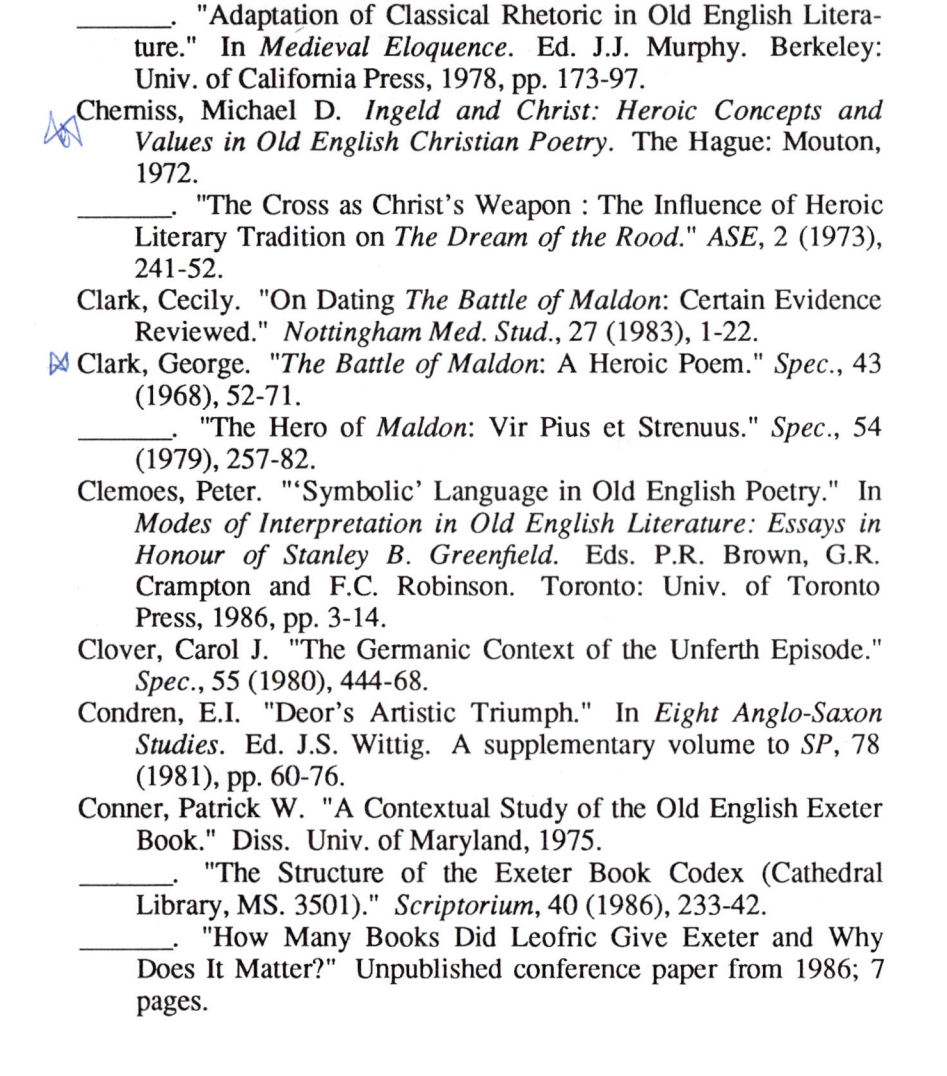

———. "The Use in *Beowulf* of Earlier Heroic Verse." In *England Before the Conquest*. Eds. P. Clemoes and K. Hughes. Cambridge: Cambridge Univ. Press, 1971, pp. 283-92.

Campbell, Jackson J. "Learned Rhetoric in Old English Poetry." *MP*, 63 (1966), 189-201.

———. "Knowledge of Rhetorical Figures in Anglo-Saxon England." *JEGP*, 66 (1967), 1-20.

———. "Adaptation of Classical Rhetoric in Old English Literature." In *Medieval Eloquence*. Ed. J.J. Murphy. Berkeley: Univ. of California Press, 1978, pp. 173-97.

Cherniss, Michael D. *Ingeld and Christ: Heroic Concepts and Values in Old English Christian Poetry*. The Hague: Mouton, 1972.

———. "The Cross as Christ's Weapon : The Influence of Heroic Literary Tradition on *The Dream of the Rood*." *ASE*, 2 (1973), 241-52.

Clark, Cecily. "On Dating *The Battle of Maldon*: Certain Evidence Reviewed." *Nottingham Med. Stud.*, 27 (1983), 1-22.

Clark, George. "*The Battle of Maldon*: A Heroic Poem." *Spec.*, 43 (1968), 52-71.

———. "The Hero of *Maldon*: Vir Pius et Strenuus." *Spec.*, 54 (1979), 257-82.

Clemoes, Peter. "'Symbolic' Language in Old English Poetry." In *Modes of Interpretation in Old English Literature: Essays in Honour of Stanley B. Greenfield*. Eds. P.R. Brown, G.R. Crampton and F.C. Robinson. Toronto: Univ. of Toronto Press, 1986, pp. 3-14.

Clover, Carol J. "The Germanic Context of the Unferth Episode." *Spec.*, 55 (1980), 444-68.

Condren, E.I. "Deor's Artistic Triumph." In *Eight Anglo-Saxon Studies*. Ed. J.S. Wittig. A supplementary volume to *SP*, 78 (1981), pp. 60-76.

Conner, Patrick W. "A Contextual Study of the Old English Exeter Book." Diss. Univ. of Maryland, 1975.

———. "The Structure of the Exeter Book Codex (Cathedral Library, MS. 3501)." *Scriptorium*, 40 (1986), 233-42.

———. "How Many Books Did Leofric Give Exeter and Why Does It Matter?" Unpublished conference paper from 1986; 7 pages.

Conquergood, Dwight. "Boasting in Anglo-Saxon England: Performance and the Heroic Ethos." *Literature in Performance*, 1 (1981), 24-35.

Creed, Robert P. "Widsith's Journey through Germanic Tradition." In *Anglo-Saxon Poetry: Essays in Appreciation*. Eds. L.E. Nicholson and D.W. Frese. Notre Dame: Univ. of Notre Dame Press, 1975, pp. 376-87.

Cross, James E. "Oswald and Byrhtnoth: A Christian Saint and a Hero who is Christian." *ES*, 46 (1965), 93-109.

―――. "Mainly on Philology and the Interpretative Criticism of *Maldon*." In *Old English Studies in Honour of John C. Pope*. Eds. R.B. Burlin and E.B. Irving, Jr. Toronto: Univ. of Toronto Press, 1974, pp. 235-53.

Dane, Joseph A. "Finnsburh and *Iliad* IX: A Greek Survival of the Medieval Germanic Oral-Formulaic Theme, the Hero on the Beach." *Neophil.*, 66 (1982), 443-49.

Doane, A.N. "Legend, History and Artifice in *The Battle of Maldon*." *Viator*, 9 (1978), 39-66.

Dodgson, John McN. "The Background of Brunanburh." *SBVS*, 14 (1953-57), 303-16.

Dumville, David N. "Some Aspects of Annalistic Writing at Canterbury in the Eleventh and Early Twelfth Centuries." *Peritia: Journal of the Medieval Academy of Ireland*, 2 (1983), 23-59.

―――. "The Anglian Collection of Royal Genealogies and Regnal Lists." *ASE*, 5 (1976), 23-50.

―――. "The West Saxon Genealogical Regnal List: Manuscripts and Texts." *Anglia*, 104 (1986), 1-32.

Eis, G. "Waltharius-Probleme." In *Britannica: Festschrift für Hermann M. Flasdieck*. Heidelberg, 1960, pp. 96-112.

Eliason, Norman E. "The Story of Geat and Mæðhild in *Deor*." *SP*, 62 (1965), 495-509.

―――. "Two Old English Scop Poems." *PMLA*, 81 (1966), 185-92.

―――. "*Deor* — a Begging Poem?" In *Medieval Literature and Civilization: Studies in Memory of G.N. Garmonsway*. Eds. D.A. Pearsall and R.A. Waldron. London: Athlone, 1969, pp. 55-61.

Engberg, Norma J. "Mod-Mægen Balance in 'Elene', 'The Battle of Maldon', and 'The Wanderer'." *NM*, 85 No. 2 (1984), 212-26.

Erickson, Jon. "The *Deor* Genitives." *Archivum Linguisticum*, 6 (1975), 77-84.

Evans, D.A.H. "*Maldon* 215." *N&Q*, 34 (1987), 5-7.

Fletcher, Alan J. "*Cald wæter, scir wæter*: A Note on Lines 91 and 98 of *The Battle of Maldon*." *NM*, 85 (1984), 435-37.

Frank, Roberta. "Viking Atrocity and Skaldic Verse: The Rite of the Blood-Eagle." *EHR*, 99 (1984), 332-43.

Frankis, P.J. "*Deor* and *Wulf and Eadwacer*: Some Conjectures." *MÆ*, 31 (1962), 161-75.

French, W.H. "*Widsith* and the Scop." *PMLA*, 60 (1945), 623-30.

Frese, Dolores W. "Poetic Prowess in *Brunanburh* and *Maldon*: Winning, Losing, and Literary Outcome." In *Modes of Interpretation in Old English Literature*. Eds. P.R. Brown, G.R. Crampton and F.C. Robinson. Toronto: Univ. of Toronto Press, 1986, pp. 83-100.

Fritz, J.M. "Chronological Impossibilities in *Widsith*." *Germanic Notes*, 6 (1975), 50-52.

Fry, Donald K. "The Hero on the Beach in *Finnsburh*." *NM*, 67 (1966), 27-31.

_____. "Old English Formulaic Themes and Typescenes." *Neophil.*, 52 (1968), 48-54.

_____. "*Finnsburh* 34a: *Hwearflicra Hwær*." *ELN*, 6 (1969), 241-42.

_____. "The Location of Finnsburh: *Beowulf* 1125-29a." *ELN*, 8 (1970), 2-3.

_____. "*Finnsburh*: A New Interpretation." *Chaucer Review*, 9 (1974), 1-14.

_____. "Two Voices in *Widsith*." *Mediaevalia*, 6 (1980), 37-56.

_____. "Launching Ships in *Beowulf* 210-16 and *Brunanburh* 32b-36." *MP*, 79 (1982), 61-66.

Garmonsway, G.N. "Anglo-Saxon Heroic Attitudes." In *Medieval and Linguistic Studies in Honour of Francis Peabody Magoun, Jr.* Eds. J.B. Bessinger, Jr. and R.P. Creed. London: George Allen and Unwin, 1965, pp. 139-46.

Gatch, Milton McC. *Loyalties and Traditions: Man and His World in Old English Literature*. New York: Pegasus, 1971.

Gillespie, George T. *A Catalogue of Persons Named in German Heroic Literature (700-1600) including Named Animals and Objects and Ethnic Names*. Oxford: Clarendon Press, 1973.

Gneuss, Helmut. *Die Battle of Maldon als historisches und literarisches Zeugnis vortragen am 4. Juli 1975*. Bayerische Akademie der Wissenschaften, Philosophisch-historische Klasse, Sitzungsberichte, No. 5, 1976. Munich: C.H. Beck, 1976.

_____. "*The Battle of Maldon* 89: Byrhtnoþ's *ofermod* Once Again." *SP*, 73 (1976), 117-37.

Goedhals, J.B. "Byrhtnoth and the Battle of Maldon." *UES*, 11 June (1973), 1-7.

Green, Martin, ed. *The Old English Elegies: New Essays in Criticism and Research.* Rutherford, Madison and Teaneck, N.J.: Fairleigh Dickinson Univ. Press, 1983.

Greenfield, Stanley B. "The Formulaic Expression of the Theme of 'Exile' in Anglo-Saxon Poetry." *Spec.*, 30 (1955), 200-06.

_____. "'Folces Hyrde', *Finnsburh* 46b: Kenning and Context." *NM*, 73 (1972), 97-102.

Harris, Joseph. "*Stemnettan*: *Battle of Maldon* Line 122A." *PQ*, 55 (1976), 113-17.

_____. "*Brunanburh* 12b-13a and some Skaldic Passages." In *Magister Regis: Studies in Honor of Robert Earl Kaske.* Eds. Arthur Groos et al. New York: Fordham University Press, 1986, pp. 61-68.

Hart, Cyril. "The East Anglian Chronicle." *JMH*, 7 (1981), 249-82.

_____. "Byrhtferth's Northumbrian Chronicle." *EHR*, 97 (1982), 558-82.

_____. "The Early Section of the *Worcester Chronicle*." *JMH*, 9 (1983), 251-315.

_____. "The Earldom of Essex." In *An Essex Tribute: Essays Presented to Frederick G. Emmison.* Ed. Kenneth Neale. London, 1987, pp. 57-84.

Hasegawa, Hiroshi. "Some Problems in *The Battle of Maldon*." *Papers on English Lang. and Lit.* (Japan), 29 (1981), 59-69.

Hatto, A.T. "Snake-swords and Boar-helms in *Beowulf*." *ES*, 38 (1957), 145-160.

Haug, Walter. "Andreas Heuslers Heldensagenmodell: Prämissen, Kritik und Gegenentwurf." *ZfdA*, 104 (1975), 273-92.

Haymes, Edward R. "Oral Poetry and the Germanic *Heldenlied*." *Rice Univ. Stud.*, 62 No. 2 (1976), 47-54.

Hill, B. "Early English Fragments and MSS Lambeth Palace Library 487, Bodleian Library Digby 4," *Proceedings of the Leeds Philosophical and Literary Society*, 14 (1972), 269-80.

Hill, Joyce. "*Widsið* and the Tenth Century." *NM*, 85 (1984), 305-15.

_____. "The Exeter Book and Lambeth Palace Library MS 149: A Reconsideration." *AN&Q*, 24 (1986), 112-16.

Hill, Thomas D. "History and Heroic Ethic in *Maldon*." *Neophil.*, 54 (1970), 291-96.

Hillman, Richard. "Defeat and Victory in 'The Battle of Maldon': The Christian Resonances Reconsidered." *ESC*, 11 (1985), 385-95.

Hofler, Otto. "Theuderich der Grosse und sein Bild in der Sage." *Anzeiger der österreichischen Akademie der Wissenschaften*, Philosophisch-historische Klasse, 111, No. 20 (1974), 349-72. Innsbruck: Universitätsverlag, 1974.

Hollowell, Ida M. "*Scop* and *Woðbora* in OE Poetry." *JEGP*, 77 (1978), 217-29.

———. "Was Widsið a *scop*?" *Neophil.*, 64 (1980), 583-91.

Hoover, David L. "Evidence for Primacy of Alliteration in Old English Metre." *ASE*, 14 (1985), 75-96.

Howe, N. *The Old English Catalogue Poems.* Anglistica 23, (1985); Chapter 5 (166-201) and Conclusion (202-08).

Howlett, D.R. "Form and Genre in *Widsith*." *ES*, 55 (1974), 505-11.

Hunter, Michael. "Germanic and Roman Antiquity and the Sense of the Past in Anglo-Saxon England." *ASE*, 3 (1974), 29-50.

Huppé, Bernard F. "The Concept of the Hero in the Early Middle Ages." In *Concepts of the Hero in the Middle Ages and the Renaissance.* Eds. N.T. Burns and C.J. Reagan. Albany: SUNY Press, 1975, pp. 1-26.

Irving, E.B., Jr. "The Heroic Style in *The Battle of Maldon*." *SP*, 58 (1961), 457-67.

Isaacs, Neil D. "Battlefield Tour: Brunanburg." *NM*, 63 (1962), 236-44.

———. "*The Battle of Brunanburh*, 13b-17a." *N&Q*, 208 (1963), 247-48.

Jacobs, Nicolas. "The Old English Heroic Tradition in the Light of Welsh Evidence." *Camb. Med. Celtic Stud.*, 2 (1981), 9-20.

John, Eric. "War and Society in the Tenth Century: The Maldon Campaign." *TRHS*, 5th ser. 27 (1976), 173-95.

Johnson, Ann S. "The Rhetoric of *Brunanburh*." *PQ*, 47 (1968), 487-93.

Johnson, Judith. "The Real Villains of the Battle of Maldon." *Michigan Academician*, 17 (1985), 409-15.

Kiernan, Kevin S. "A Solution to the Mæðhild-Geat Crux in *Deor*." *ES*, 56 (1975), 97-99.

_____. "*Deor*: The Consolation of an Anglo-Saxon Boethius." *NM*, 79 (1978), 333-40.

Kleinschmidt, Harald. "Das Problem des Geschichtlichen in der *Battle of Maldon*." *Poetica* (Tokyo), 10 (1978), 12-34.

Koike, Kazuo. "On the Connection between Anglo-Saxon England and the Vikings: Focussing on *The Battle of Maldon*." *International Culture* (Obirin Univ.), 2 (1980), 143-69.

_____. "On the Vocabulary for Byrhtnoth in *The Battle of Maldon*." *Obirin Stud. in Eng. Lit.*, 24 (1984), 209-19.

Kossick, Shirley G. "The Old English *Deor*." *UES*, 10 No. 1 (1972), 3-6.

Laborde, Edward D. "The Site of the Battle of Maldon." *EHR*, 40 (1925), 161-73.

Langenfelt, Gösta. "Some Widsith Names and the Background of Widsith." In *VI. Internationaler Kongress für Namenforschung*; München 24-28 August 1958. Eds. G. Rohlfs and K. Puchner. Munich, 1960-61. Vol. III, pp. 496-510.

Lapidge, Michael. "Some Latin Poems as Evidence for the Reign of Athelstan." *ASE*, 10 (1981), 83-93.

_____, and Helmut Gneuss, eds. *Learning and Literature in Anglo-Saxon England*. Cambridge: Cambridge Univ. Press, 1985.

Lawler, Traugott. "*Brunanburh*: Craft and Art." In *Literary Studies: Essays in Memory of Francis A. Drumm*. Ed. J.A. Dorenkamp. Wetteren, Belgium: 1973, pp. 52-67.

Lipp, Frances R. "Contrast and Point of View in *The Battle of Brunanburh*." *PQ*, 48 (1969), 166-77.

Locherbie-Cameron, Margaret A.L. "Ælfwine's Kinsmen and *The Battle of Maldon*." *N&Q*, 25 (1978), 486-87.

_____. "Two Battles of Maldon." *Trivium*, 19 (1984), 55-59.

Loyn, Henry R. "The King and the Structure of Society in Late Anglo-Saxon England." *History*, 42 (1957), 87-100.

_____. "Kinship in Anglo-Saxon England." *ASE*, 3 (1974), 197-209.

_____. *The Governance of Anglo-Saxon England 500-1087*. London: Edward Arnold, 1984.

Macrae-Gibson, O.D. "*Maldon*: The Literary Structure of the Later Part." *NM*, 71 (1970), 192-96.

Magoun, Francis P., Jr. "Theme of the Beasts of Battle in Anglo-Saxon Poetry." *NM*, 56 (1955), 81-90.

———. "Two Verses in the OE *Waldere* Characteristic of Oral Poetry." *BGdSL* (Tübingen), 80 (1958), 214-18.

———, and H.M. Smyser. *Walter of Aquitaine: Materials for the Study of his Legend*. Connecticut College Monographs No. 4. New London, Conn.: 1950.

Malone, Kemp. "On *Deor* 14-17." *MP*, 40 (1942), 1-18.

———. "The Franks Casket and the Date of *Widsith*." In *Nordica et Anglica: Studies in Honour of Stefán Einarsson*. Ed. A.H. Orrick. The Hague: Mouton, 1968, pp. 10-18.

———. "The Rhythm of *Deor*." In *Old English Studies in Honour of John C. Pope*. Eds. R.B. Burlin and E.B. Irving, Jr. Toronto, Univ. of Toronto Press, 1974, pp. 165-69.

Mandel, Jerome. "Exemplum and Refrain: The Meaning of *Deor*." *YES*, 7 (1977), 1-9.

———. "Audience Response Strategies in the Opening of *Deor*." *Mosaic*, 15 (1982), 127-32.

Markland, Murray F. "Boethius, Alfred and *Deor*." *MP*, 66 (1968), 1-4.

———. "*Deor*: þæs ofereode; þisses swa mæg." *AN&Q*, 11 (1973), 35-36.

Marold, Edith. "Hunwil." *Die Sprache*, 17 (1971), 157-63.

McKinnell, John. "On the Date of *The Battle of Maldon*." *MÆ*, 44 (1975), 121-36.

Meier, Hans H. "Old English Style in Action: The Battle Scene (with a hint of *Hildebrand*." In *Studies in Honour of René Derolez*. Ed. A.M. Simon-Vandenbergen. Gent: Seminarie voor Engelse en Oud-Germaanse Taalkunde, Rijksuniversiteit Gent, 1987, pp. 334-50.

Meindl, R.J. "The Artistic Unity of *Widsith*." *Xavier University Studies*, 3 (1964), 19-28.

Mills, Carl R. "Stylistic Applications of Ethnosemantics: Basic Color Terms in *Brunanburh* and *Maldon*." *Language and Style*, 9 (1976), 164-70.

Mitchell, B. and F. Robinson, eds. *A Guide to Old English*. 4th ed. Oxford: Blackwell, 1986.

Moisl, Hermann. "Anglo-Saxon Royal Genealogies and Germanic Oral Tradition." *JMH*, 7 (1981), 216-48.

Molinari, Maria Vittoria. "Il 'Frammento di Finnsburg': proposta di rilettura." *AIUON*, Filologia germanica, 24 (1981), 27-50.

Nelson, Marie. "*The Battle of Maldon* and *Juliana*: The Language of Confrontation." In *Modes of Interpretation in Old English*

Literature. Eds. P.R. Brown, G.R. Crampton and F.C. Robinson. Toronto: Univ. of Toronto Press, 1986, pp. 137-50.

Niles, John D. "Skaldic Technique in *Brunanburh*." *Scandinavian Studies*, 59 (1987), 356-66.

Nolan, Barbara, and Morton W. Bloomfield. "Beotword, Gilpcwidas, and the Gilphlæden Scop of *Beowulf*." *JEGP*, 79 (1980), 499-516.

Norman, Frederick. "Problems in the Dating of *Deor* and its Allusions." In *Medieval and Linguistic Studies in Honour of Francis Peabody Magoun, Jr.*. Eds. J.B. Bessinger, Jr. and R.P. Creed. London: George Allen and Unwin, 1965, pp. 205-13.

———. "The Evidence for the Germanic Walter Lay." *Acta Germanica*, 3 (1968), 21-35.

———. "The OE *Waldere* and Some Problems in the Story of Walther and Hildegunde." In *Mélanges pour Jean Fourquet*. Eds. P. Valentin and G. Zink. Paris: Klincksieck, 1969, pp. 261-71.

———. "Early Germanic Background to Old English Verse." In *Medieval Literature and Civilization: Studies in Memory of G.N. Garmonsway*. Eds. D. Pearsall and R.A. Waldron. London: Athlone, 1969, pp. 3-27.

Opland, Jeff. *Anglo-Saxon Oral Poetry: A Study of the Traditions*. Ann Arbor: Edwards Brothers, 1980.

———. "From Horseback to Monastic Cell: The Impact on English Literature of the Introduction of Writing." In *Old English Literature in Context*. Ed. J.D. Niles. Cambridge: D.S. Brewer, 1980, pp. 30-43.

Ortoleva, Grazia. "Waldere II, 21b: *þonne ha[n]d wereð*." *AIUON*, Filologia germanica, 22 (1979), 117-18.

Orton, P.R. "'The Battle of Brunanburh', 40B-44A: Constantine's Bereavement." *Peritia*, 4 (1985), 243-50.

Osborn, Marijane. "The Finnsburg Raven and *Guðrinc Astah*." *Folklore*, 81 (1970), 185-94.

———. "The Text and Context of *Wulf and Eadwacer*." In *The Old English Elegies: New Essays in Criticism and Research*. Ed. M. Green. Rutherford, Madison and Teaneck, N.J.: Fairleigh Dickinson Univ. Press, 1983, pp. 174-89.

Page, Raymond I. "The Audience of *Beowulf* and the Vikings." In *The Dating of Beowulf*. Ed. Colin Chase. Toronto: Univ. of Toronto Press, 1981, pp. 113-22.

_____. "A Tale of Two Cities." *Peritia: Journal of the Medieval Academy of Ireland*, 1 (1982), 335-51.

Parkes, Malcolm. "The Palaeography of the Parker Manuscript of the *Chronicle* laws, and Sedulius, and Historiography at Winchester in the Late Ninth and Tenth Centuries." *ASE*, 5 (1976), 149-71.

Parks, Ward. "Flyting and Fighting - Pathways in the Realization of the Epic Contest." *Neophil.*, 70 (1986), 292-306.

_____. "The Flyting Speech in Traditional Heroic Narrative." *Neophil.*, 71 (1987), 285-95.

_____. "The Traditional Narrator and the 'I heard' Formulas in Old English Poetry." *ASE*, 16 (1987), 45-66.

Petty, George R., Jr., and Susan Petty. "Geology and *The Battle of Maldon*." *Spec.*, 51 (1976), 435-46, ill.

Pheifer, J.D. "*Waldere* I 29-31." *RES*, NS 11 (1960), 183-86.

Piccolini, Antonio. "Sui presunti influssi nordici nel *Waldere*." *AIUON*, Filologia germanica, 23 (1980), 159-80.

Pope, John C. "The Lacuna in the Text of Cynewulf's *Ascension* (*Christ* II, 556 b)." In *Studies in Language, Literature and Culture of the Middle Ages and Later in Honor of Rudolph Willard*. Eds. E.B. Atwood and A.A. Hill. Austin, Texas: Univ. of Texas Press, 1969, pp. 210-19.

_____. "An Unsuspected Lacuna in the Exeter Book: Divorce Proceedings for an Ill-Matched Couple in the Old English Riddles." *Spec*, 49 (1974), 615-22.

Raffel, Burton. "Scholars, Scholarship, and the Old English *Deor*." *Notre Dame English Journal*, 8 (1972), 3-10.

Raw, Barbara C. *The Art and Background of Old English Poetry*. London: Edward Arnold, 1978.

Regan, C.L. "*Deor*: Q.E.D." In *Inscape: Studies presented to Charles F. Donovan, S.J.* Eds. M.J. Connolly and L.G. Jones. Maine: 1977, pp. 146-48.

Renoir, Alan. "Crist Ihesu's Beasts of Battle: A Note on Oral-Formulaic Theme Survival." *Neophil.*, 60 (1976), 455-59.

_____. "Old English Formulas and Themes as Tools for Contextual Interpretation." In *Modes of Interpretation in Old English Literature: Essays in Honour of Stanley B. Greenfield*. Eds. P.R. Brown, G.R. Crampton and F.C. Robinson. Toronto: Univ. of Toronto Press, 1986, pp. 65-79.

Richards, Mary P. "*The Battle of Maldon* in Its Manuscript Context." *Mediaevalia*, 7 (1984 for 1981), 79-89.

Roberts, Jane. "*Maldon* 189b: *Þe hit riht ne wæs.*" *N&Q*, 29 (1982), 106.
Robinson, Fred C. "Some Aspects of the *Maldon* Poet's Artistry." *JEGP*, 75 (1976), 25-40.
―――――. "God, Death and Loyalty in *The Battle of Maldon.*" In *J.R.R. Tolkien, Scholar and Storyteller: Essays 'In Memoriam'*. Eds. M. Salu and R.T. Farrell. London: Cornell Univ. Press, 1979, pp. 76-98.
―――――. *Beowulf and the Appositive Style*. Knoxville: Univ. of Tennessee Press, 1985.
―――――. "Literary Dialect in *Maldon* and the Casley Transcript." *AN&Q*, 24 (1986), 103-04.
Rogers, H.L. "*The Battle of Maldon*: David Casley's Transcript." *N&Q*, 32 (1985), 147-55, ill.
Rollman, David A. "*Widsith* as an Anglo-Saxon Defense of Poetry." *Neophil.*, 66 (1982), 431-39.
Russchen, A. "Finnsburg — A Critical Approach." In *Miscellanea Frisica*. Eds. Nils Arhammar et al. Assen: 1984, pp. 349-56.
Russom, Geoffrey R. "Artful Avoidance of the Useful Phrase in *Beowulf, The Battle of Maldon*, and *Fates of the Apostles.*" *SP*, 75 (1978), 371-90.
Scattergood, John. "*The Battle of Maldon* and History." In *Literature and Learning in Medieval and Renaissance England: Essays Presented to Fitzroy Pyle*. Ed. John Scattergood. Blackrock, Co. Dublin: 1984, pp. 11-24.
Schibsbye, Knud. "*þæs ofereode; þisses swa mæg.*" *ES*, 50 (1969), 380-81.
Schlauch, Margaret. "Widsith, Vithförull, and Some Other Analogues." *PMLA*, 46 (1931), 969-87.
Schneider, C. "Cynewulf's Devaluation of Heroic Tradition in *Juliana.*" *ASE*, 7 (1978), 107-18.
Schücking, Levin. "*Waldere* und *Waltharius.*" In *Waltharius und Walthersage: eine Dokumentation der Forschung*. Ed. E.E. Ploss. Hildesheim: Olms, 1969, pp. 307-26.
Schulze, Fritz W. "Germanische Bindungen vergleichende compositio in Tacitus *Germania.*" In *Studien zur englischen Philologie: Edgar Mertner zum 70. Geburtstag*. Eds. H. Mainusch and D. Rolle. Frankfurt: 1979, pp. 11-25.
Schwab, Ute. "Nochmals zum ags. *Waldere* neben dem *Waltharius.*" *BGdSL*, 101 (1979), 229-51, 347-68.

Sedgefield, W.J. "Scilling." *MLR*, 26 (1931), 75.

Shippey, Thomas A. *Old English Verse*. London: Hutchinson, 1972.

———. *Poems of Wisdom and Learning in Old English*. Cambridge: D.S. Brewer, 1976.

———. "Maxims in Old English Narrative: Literary Art or Traditional Wisdom?" In *Oral Tradition, Literary Tradition: A Symposium*. Eds. H. Bekker-Nielsen et al. Odense: Odense Univ. Press, 1977, pp. 28-46.

———. "Boar and Badger: An Old English Heroic Antithesis?" In *Sources and Relations: Studies in Honour of J.E. Cross*. Leeds Studies in English, NS 16. Eds. Marie Collins et al. Leeds: Moxon Press, 1985, pp. 230-39.

Sims-Williams, Patrick. "'Is It Fog or Smoke or Warriors Fighting?': Irish and Welsh Parallels to the *Finnsburg Fragment*." *BBCS*, 27 (1976-78), 505-14.

Sklar, Elizabeth S. "*The Battle of Maldon* and the Popular Tradition: Some Rhymed Formulas." *PQ*, 54 (1975), 409-18.

Stanley, Eric G. *The Search for Anglo-Saxon Paganism*. Cambridge: D.S. Brewer, 1975.

———. "Old English '-calla', 'ceallian'." In *Medieval Literature and Civilization: Studies in Memory of G.N. Garmonsway*. Eds. D.A. Pearsall and R.A. Waldron. London: Athlone, 1969, pp. 94-99.

Stuart, Heather. "The Meaning of *Maldon*." *Neophil.*, 66 (1982), 126-39.

Swanton, Michael. "*The Battle of Maldon*: A Literary Caveat." *JEGP*, 67 (1968), 441-50.

———. "Heroes, Heroism and Heroic Literature." *Essays and Studies*, 30 (1977), 1-21.

Thundyil, Zacharias. "*The Battle of Maldon*: A Christian Heroic Poem." *HUSL*, 3 (1975), 101-34.

Tristram, Hildegard L.C. "Ohthere, Wulfstan, und der Aethicus Ister." *ZfdA*, 111 (1983), 153-68.

Tuggle, Thomas T. "The Structure of *Deor*." *SP*, 74 (1977), 229-42.

Valentine, Virginia. "Offa and the 'Battle of Maldon'." *Explicator*, 44.3 (1986), 5-7.

Van't Hul, Bernard, and Dennis S. Mitchell. "'Artificial Poetry' and Sea Eagles: A Note on *þane hasupadan / earn æftan hwit*,

Lines 62b and 63a of *The Battle of Brunanburh*." *NM*, 81 (1980), 390-94.
Wenisch, Franz. "Sächsische Dialektwörter in *The Battle of Maldon*." *IF*, 81 (1976), 181-203.
Wentersdorf, Karl P. "On the Meaning of O.E. *dreorig* in *Brunanburh* 54." *NM*, 74 (1973), 232-37.
Whitaker, Ian. "Scridefinnas in *Widsith*." *Neophil*., 66 (1982), 602-08.
Whitbread, Leslie. "The Pattern of Misfortune in *Deor* and Other Old English Poems." *Neophil*., 54 (1970), 167-83.
Whitelock, Dorothy. "Anglo-Saxon Poetry and the Historian." *TRHS*, 4th ser. 31 (1949), 75-94; rep. in *From Bede to Alfred: Studies in Early Anglo-Saxon Literature and History*. London: Variorum Reprints, 1980.
Wienold, Gotz. "*Deor*: Über Offenheit und Auffüllung von Texten." *Sprachkunst*, 3 (1972), 285-97.
Wood, Michael. "Brunanburh Revisited." *SBVS*, 20.3 (1980), 200-17.
Woolf, Rosemary. "The Ideal of Men Dying with their Lord in the *Germania* and in *The Battle of Maldon*." *ASE*, 5 (1976), 63-81.
York, Lamar. "A Reading of *Widsith*." *Midwest Quarterly*, 20 (1979), 325-31.

ONE: WIDSITH

INTRODUCTION

Manuscript

The *Exeter Book* (or Liber / Codex Exoniensis) bears the press mark 3501 in the Library of the Dean and Chapter, Exeter Cathedral.

Date: Late tenth century.

Provenance: It cannot be said for certain which Anglo-Saxon scriptorium produced the *Exeter Book*, but recent investigations suggest that it may have actually been produced at Exeter.[1]

History: There is no record of the *Exeter Book* manuscript until it was given to the Cathedral Library by the first bishop of Exeter, Leofric, who died in 1072. Scholars agree that it is the manuscript described in the list of his donations as *.i. mycel Englisc boc be gehwilcum þingum on leoðwisan geworht*; this list is found both at the beginning of the *Exeter Book* (ff 1r-2v) and in Bodleian MS Auct. D.2.16 (ff 1r-2v).[2] The *Exeter Book* has remained in the

---

[1] From a reconsideration of the historical and archaeological evidence available for the period prior to the appointment of Leofric as first bishop of Exeter, Conner (1986) argues cogently that there is great likelihood that there was a scriptorium at Exeter capable of producing the *Exeter Book* and the other manuscripts associated with it, Lambeth Palace Library MS 149, Bodleian Library MS 319, and perhaps Exeter, Dean and Chapter MS 3507, Bodleian Library MS 718 and Paris, Bibliothèque Nationale, ms lat 943.

[2] The latter has been edited several times (see Chambers et al. (1933, 10; henceforth *EBOEP*)), most recently by Lapidge and Gneuss (1985, 64-69); Förster edited and annotated the *Exeter Book* version (*EBOEP*, 18-30).

possession of the Library of the Dean and Chapter, Exeter Cathedral, since the eleventh century, and perhaps since it was first compiled in the tenth.

Description: [The *Exeter Book* manuscript has been described in exhaustive detail on many occasions, and the reader is directed in particular to the editions of Chambers et al. (1933) and of Krapp and Dobbie (1936) for complete codicological analyses.] The original book of poetry which Leofric gave to the Library of Exeter Cathedral comprises folios 8-130 as the manuscript now stands; there is a blank (unnumbered) leaf at the beginning, followed by folios numbered 1 to 7 containing documents and records in English and Latin from the eleventh century and later.[3] The average size of each folio is 310-20 × 218-25 mm, with an average writing area of 240 × 160 mm. There are now seventeen gatherings (without signatures) in the manuscript, containing from 5 to 8 folios; these were evidently ruled individually as work on the manuscript progressed, and contain from 21 to 23 long lines.[4] From folio 119 on there is increasingly severe damage to the text of the codex caused by a brand which was placed on the back of the manuscript at some stage; folios 8-12 are disfigured in varying degrees by a stain caused by a spilled liquid, but the text is mostly legible.[5] Other than some simple decoration of some of the large capitals, the only ornamentation in the manuscript is some sporadic drypoint etching on seven folios.[6]

The script is Anglo-Saxon minuscule, and was described by Robin Flower as "the noblest of Anglo-Saxon hands". It is quite consistent in appearance, but opinion varies as to whether one or more scribes shared the work of copying the texts in the codex.[7]

---

[3] Förster has identified and annotated these (*EBOEP*, 44-54).

[4] The structure and arrangement of the gatherings have been fully described by Förster (*EBOEP*, 56-60) and by Krapp and Dobbie (1936, xi-xiii; henceforth *EB*). From textual and codicological investigations, it is now apparent that a considerable amount of the *Exeter Book* has been lost; see *EB*, xi-xii, Pope (1969 and 1974) and Bliss/Frantzen (1976).

[5] The damaged sections of the codex have been transcribed and annotated by R.W. Chambers and R. Flower (*EBOEP*, 68-82). Krapp and Dobbie (*EB*) summarize textual emendations advanced by various critics prior to 1936. I am at present working on a new edition of the *Exeter Book* which will take subsequent textual criticism into account.

[6] Conner (1985, 236-37 and *Table 2*), describes these in some detail, and observes that, contrary to what Förster concluded (*EBOEP*, 60), these etchings were made before the text was written.

[7] The field of critical opinion ranges from Flower, ". . . for there is, despite the general identity of letter forms, such variety in the quality of the script that we must

Compilation: Until recently, scholars generally agreed that the *Exeter Book* was a fair copy of an unstructured miscellany.[8] However, in a recent unpublished contextual study of the codex, Patrick Conner presents a different view, arguing that the "principle behind the selection of the poems in the manuscript . . . was a didactic one, and that the Exeter Book was intended to be an instructional manual" (1975, 10-11). He agrees with Sisam and other scholars that the *Exeter Book* is most likely a fair copy of an earlier collection (1975, 11), but goes further, arguing that whoever compiled it deliberately integrated two pre-existing (structured) collections which he designates the 'Church Group' and the 'Native Group'.[9] He contends that the Church Group was added to the Native Group, but that the overall codex "is not nearly so well controlled as was the structure of the Native Group" (1975, 67). In light of further codicological, palaeographical and textual research, he has adopted a new thesis, and now argues that the texts of the codex were originally contained in three discrete 'booklets'.[10]

---

suppose several scribes to have been employed on the writing . . ." (*EBOEP*, 83) to Ker and Sisam, who favoured the hypothesis of a single scribe, to Conner, who takes up an intriguing position of compromise, but one founded on detailed examination of the whole manuscript: "One scribe probably did write the manuscript, but at different times" (1985, 238).

[8] In 1964, N.F. Blake wrote, "The Exeter Book differs from the other three poetic codices in that it is a poetic miscellany in which there does not appear to be a recognisable principle of selection" (*The Phoenix*, Manchester Univ. Press, 2); and as late as 1969, J.P. Dunning and A.J. Bliss wrote [in reaction to Sisam's observation that the stately even style of the Exeter Book indicated "that it was transcribed continuously from a collection already made" (*Studies in the History of Old English Literature*, Oxford: 1953, 97)], "If the scribe of the Exeter Book had had before him a complete exemplar it would have been both easy and obviously desirable to rearrange the contents into a more systematic order; even if we allow him only a minimum of intelligence and acumen, he would surely at least have brought the two sets of *Riddles* together . . . . It seems likely that the Exeter Book was compiled over a period of years" (*The Wanderer*, London: Methuen, 3-4).

[9] Conner (1975, 62 ff). The Native Group comprises *Wanderer, Gifts of Men, Precepts, Seafarer, Vainglory, Widsith, Fortunes of Men, Maxims I, Order of the World, Riming Poem, Deor, Wulf and Eadwacer, Wife's Lament, Resignation, Husband's Message,* and *Ruin*; the Church Group comprises *Christ, Guthlac, Azarias, Phoenix, Juliana, Panther, Whale, Partridge, Soul and Body II, Judgment Day I, Descent into Hell, Almsgiving, Pharaoh, Lord's Prayer I,* and *Homiletic Fragment II*. "Because the riddles make up a formally derived structure, there is no structuralistic means for determining when they became part of the manuscript with relationship to the Church and Native groups of poems" (67). In his analysis, he breaks down the Native Group into three sub-groups of 5, 5 and 6 poems respectively, and isolates individual major themes within these smaller divisions, showing tensions of opposing statements on these themes among the poems; his methodology is the same when dealing with the Church Group.

[10] He gives the following analysis of the contents of each booklet in his *Table 1*:

Text

The poem has no title in the codex, but is today generally referred to as *Widsith*;[11] its edited length is 143 lines. It appears in the eleventh gathering (ff 83-90) on ff 84^r-87^r, following *Vainglory* and preceding *The Fortunes of Men*; the text is undamaged, but a few lines as they stand are in need of rearrangement (see the commentary for lines 85-87).

Structure, theme, and genre: *Widsith* consists of a prologue (1-9), the speech of the poet Widsith [consisting of an introduction (10-13), three fitts (14-49, 50-108, 109-130), and a conclusion (131-34)], and an epilogue (135-43).[12]

At first glance, it seems as if *Widsith* is about a poet of that name whose speech makes up the major part of the poem. It was probably never intended that the persona 'Widsith' be understood to be an historical figure, as his name, apparently more fictional than real, seems to indicate.[13] However, the poem might also be about the poet who utters the complete poem including the prologue and epilogue, and

---

i) *Christ I-Guthlac B*; ii) *Azarias-Partridge* (to line 2a); and iii) *Homiletic Fragment III* (traditionally lines 3-16 of *Partridge*)-*Riddle 95*. A careful evaluation of the palaeographic evidence (especially the use of ligatures and certain letter forms) leads him to conclude that the booklets were copied in the order ii, iii, i (1985, 233-34 and 238-40).

[11] The first line of the text in the manuscript consists of the first two words of the poem, *Widsið maðolade*, written in capitals, their height taking up the space of two regular lines of script (except for the final 'e' (which is normal size) and the initial *wynn* (which is seven lines in height); see Plate 1. The use of capitals is rather to indicate the beginning of a new poem than to designate the intended title of a text.

[12] Noting the symmetry of the prologue and epilogue (both of 9 lines) and of the introduction and conclusion (both of 4 lines), Malone and others designate as interpolations certain lines of the poem which spoil the perfect symmetry of the original poem as they conceive it to have been. This attitude towards the poems as they have come down to us, and as they were copied into the manuscript in the tenth century, prevents such critics from appreciating the full artistry of the poet who moulded his traditional material into its final form; see Hill (1984) for a discussion of *Widsith* and its tenth century audience.

[13] The persona 'Widsith' is regarded as fictitious primarily because of his claim to have associated with various people who are known to have lived over a period spanning a few centuries, a biological impossibility. Malone observes:
> When the *Widsith* poet conceived the idea of making a poem about the Germanic heroic age, a poem to which the figure of a fictitious scop was to give the needful unity, he began his work of composition by putting into the scop's mouth these three thulas, and about the thulas he built up the rest of the poem. (1962, 27)

The name literally means 'far-traveller', or some equivalent.

describe the career of such a poet, his attitudes towards his position in his society, and such things as patronage and reward for service.[14] One critic has recently advanced the most attractive theory that *Widsith* is actually a poem about poetry itself, that is, that it is an Anglo-Saxon 'ars poetica'.[15]

Although *Widsith* deals with traditional legendary and historical material from early heathen times, it was, like most surviving Anglo-Saxon poetry, recorded in the form in which it has come down to us by an educated Christian, perhaps a cleric. It emphasizes that the kind of *lof* and *dom* that kings (who govern because God allows them to) earn here, and which is celebrated and immortalised by poets (*gleomen*), is that *dom* often mentioned in other heroic poetry, that is, immediate and lasting fame and recognition in their society in this temporal world.[16] And though the poem is primarily about the poet and poetry, it is also a celebration of the society in which he functions, with special emphasis on the proper and ideal nature and role of the king; the aphorism of lines 10-13, for example, probably encapsulates traditional wisdom concerning the most judicious and prudent way for those in power to act.

The three fitts of the speech draw upon traditional mnemonic metrical name lists (sometimes called 'thulas') for their substance, the first a list of kings (with the structure "W ruled X, and Y Z"), the second of tribes (with the structure "I was with X and Y and Z"), and the third of heroes (with the structure "X I sought, and Y and Z"). These fitts combine mnemonic and narrative passages in varying proportions throughout the poem; the artistry of the poet is to be seen in how he creates his poem from this mixture of historical and fictional ingredients.

---

[14] For various interpretations of the poem see Creed (1975), Eliason (1965), French (1945), Hill (1984), Hollowell (1978 and 1980), Howlett (1974), Meindl (1964), and York (1979).

[15] Rollman writes:
Widsith is, I think, a poem about the powers of poetry itself, a celebration of the ability of art to influence life. Poetry has three vital functions, the *Widsith*-poet proposes: the didactic, the experiential, and the ability to add something to life itself by endowing immortality. These three functions of poetry govern the construction of the poem, determine the contents and form of the lists, and finally form the basis of the poet's plea, which is not for himself but for his art. (1982, 432)

[16] Various words are used to describe it: *dom, lof, blæd, tir*; see, for example, 2.31b-34a, 3.8-11, 5.3, 6.129, and throughout *Beowulf* (eg 18, 885 ff, 2664-66a, and especially Beowulf's advice to Hrothgar at 1384-89).

Language: The language of *Widsith* has been analysed on a number of occasions, and has been found to be a mixture of West Saxon, Anglian, Mercian, Northumbrian and Kentish forms. The presence of various dialectal elements in a text is the norm in the surviving Anglo-Saxon poems, and is usually interpreted as evidence either for a long and complex history of textual transmission or for the existence of a poetic language of mixed dialect used throughout the period when the surviving texts were recorded.[17] There are some orthographic features in *Widsith* which indicate that it was composed quite early, unless these are deliberate archaisms, which does not seem to be the case.[18] Most noteworthy of these are: *mearchealf* (23), *moidum* (84) and *amothingum* (85).[19] Some typical non-West-Saxon forms are:

Kentish
meaca (23), *breoca* (25), *wiolane* (78), *sprecan* (107);

Anglian
maðolade (1), *becca* (19), *merce* (42) *wærnum* (59), *innweorud* (111), *beccan* (115);

Mercian
heaðo- (49, 63, 116), *beadecan* (112), *seafolan* (115), *alewih* (35);

Northumbrian
bidæled (52), *eatule* (70), *bicwōm* (94), *earmanrīces* (111).

Some of these may, however, merely be either early or late forms, and not dialectal characteristics; it is often hard to distinguish between these.

---

[17] Malone (1962, 115) considers the mixture of forms in *Widsith* to be evidence for the former theory; a great number of scholars (following Sisam, *Studies*, p. 138) favour the view that there was in all likelihood a 'poetic language' (or *koine*) used by Anglo-Saxon poets that was "not closely related to any of the major dialects, but which contained elements otherwise characteristic of these dialects" (Blake, *The Phoenix*, 4).

[18] See Malone (1962, 115-16).

[19] Malone gives a complete summary of these (1962, 112-16).

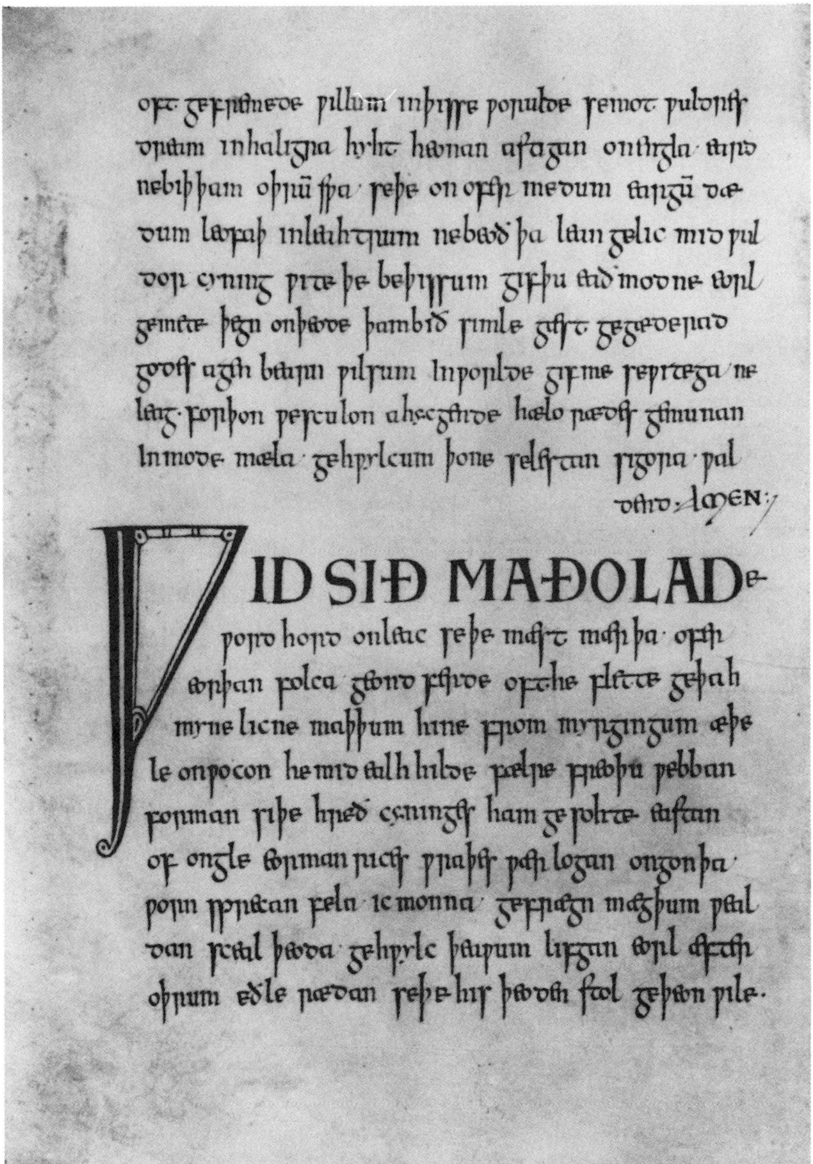

PLATE 1 Exeter, Dean and Chapter MS 3501, 84ᵛ. The opening lines of *Widsith*.

WIDSITH

      Widsið maðolade,   wordhord onleac,
      se þe [monna] mæst   mægþa ofer eorþan
3 folca geondferde;   oft he [on] flette geþah
      mynelicne maþþum;   hine from Myrgingum
      æþele onwocon;   he mid Ealhhilde,
6 fælre freoþuwebban,   forman siþe
      Hreðcyninges   ham gesohte
      eastan of Ongle,   Eormanrices,
9 wraþes wærlogan;   ongon þa worn sprecan:
      "Fela ic monna gefrægn   mægþum wealdan -
      sceal þeoda gehwylc   þeawum lifgan,
12 eorl æfter oþrum   eðle rædan,
      se þe his þeodenstol   geþeon wile - /
      þara wæs [H]wala   hwile selast
15 ond Alexandreas   ealra ricost
      monna cynnes   ond he mæst geþah
      þara þe ic ofer foldan   gefrægen hæbbe:
18 Ætla weold Hunum,   Eormanric Gotum,
      Becca Baningum,   Burgendum Gifica;
      Casere weold Creacum   ond Cælic Finnum,
21 Hagena Holmryc[g]um   ond Henden Glommum;
      Witta weold Swæfum,   Wada Hælsingum,
      Meaca Myrgingum,   Mearchealf Hundingum;
24 Þeodric weold Froncum,   Þyle Rondingum,
      Breoca Brondingum,   Billing Wernum;
      Oswine weold Eowum   ond Ytum Gefwulf,
27 Fin Folcwalding   Fresna cynne;
      Sigehere lengest   Sædenum weold,
      Hnæf Hocingum,   Helm Wulfingum,
30 Wald Woingum,   Wod Þyringum,
      Sæferð Sycgum,   Sweom Ongendþeow,
      Sceafthere Ymbrum,   Sceafa Longbeardum,

---

  2 *monna*] Supp. ed. MS *mærþa*.
  3 *on*] Supp. ed.
  14 MS *wala*.
  21 MS *holm rycum*.

WIDSITH

33 Hun Hætwerum ond Holen Wrosnum;
Hringweald wæs haten Herefarena cyning,
Offa weold Ongle, Alewih Denum
36 se wæs þara manna modgast ealra,
no hwæþre he ofer Offan eorlscype fremede,
ac Offa geslog ærest monna,
39 cnihtwesende cynerica mæst;
nænig efeneald him eorlscipe maran
onorette: ane sweorde
42 merce gemærde wið Myrgingum
bi Fifeldore; heoldon forð siþþan
Engle ond Swæfe swa hit Offa geslog;
45 Hroþwulf ond Hroðgar heoldon lengest
sibbe / ætsomne suhtorfædran   85^v
siþþan hy forwræcon Wicinga cynn
48 ond Ingeldes ord forbigdan,
forheowan æt Heorote Heaðobeardna þrym.
   Swa ic geondferde fela fremdra londa
51 geond ginne grund, godes ond yfles
þær ic cunnade, cnosle bidæled,
freomægum feor folgade wide;
54 forþon ic mæg singan ond secgan spell,
mænan fore mengo in meoduhealle
hu me cynegode cystum dohten.
57   Ic wæs mid Hunum ond mid Hreðgotum,
mid Sweom ond mid Geatum ond mid Suþdenum,
mid Wenlum ic wæs ond mid Wærnum ond mid Wicingum,
60 mid Gefþum ic wæs ond mid Winedum ond mid Gefflegum,
mid Englum ic wæs ond mid Swæfum ond mid Ænenum,
mid Seaxum ic wæs ond [mid] Sycgum ond mid Sweordwerum,
63 mid Hronum ic wæs ond mid Deanum ond mid Heoþoreamum,
mid Þyringum ic wæs ond mid Þrowendum
ond mid Burgendum: þær ic beag geþah,
66 me þær Guðhere forgeaf glædlicne maþþum
songes to leane - næs þæt sæne cyning;
mid Froncum ic wæs ond mid Frysum ond mid Frumtingum,
69 mid Rugum ic wæs ond mid Glommum ond mid Rumwalum;
swylce ic wæs on Eatule mid Ælfwine:

---
62 *mid*] Supp. ed.
65 MS *geþeah*.

LEOÐ

```
         se hæfde moncynnes,   mine gefræge,
72   leohteste hond   lofes to wyrcenne,
     heortan unhneaweste   hringa gedales, /                86ʳ
     beorhtra beaga,   bearn Eadwines;
75   mid Sercingum ic wæs   ond mid Seringum,
     mid Creacum ic wæs ond mid Finnum   ond mid Casere
     se þe winburga   geweald ahte
78   wiolena ond wilna   ond Wala rices;
     mid Scottum ic wæs ond mid Peohtum   ond mid Scridefinnum,
     mid Lidingum ic wæs ond mid Leonum   ond mid Longbeardum,
81   mid Hæðnum ond mid Hæleþum   ond mid Hundingum,
     mid Israhelum ic wæs   ond mid Exsyringum,
     mid Ebreum ond mid Indeum   ond mid Egyptum,
84   mid Moidum ic wæs ond mid Persum   ond mid Myrgingum,
     [mid] Ongendmyrgingum   ond mid Amothingum,
     mid Eastþyringum ic wæs   ond m[id] Ofdingum,
87   mid Eolum ond mid Istum   ond [mid] Idumingum;
     ond ic wæs mid Eormanrice   ealle þrage:
     þær me Gotena cyning   gode dohte,
90   se me beag forgeaf   burgwarena fruma,
     on þam siex hund wæs   smætes goldes
     gescyred sceatta   scillingrime;
93   þone ic Eadgilse   on æht sealde
     minum hleodryhtne   þa ic to ham bicwom,
     leofum to leane   þæs þe he me lond forgeaf,
96   mines fæder eþel,   frea Myrginga;
     ond me þa Ealhhild   oþerne forgeaf
     dryhtcwen duguþe,   dohtor Eadwines -
99   hyre lof lengde   geond londa fela
     þonne ic be songe   secgan sceolde
     hwær ic under swegl[e]   selast wisse
102  goldhrodene cwen /   giefe bryttian;                   86ᵛ
     ðon[ne] wit Scilling   sciran reorde
     for uncrum sigedryhtne   song ahofan,
105  hlude bi hearpan   hleoþor swinsade,
```

---
78   MS *wiolane*.
80   MS *lidwicingum*.
85   See *Commentary* for a discussion of the rearrangement of the next three lines.
101 MS *swegl*.
103 MS *don*.

WIDSITH

    þonne monige men   modum wlonce
    wordum sprecan   - þa þe wel cuþan -
108 þæt hi næfre song   sellan ne hyrdon.
    Đonan ic ealne geondhwearf   eþel Gotena,
    sohte ic a [ge]siþa   þa selestan -
111 þæt wæs innweorud   Earmanrices;
    Hehcan sohte ic ond Beadecan   ond Herelingas,
    Emercan sohte ic ond Fridlan   ond Eastgotan
114 frodne ond godne   fæder Unwenes,
    Seccan sohte ic ond Beccan,   Seafolan ond Þeodric,
    Heaþoric ond Sifecan,   Hliþe ond Incgenþeow,
117 Eadwine sohte ic ond Elsan,   Ægelmund ond Hungar
    ond þa wloncan gedryht   Wiþmyrginga;
    Wulfhere sohte ic ond Wyrmhere: ful oft þær wig ne alæg
120 þonne Hræda here   heardum sweordum
    ymb Wistla wudu   wergan sceoldon
    ealdne eþelstol   Ætlan leodum;
123 Rædhere sohte ic ond Rondhere,   Rumstan ond Gislhere,
    Wiþergield ond Freoþeric,   Wudgan ond Haman -
    ne wæran þæt gesiþa   þa sæmestan
126 þeah þe ic hy a nihst   nemnan sceolde:
    ful oft of þam heape   hwinende fleag,
    giellende gar   on grome þeode;
129 wræccan þær weoldan   wundnan golde,
    werum ond wifum,   Wudga ond Hama.
    Swa ic þæt symle onfond / on þære feringe   87[r]
132 þæt se biþ leofast   londbuendum
    se þe him God syleð   gumena rice
    to gehealdenne   þenden he her leofað."
135   Swa scriþende   gesceapum hweorfað
    gleomen gumena   geond grunda fela,
    þearfe secgað,   þoncword sprecaþ,
138 simle suð oþþe norð   sumne gemetað
    gydda gleawne,   geofum unhneawne
    se þe fore duguþe wile   dom aræran,
141 eorlscipe æfnan   oþþæt eal scæceð,
    leoht ond lif somod;   lof se gewyrceð,
    hafað under heofonum   heahfæstne dom.

---
110 MS *siþa*.
112 MS *heðcan*.

COMMENTARY

1 Howlett observes that the structure of *Widsith* "can scarcely be perceived from oral recitation, though it is obvious on a written page", that though it "may preserve the most ancient lines of English verse, the present shape of the poem (except four lines) is probably the work of a single literate man" (1974, 510).

Malone argues that the *Widsith* poet based his poem on the three pre-existing thulas, reworking these and incorporating episodic passages into them; this largely ignores the fact that only the first of these thulas retains what was probably its original structure. In the second and the third the poet uses the verbs *wæs* and *sohte* (respectively) with the pronoun *ic*, thus subjectifying and specifying the material in the lists, and reshaping their content to meet his predetermined needs. Howe suggests "the poet recast the historical material he found in the source thulas in such a way as to accommodate these two verbs" (1985, 172). [The possibility that many of the 'proper names' in the poem may have little or no significance adds weight to this argument; see 18 note and 62 note.] It is also apparent from Howe's research that critical discussions of this poem and *Deor* must take into account the fact that they are catalogue poems.

maðolade: Robinson examines how the *Beowulf* poet rejuvenates this word semantically by first using its root *mæðel* in the compound *meþelwordum* (236b) and later in the poem by defining it: *Wealhðeo maþelode, heo fore þæm werede spræc* (1215) and *Wiglaf maðelode, wordrihta fela / sægde gesiðum* (2631-32a) (1985, 66-67).

It seems as if the *Widsith* poet shares the same awareness of the etymology of this word and intends his poem to be a formal exposition of the art and powers of poetry and the function of the poet in society. The use of this word in conjunction with the off-verse *wordhord onleac* may be of even more significance given that it occurs only once in *Beowulf*, in the narrator's first introduction of the hero of the poem (259b); later in the poem, after Beowulf has shown his ability to fulfil his *beot*, Hrothgar refers to him as *wis wordcwida* (1845a), suggesting that an awareness of the power of speech and of the responsibilities inherent in undertaking a social obligation (through the utterance of a *beot*) are characteristics of a hero. For further argument to this effect, see Howe (1985, 173).

In light of this evidence, it should be noted that the first recorded speeches of Waldere, Byrhtnoth, and Byrhtwold are all introduced by *maþelode* (at 3.43, 6.42 and 6.309 respectively); however, that these poems are both fragments must also be borne in mind when considering these as 'first' speeches.

2 *monna*: [Grein]; some early editors supplied a verb to complete the sense of the line (see Krapp and Dobbie, *EB* p. 300, for details).

mægþa: [Kemble]; but cf. *Beowulf* 2645 *forðam he manna mæst mærða gefremede* and *Seafarer* 84 *þonne hi mæst mid him mærþa gefremede*; see also Creed's discussion of this emendation in which he struggles to justify retaining the MS reading. Creed (who has an interest in the performance of Anglo-Saxon poetry) prefers a defective line 2a because it allows him time for an extra stroke on his lyre (1975, 386). The emendation is accepted here because it makes better sense than the original reading; it is easy to see how the scribe might have unconsciously substituted *mærþa* for the proposed *mægþa* since the analogues cited suggest the influence of a traditional formula here.

4b-5a In introducing speeches, Anglo-Saxon poets customarily give the speaker's lineage (this seems even more important than revealing his name) and, if the speech is made in the context of confrontation, it is preceded by some form of brandishing of weapons. For the formula expressing Widsith's inherent nobility, cf. 5.6b-7a. In his discussion of the symbolic language of Old English poetry, Clemoes observes with reference to the epithets used for Wiglaf in *Beowulf*, "Information such as what training in wielding a sword Wiglaf had received is not worthy of mention: what really matters is his revelation of innate 'ellen,' 'cræft' and 'cenðu'" (1986, 6; and see also pages 8-9).

5 *mid Ealhhilde*: The queen is to be understood to be with Eormanric, not Widsith; see Malone (1962, 140-41).

6 *freoþuwebban*: See 45-48 note.

forman siþe: "to start with"; cf. 4.19, *Beowulf* 740b and 2268b, which are identical, indicating the formulaic nature of this verse.

7-9 Malone is at pains to reconcile the apparently contradictory characterizations of Eormanric in the poem, as *wraþes wærlogan* ('hostile pledge-breaker') here and as an ideal king below, 88-92 (1962, 29-35); Fry demonstrates that there is no contradiction if it is recognized that "the poet and his fictional *scop* Widsith speak in different voices, varying their estimates of Ermanric" (1980,39). Malone understands the *-an* suffix to be a reduced dative plural for usual *-um*, and translates "foe to traitors" (1962, 33). Compare *Beowulf* 2847a where *treowlogan* describes Beowulf's followers who failed to support him in his greatest need; (*wraþes*) *wærlogan*, a close analogue for the *Beowulf* reading (if not synonymous) is reserved exclusively for the Devil elsewhere.

It should be noted that *Deor* refers to Eormanric as *grim cyning* (2.23b), and to his *wylfenne geþoht* (2.22a), which is consistent with the pejorative interpretation of *wraþes wærlogan*; see also *Beowulf* 1197-1201 which refer to the *searoniðas* ('treacherous hostilities') of Eormanric.

10 Fry's interpretation of this passage, which first adopts a hypothetical reading (in this case *monna* of line 2) and then uses this as part of his premiss for further argument (1980, 40 and note 12), should be regarded with some scepticism.

ic . . . gefrægn: Chambers regards this as "an epic formula with little meaning" (1912, 127-28); however, Howe is probably closer to the truth in assessing the poet's use of this traditional formula in this instance:

> Since the speaker claims no personal knowledge of those he names through l. 49, he could know of them only by having heard of them, probably from other poets. For this reason, *ic gefrægn* has the power here of literal statement; it is the speaker's candid acknowledgement for the sources of his knowledge. (1985, 175)

See also 50-56 note.

11-13 As stated in the Introduction, this seems to be either a maxim or some sort of traditional gnomic utterance; in *Beowulf*, there are a number of references to living properly according to tradition, eg:

> Ic þæt leode wat
> ge wið feond ge wið freond fæste geworhte,
> æghwæs untæle ealde wisan (1863b-65)

> [I know that people to be steadfast to both foe and friend, in every way blameless in the traditional manner];

and,

Swa se ðeodkyning þeawum lyfde (2144)

[Thus the people's king lived according to custom].

Note also 359b (*cuþe he duguðe þeaw*) and 613b (*cynna gemyndig*). Structurally, 10-13 are parallel to 131-34, also a reflection on kingship, a central theme of this poem.

Gnomic utterances, often in the form of a maxim, pervade Anglo-Saxon literature, and are especially common in *Beowulf*; eg,

Fela sceal gebidan
leofes and laþes se þe longe her
on ðissum windagum worolde bruceð (1060b-62)

[He who partakes of this worldly life here in these days of strife must endure a great deal of both desirable and unwanted experiences].

14-17 Malone rejects these lines along with 82 on the grounds that 15 and 82 share the same unusual vocalic alliteration, and because they are not concerned with Germanic legend or history. Such a mingling of Germanic and classical or Christian references, however, was a commonplace in Christian Anglo-Saxon England; see Fry (1980) 40-42. The so-called Franks Casket, which, interestingly, Malone discusses with reference to the date of *Widsith* (1968), is an example of such thematic integration. It should also be noted that the exact significance of the apposition of certain scenes on the casket (a three dimensional text) has not yet been determined.

18 Discussing the three thulas incorporated in *Widsith*, Hill argues that many names cited have little or no significance in surviving Germanic legend cycles, and that by the tenth century when the poem was recorded in its present form by the compiler of the *Exeter Book* "part of the poem's appeal lay in the total impression created by the catalogues" (1984, 305). She supposes it was anthologized because of its encyclopaedic nature, whereas Rollman argues that it is best understood as an 'ars poetica' and that its display of erudition illustrates one of the three vital functions of poetry, the didactic (see Introduction, note 15).

Hill further argues that whether the names were factual or fictional was not the point; it was the overall effect of such apparently comprehensive lists, reflecting the tremendous erudition of the poet, that was important. Even when first composed, the catalogues must have been "impressionistic":

> The accumulative effect of the catalogues in creating a general sense of a wealth of legendary matter as a background to the main stories remains the same, at a time when fewer of the allusions may be understood. (1984, 313)

The episodes celebrating certain kings and heroes in detail throughout *Widsith* (such as Offa, Eormanric, Wudga and Hama) illustrate how the other characters listed in the thulas in which they appear were to be regarded (even if nothing more was known of them than their names).

21 *holmrycgum*: [Grimm].

24-48 It is remarkable how many of the kings and tribes mentioned here also appear in *Beowulf;* in the following alphabetically arranged list the first number refers to the first mention of the name in *Widsith* and the second to its first appearance in *Beowulf* (forms followed by an asterisk are common to both, but do not designate the same person / tribe):

> Breoca 25-506; Brondings 25-521; Danes 35-(throughout *Beowulf* in various compounds); Eadgils* 93-2392; Eormanric 8-1201; Finn 27-1068; Finns 20-580; Folcwalda 27-1089; Franks 24-1210; Frisians 27-1093; Geats 58-205; Gibids 60-2494; Hætwere 33-2363; Hama 130-1198; Heathobards 49-2032; Heathoræmas 63-519; Helm 29-620 (Helming); Hnæf 29-1069; Hocings 29-1076 (Hoc); Hrothgar 45-61; Hrothwulf 45-1017; Ingeld 48-2064; Jutes 26-1072; Offa 35-1949; Ongendtheow 116-1968; Sceafa* 32-4 (Scefing); Swedes 31-2472; Wendlas 59-348; Withergield 124-2051;

see Campbell's discussion of the *Beowulf* poet's use of earlier heroic verse (1971).

26 *Eowum*: Bliss (1985) attempts to account for this difficult form; the complexity of his argument is a disturbing reminder of how much work still remains to be done on the many names in this poem. See 62 note for further discussion of this point.

35 *Beowulf* alludes to the story of the famous continental king of the Angles, Offa, and his queen, Modþryð (1931-62). The possibility that this Offa is praised in order to allow his descendant, the eighth century insular Anglian king Offa, to participate in his glory has been entertained and rehearsed on many occasions. The inference is

that *Beowulf* was perhaps written during the eighth century at the court of the English king, who is thus being praised indirectly. Though this is quite plausible, it obviously cannot be advanced as anything more than conjecture.

37 *eorlscipe*: This word, and others of similar formation (like *dryhtscipe* or *dryhtlice*), appear to be very important and meaningful in Anglo-Saxon verse. It is used here again at 40b and 141a, and appears throughout *Beowulf*, often in the phrase *eorlscipe æfnan*. *Eorlscipe* seems to offer a characterization of all those accomplishments and qualities deemed desirable in an *eorl*. That this and other words denoting rank are important is indicated by the fact that the *Beowulf* poet on two occasions explicitly defines them with reference to his characters and their behaviour:

> Dead is Æschere,
> Yrmenlafes yldra broþor,
> min runwita ond min rædbora,
> eaxlgestealla, ðonne we on orlege
> hafelan weredon, þonne hniton feþan,
> eoferas cnysedan. Swy(lc) scolde eorl wesan
> [æþeling] ærgod, swylc Æschere wæs.
> (1323b-29)

[Æschere, the older brother of Yrmenlaf is dead, my secret advisor and my counsellor, my close companion at arms, when we protected our lives in battle, when footsoldiers clashed together and struck upon boar-helmets. Such ought an *eorl* to be, a prince proven of old, such was Æschere]

and,

> Feond gefyldan -ferh ellen wræc-
> ond hi hyne þa begen abroten hæfdon,
> sibæðelingas; swylc sceolde secg wesan,
> þegn æt þearfe. (2706-09a)

[They had felled the enemy — their valorous deed drove out his life — and they both together, princely relations, had destroyed him; such (as Wiglaf) ought a *secg* to be, a thane in time of need].

It is noteworthy that both of these are formulated like maxims or gnomic utterances. At 6.289-94, the *Maldon* poet defines *ðegenlice*. See also 4.13 note on *ðegn*.

38-44 Short episodes in Anglo-Saxon poetry (as here) often seem to begin and close with the name of the character (or some equivalent term), in this instance Offa (38 and 44). This is referred to here as a 'framing device'. The poet uses it again in 70-74, 93-96, and in the Wudga and Hama episode (124b-130). Among the other poems edited here, it is also found at: i) 3.6-11 (where Waldere is not referred to by name at all, but as *Ætlan ordwyga* (6a) and *Ælfheres sunu* (11b)); and ii) 5.1-7 (where the king and prince are referred to individually by name at the opening, and collectively as *afaran Eadweardes* (7a) at the close). In *Beowulf*, an example is found in Hrothgar's speech as he gazes upon Grendel's grip (928-56), where *Alwealda* appears at the beginning and the end. Such use of a framing device might be regarded technically as a form of epanalepsis.

41 *onorette*: Malone glosses this 'win, achieve by fighting' after Bosworth-Toller. Robinson examines the etymological force of the words *oretta* and *oretmecg* which are derived from the root **or-hat* (related to *hatan* ('vow, promise, be called') in *Beowulf*, and suggests that it is probably used consciously by the poet to designate a "man of the ultimate (or primal) vow" (1985, 67); additional aspects of the character of Offa and the exact nature of the *eorlscipe* he embodies are suggested here if he is understood to be a man who makes such a boast and performs it better than any of his contemporaries.

45-48 As is known from Scandinavian sources and *Beowulf*, Hrothgar was Hrothulf's uncle (hence *suhtorgefædran*). The feud with the Heathobards alluded to here arose after Ingeld's father, Froda, was killed in a clash with the Saxons (the nationalities of the two parties are confused in the sources); Ingeld was given the hand of a Saxon princess in an attempt to avert revenge being sought by her brothers. In the end, Ingeld is egged on to avenge his father by an old companion (much as Hengest is in *Beowulf* 1136b-45), and he kills his father's murderers, including his wife's brothers. Note that there is no suggestion here, as there is in *Beowulf* (81b-85), that Heorot was destroyed by flames during the course of this feud.

In Germanic lore, there are many examples of politically contracted marriages which failed; a few of them are alluded to in the poems edited here: Hrothulf, who ultimately overthrew Hrothgar's heir (and his cousin), Hrethric, is the product of a marriage between Healfdene's daughter Yrse (?) and the Swede Onela. The woman involved in the relationship is often known as a 'peace-weaver', or some equivalent term, as Ealhhild is in *Widsith* (*freoþuwebban*, 6) and Wealhtheow in *Beowulf* (1942a). Beowulf himself is sceptical about the likely success of such marriages (*Beowulf* 2057-69a), and Hildeburh's tragic story is also told in the epic (1068-1159a) as a further example of the doomed nature of such enterprises; it is noteworthy that the so-called Finnsburh Episode in *Beowulf* is framed by allusions to the future treacherous activities of Hrothulf (see 1013-19 and 1162b-65a). Anderson's analysis (1980) of the type-scene he calls 'tragic court flyting' is of interest here since there he discusses the breakdown of political marriages arranged to settle feuds or confirm treaties in Germanic literature. In the two instances of this type-scene in *Beowulf*, hostilities are renewed after a "particularly provocative weapon" which brings to mind an old feud (or which anticipates it as in the second instance as Creed notes (1980, 298)) is placed on someone's lap (see 1142-44 and 2029b-31).

48 *Ingeldes ord*: Cf. 6.69, *Eastseaxena ord*.

50-56 The poet relates how he has learned many things by asking and listening (10a, 17b) and then learned others through his own experiences while travelling widely; cf. *Beowulf* 2105b-06 (*Gomela Scilding / fela fricgende, feorran rehte*) and 867b-870a (*Hwilum cyninges þegn / guma gilphlæden, gidda gemyndig, / se ðe ealfela ealdgesegena / worn gemunde*). That this is the central theme of *Widsith* is argued at length by Howe (1985). As Howe notes,

> In his use of *ic*, the poet maintains a strict integrity of voice; for it is surely deliberate that *ic* should appear but once through l. 49 and should then be littered throughout the remainder of the poem. Widsith has earned his right to personal statement because he has demonstrated his historical knowledge. (1985, 180)

51b-53 A number of so-called elegiac and wisdom poems in the *Exeter Book* contain the (not exclusively or necessarily Boethian) reflection that each man must experience reversals and changes of fortune during his life (eg, 2.28-34 below; see also *Beowulf* 1060b-62 quoted above, 11-13 note). The vocabulary used here to explore this theme is characteristic of these elegies, as might be expected (see Greenfield, 1955). It should be noted that the narrator says that experiencing such reversals is a fundamental constituent element of his development as a poet (. . . *forþon ic mæg singan ond secgan spell . . .*, 54); he can function now as a poet only because of these experiences.

62 *sweordwerum*: Chambers-Malone are followed here in identifying this tribe with the *Suardones* of Tacitus. Hill is right to suggest that such words can also be understood simply as common nouns (ie, 'swordsmen'; cf. *hæðnum* 'heathens' and *hælebum* 'heroes' in 81), and the possibility that this is the case in *Widsith* should be considered by critics. If such is the case, then the thulas contain much more contamination and reworking than has been recognized by earlier critics.

75 It is possible that the same tribe is mentioned twice in this line; see Hill's summary of the critical literature on this (1984, 308-09). Latin *Seres/Serae* in post-classical times was applied to Central Asia, not the far East as earlier.

78 *wiolena*: [first taken as 'riches' by Rieger; before him, MS *wiolane* was understood to be a proper name.].

79 *Scridefinnum*: These are the *Scrithiphini* of Procopius' *History of the Wars of Justinian* (6.15.16-26), and the *Scritobini* of Paulus Diaconus' *History of the Langobards*; for further discussion of this and other early references to the Lapps, see Whitaker (1982, 602-03). They are called the 'sliding-Finns' because of their use of skis.

85-87 These lines, which depart so radically from the pattern of the thula in the manuscript, yet suggest they were once in the same pattern as those around them, are obviously corrupt. They are left to stand in Krapp and Dobbie (1936), but are rearranged and emended here following Malone (1962). The MS reads,

> ... *ond* mofdingum *ond* ongend myrgingum and mid amothingum mid eastþyringum ic wæs *ond* mid eolum *ond* mid istum *ond* idumingum ...

91-92 "in which there was 600 coins worth of pure gold, counted by shillings."

93-96 Cf. *Beowulf* 2490-91:

> Ic him þa maðmas, þe he me sealde,
> gealde æt guðe, swa me gifeðe wæs ...

[I repaid him (Hygelac) in battle for the treasures he had given me, as it was granted me];

Robinson observes that these lines state "in clearest possible terms the contractual importance of accepting royal generosity" (1985, 75).

Beowulf also received ancestral lands as reward for his dutifully heroic behaviour (*lond gecynde, / eard eðelriht* 2197b-98a), and later in the poem Wiglaf predicts that now that their lord is dead each of the Geats will be deprived of his *londriht* (2886b) by their enemies. Note that Deor was stripped of his right to this (*londrhyt* 2.40) when he fell from his lord's favour.

103 *scilling*: This may be the name of Widsith's partner in a duet performance (Malone, 50 and 194) or the name of his harp (Sedgefield, 1931, 75; cf. *scyl wæs hearpe* in *Riming Poem*, 27b); as Opland notes, "there seems no way of conclusively resolving the crux" (1980, 211). Fry notes that it is "probably an ironic pun tc remind us of the *scop*'s primary motivation" (1980, 44).

110 *gesiþa*: [Ettmüller]; cf. 125.

112 *hehcan*: [Malone].

124 *Wudga*: (Widia) A famous adventurer in Germanic lore; see 2.1-13 note and 3.36-42.

129 *wræccan*: In this context, 'adventurers' rather than 'exiles'; cf. the reference to Sigemund in *Beowulf*:

> Se wæs wreccena wide mærost
> ofer werþeode, wigendra hleo,
> ellendædum . . . (898-900a)

[He, the protector of warriors, was the most widely renowned among the nations of men for his deeds of valour];

and see also 4.25.

134 *þenden he her leofað*: The opposition between life here in this world, as stressed by the metre here (*her* alliterates with *gehealdenne* in the a-verse) and life in the next world is a commonplace in Anglo-Saxon literature, often expressed formulaically; cf. 2.31 and *Christ III* 1574b, *þenden her leofað*. This opposition is stressed again by *under heofonum*, 143 (see note).

135-43 Both *Widsith* and *Beowulf* celebrate the heroic life in this world to some extent. However, Robinson demonstrates that the *Beowulf* poet regarded the condition and aims of his heroic characters as admirable (note line 1865, "in every way blameless according to the ancient way") but hopeless because they lived in pre-Christian times, and so in spite of how well any of them lived he could not be saved — something essential for the poet and his audience (1985, 7-

10 *et passim*). Fry observes the same thing with regard to *Widsith*, noting the difference between the voice of the poet and of his fictional character Widsith, the latter exulting in the joys of heroic life while the former reminds the reader / listener of the larger scheme of man's universe, that secular affairs are transacted *under heofonum*, and that these are transitory compared with the stability to be found in heaven; cf. *Wanderer* 106-115, and see Fry 1980, 46-52.

137 *þearfe secgað*: This phrase has a number of possible meanings, "speaking out of need" being, it would appear, the least consonant with the general argument of the poem which is concerned with the function and power of poetry and the role of the poet (see Rollman, 1982, and note 15 to the Introduction here); either Malone's "say what is needful" or Rollman's "they address a need" is probably closer to what is meant.

140 As indicated above (135-43 note), Anglo-Saxon poets acknowledge the value of the earthly heroic life (though there is some indication that they feel its ethos and aims inadequate ultimately for Christians). The chief goal of the characters in such poems is the attainment of enduring fame and reputation in this world. Hrothgar says to Beowulf,

> Þu þe self hafast
> dædum gefremed, þæt þin [dom] lyfað
> awa to aldre (953b-55a)

[You yourself have ensured by your deeds that your glory will endure forever];

although this citation supplies the key word by means of emendation, Beowulf's own words to Hrothgar later in the poem confirm that the emendation — which conforms to normal alliterative patterns — is a good and reasonable offering, and in the spirit of the poetry:

> Ne sorga, snotor guma. Selre bið æghwæm
> þæt he his freond wrece, þonne he fela murne.
> Ure æghwylc sceal ende gebidan
> worolde lifes; wyrce se þe mote
> domes ær deaþe; þæt bið drihtguman
> unlifgendum æfter selest (1384-89)

[Sorrow not, wise man. It is better for each man to avenge his friend than to mourn inordinately. Each of us must await the end of this worldly life; let him who has the opportunity achieve glory before his death; that is the best thing for a dead retainer afterwards].

(*se þe mote* is essential to the overall interpretation of the poem, and could also be translated '(let) him who can' or '(let) him who is allowed', the latter being more consonant with the narrator's point of view than with Beowulf's. See 3.57-61 note and Robinson, 1985.)

Among the poems presented here, similar sentiments are expressed at 3.8b-11 and 6.127-29, and encapsulated by the *Maldon* poet in the words, *Þa wæs feohte neh, / tir æt getohte* (103b-04a). In this context, it should be noted that Wiglaf describes the disgraceful flight of Beowulf's retainers as *domleasan dæd* (2890a), and that the narrator remarks that Unferth forsook the opportunity to win enduring fame through deeds of valour by not risking his life beneath the waves of the mere:

> selfa ne dorste
> under yða gewin aldre geneþan,
> drihtscype dreogan; þær he dome forleas,
> ellenmærþum (1468b-71a)

[He himself did not dare to risk his life, to act in a lordly manner, beneath the tossing of the waves; in that he abandoned his reputation concerning notable deeds of valour].

142b-43 A glance at the many translations proffered for these lines reveals their elusiveness: does the *se* refer to the leader *gydda gleawne* (139a) or to the poet? Or is it a maxim or gnomic utterance referring to any king or poet (both the concerns of the poem) who wishes to earn the praise of others?

Howe observes,

> In return for drawing so prodigiously on his poetic and historical reserves, the poet offers the gift of *lof* and *dom*. When light and life together depart, he reminds us, all that remains is the collective memory of the culture as it is held by the poet. As the final stay against oblivion, the poet earns the earthly rewards he receives, but he earns them as historian and not as court-flatterer (1985, 188).

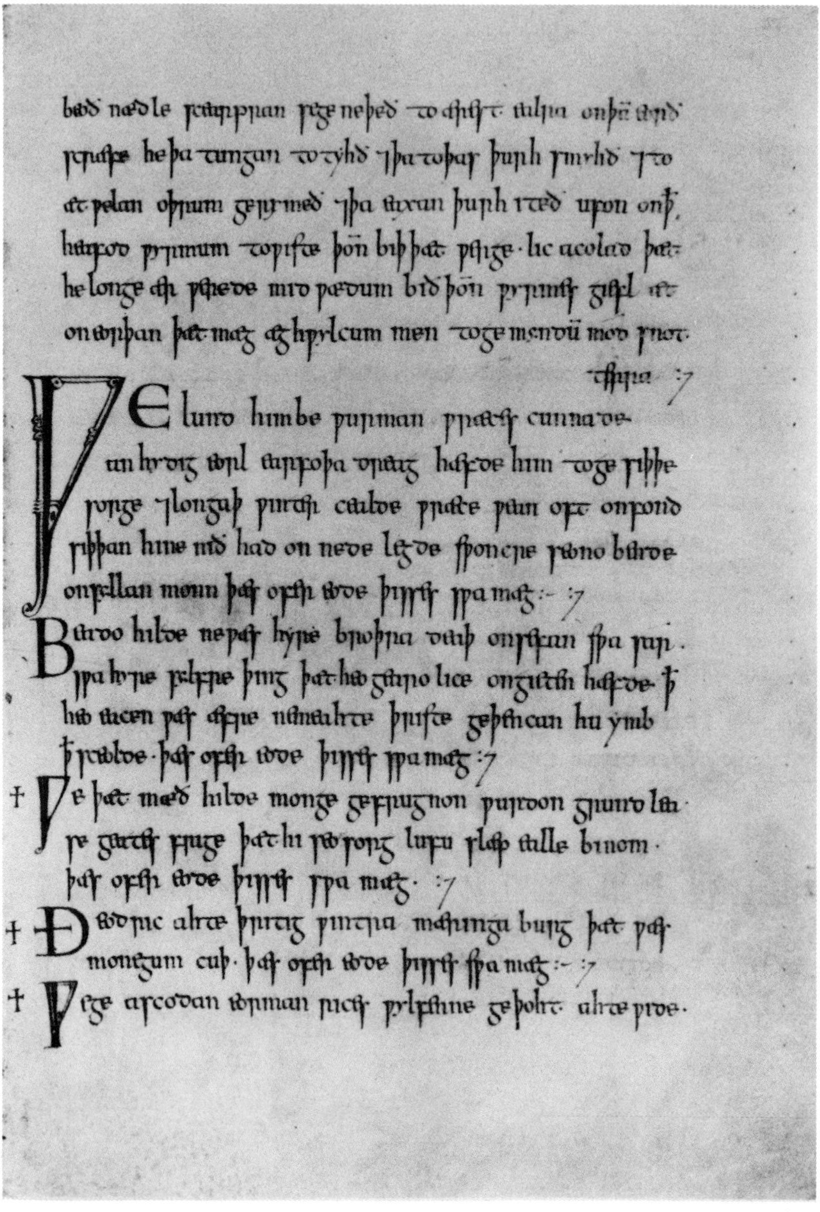
on worþan þæt mæg æghwylcum men to ge mendū mod snot-
tera :7
WElund him be wurman wræces cunnade
anhydig eorl earfoþa dreag hæfde him to gesiþþe
sorge ond longaþ wintercealde wræce wean oft onfond
siþþan hine niðhad on nede legde swoncre seonobende
onsyllan monn þæs ofereode þisses swa mæg :- :7
Beadohilde ne wæs hyre broþra deaþ on sefan swa sar
swa hyre sylfre þing þæt heo gearolice ongieten hæfde þæt
heo eacen wæs æfre ne meahte þriste geþencan hu ymb
þæt sceolde· þæs ofereode þisses swa mæg :7
We þæt mæðhilde monge gefrugnon wurdon grundlea·
se geates frige þæt hi seo sorglufu slæp ealle binom·
þæs ofereode þisses swa mæg· :7
Ðeodric ahte þritig wintra mæringa burg þæt wæs
monegum cuþ· þæs ofereode þisses swa mæg :- :7
We geascodan eormanrices wylfenne geþoht ahte wide·

PLATE 2 Exeter, Dean and Chapter MS 3501, 100r. Lines 1-22 of *Deor*.

TWO: DEOR

INTRODUCTION

Manuscript

The Library of the Dean and Chapter, Exeter Cathedral, MS 3501; see the Introduction to *Widsith* for details concerning this manuscript.

Text

The poem has no title in the codex, but is today generally referred to as *Deor* after the name of the poet who is its narrator;[1] its edited length is 42 lines. It appears in the thirteenth gathering (ff 98-105) on ff 100^{r-v}, following *Soul and Body II* and preceding *Wulf and Eadwacer*; the text is undamaged.

Structure, theme and genre: *Deor* consists of six stanzas of varying length, each of which is clearly distinguished from the others in the MS by punctuation, capitalization and spacing. Each of these stanzas is followed by the refrain *Þæs ofereode, þisses swa mæg*. The use of stanzas regularly marked by a refrain is unique in Anglo-Saxon literature; only one other poem, *Wulf and Eadwacer*, also in the

---

[1] The poem begins with an angular, modestly decorated, capital *wynn* 6 spaces in height followed by a 2-space high 'e'; the rest of the line consists of letters of normal size. Each of the remaining stanzas begins with a lightly decorated 2-space high capital letter, those for the second to fourth stanzas having a cross in the margin to the left of them; see Plates 2 and 3.

Exeter Book and, interestingly, following *Deor* directly, has a line repeated as a refrain (*Ungelic is us*).

The subjects of the first five stanzas are, i) the hamstringing of Weland and his revenge; ii) the troublesome pregnancy of Beadohild (part of Weland's revenge); iii) the ill-starred love of Mæthhild and Geat; iv) the reign of Theodoric; and v) the tyrannical reign of Eormanric. In the sixth stanza, the poet reflects upon fate, providence, and the unforeseeable reversals man is subject to in this life, and how this can be reconciled with an acceptance of God's prescience. He then discloses a reversal he himself has suffered as a professional poet (*scop*).

The readings of this poem have been varied and manifold. Contextually, it is associated with *Wulf and Eadwacer*, surely the most enigmatic poem surviving from the Anglo-Saxon period, which is followed by the first group of riddles, and sometimes associated with them. It has been read as a list of examples drawn from Germanic history and lore of the misfortunes suffered by others in this world, a pattern into which the poet sees his own life falling (one of the early titles of the poem, 'Deor's Lament', registers acceptance of the reading of the poem as pessimistic). Another has discerned a philosophical optimism in the refrain indicating that, although the poet sees himself as just another victim of fate or of the sometimes mysterious way in which God intervenes in man's world, he expects better things in the future, or at least entertains the possibility that a subsequent, equally unpredictable, reversal will improve his lot. Another has noted that although these episodes at first appear to be examples of misfortune, when they are examined more closely in context, it becomes apparent that most of the crises alluded to were ultimately resolved and worked out for the better; for example, Beadohild, who was raped by Weland, bore a son named Widia who became a famous hero, and thus a source of consolation for her earlier grief. (Widia also appears in *Widsith* and *Waldere* among the poems edited here). Another sees it as a begging poem by a professional Anglo-Saxon poet. Its structural resemblance to an Anglo-Saxon charm has been investigated. Needless to say, the probable influence of Boethius' *Consolation of Philosophy* on it has also been noted.[2]

---

[2] See the Commentary (§ 1) for an indication of which critics have advanced these views, and for cross-references to the Bibliography.

Deor has much in common with *Widsith*: both are apparently written by poets who are interested in discussing poetry and the poet and his role in society; both treat of Germanic history and lore in an elliptical manner which assumes a wide knowledge of traditional material on the part of the audience; both have perceivable structural principles; both are monologues; and both are concerned with speculation on man's role in his world and the impact of fate and providence on him.

Language: *Deor* is written for the most part in the West-Saxon dialect. Some non-West-Saxon forms are:

Anglian
> *heodeninga* (36), and the unsyncopated verbal forms of the 3 sg pres ind (*siteð* (28), *sweorceð* (29), *þinceð* (29), *wendeþ* (32)).

These and the few other traces of forms possibly not West-Saxon that Malone and others discern do not argue convincingly for an earlier Anglian or Kentish version of the poem, as Malone readily concedes (1977, 18-19).

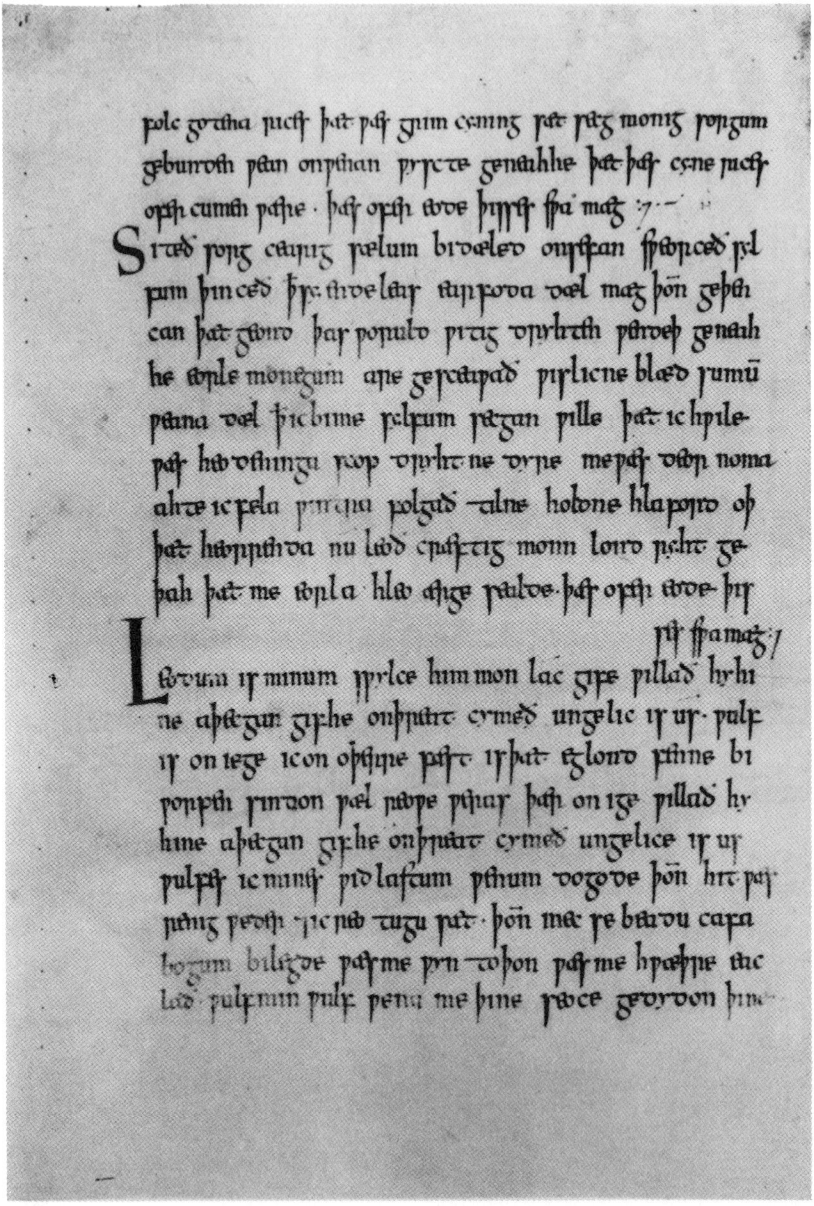

PLATE 3 Exeter, Dean and Chapter MS 3501, 100ᵛ. Lines 22-42 of *Deor*.

DEOR

     Welund him be wurman   wræces cunnade,   100ʳ
     anhydig eorl   earfoþa dreag,
  3 hæfde him to gesiþþe   sorge ond longaþ,
     wintercealde wræce,   wean oft onfond
     siþþan hine Niðhad   on nede legde,
  6 swoncre seonobende   on syllan monn.
           Þæs ofereode,   þisses swa mæg.

     Beadohilde ne wæs   hyre broþra deaþ
  9 on sefan swa sar   swa hyre sylfre þing -
     þæt heo gearolice   ongieten hæfde
     þæt heo eacen wæs;   æfre ne meahte
 12 þriste geþencan   hu ymb þæt sceolde.
           Þæs ofereode,   þisses swa mæg.

     We þæt Mæðhilde   monge frugnon:
 15 wurdon grundlease   Geates frige
     þæt hi[m] seo sorglufu   slæp ealle binom.
           Þæs ofereode,   þisses swa mæg.

 18 Ðeodric ahte   þritig wintra
     Mæringa burg -   þæt wæs monegum cuþ.
           Þæs ofereode,   þisses swa mæg.

 21 We geascodan   Eormanrices   100ᵛ
     wylfenne geþoht;   ahte wide / folc
     Gotena rices -   þæt wæs grim cyning;
 24 sæt secg monig   sorgum gebunden,
     wean on wenan,   wyscte geneahhe
     þæt þæs cynerices   ofercumen wære.
 27   Þæs ofereode,   þisses swa mæg.

     Siteð sorgcearig   sælum bidæled,
     on sefan sweorceð,   sylfum þinceð

---
14 MS *gefrugnon*.
16 MS *hi*.

30 þæt sy endeleas   earfoða dæl;
   mæg þonne geþencan   þæt geond þas woruld
   witig Dryhten   wendeþ geneahhe,
33 eorle monegum   are gesceawað
   wislicne blæd,   sumum weana dæl.
   Þæt ic bi me sylfum   secgan wille
36 þæt ic hwile wæs   Heodeninga scop,
   dryhtne dyre -   me wæs Deor noma;
   ahte ic fela wintra   folgað tilne,
39 holdne hlaford   oþþæt Heorrenda nu,
   leoðcræftig monn,   londryht geþah
   þæt me eorla hleo   ær gesealde.
42   Þæs ofereode,   þisses swa mæg.

---

30 MS *earfoda*.

COMMENTARY

The following list identifies recent interpreters of the poem and what some of their conclusions have been: Anderson (1983, riddle-like; explores the contextual significance of its position next to *Wulf and Eadwacer*), Bloomfield (1964, form similar to a charm, 1986, a reaffirmation of 1964's thesis); Bolton (1972, a *consolatio*); Boren (1975, wisdom literature: examines the possibility of escape from misery through the agency of art); Condren (1981, the poem itself is evidence of Deor's triumph over adversity through art); Eliason (1966, a begging poem); Frankis (1962, a dramatic monologue); Jacobs (1981, a reconciliation poem); Kiernan (1978, examines the Alfredian Boethius as a source for *Deor*); Markland (1968, a *consolatio*); Whitbread (1970, examines general influence of Boethius' *Consolation* on Anglo-Saxon poems).

Bolton argues that Boethius' *Consolation of Philosophy* was the source, but that the *Deor* poet drew material from it selectively:

> Not all of the *Consolation* can be traced in the brief lyric, to be sure, but all the chief constituents of *Deor* can be traced to Boethius' work: the overall fiction of the unfortunate poet, the fivefold view of human ambition [see next paragraph], the viewpoint and language of the refrain, the implementation of literary tradition for exemplary ends, perhaps even the symbolic name of the narrator's persona. (1972, 227) (See 28-42 note.)

[Bolton notes that the first five stanzas can be seen as illustrations/exempla of "the five false goods of Philosophy's discussion": in this system, Weland = wealth, Beadohild = honour, Mæthhild and Geat = pleasure, Theodoric = fame, and the Ostrogoths = power (1972, 224-25).]

1-13 These first two stanzas relate two episodes of a single story recounted with some differences in two Scandinavian poems, *Volundarkviða* and *Þiðrekssaga*. The artificer Weland is well-known from Germanic legend as a forger of renowned arms (and can be compared with Daedalus of classical legend); he is said to have fashioned Beowulf's corselet (454b-55) and Waldere's arms (3.2-4a). Nithhad had ensured that Weland would remain in his service by hamstringing him. Weland got his revenge for that by killing Nithhad's two sons and making jewelled cups from their skulls, brooches from their teeth, and jewels from their eyes. Then he ravished Beadohild, Nithhad's daughter, before escaping by flying off using a pair of wings he had made; a scene from this story is found on the front panel of the Franks Casket. The child born of this violence was Widia / Wudga, a famous adventurer in Germanic legend (see 1.124-30 and 3.36-42).

Mandel, concerned with the oral delivery of the poem and the way a listener would have perceived it at a first hearing, analyses the strategies of the poet in these opening lines, the way he creates suspense and suggests concern for the subject of each exemplum before undercutting it with the refrain and moving on to the next stanza. He finds *Deor* "remarkable among Old English poems for the way in which it involves the listeners, asking them to recognize first their own suffering in terms of the suffering of others and then their own lives in terms of a principle of transience" (1982, 132).

1 *be wurman*: This has been emended by some editors, but makes perfect sense when understood as a poetic way of saying 'by the sword / knife'; knives and swords are often described in Anglo-Saxon literature as being decorated with serpentine patterns (eg, *wyrmfah*, *Beowulf* 1698a). For further discussion, see Hatto's examination of the use of serpent and boar motifs in Germanic art and literature; he concludes,

> ... it is hoped that enough has been said here to show that the choice of snake and boar was determined by considerations of agressive and defensive magic of the same kind, say, as occurs in the Ainu epic, where the animals depicted on the sword sheaths leap off to join in the fray. Magic of this sort has strong artistic potentialities, and it is suggested here that qualities of this order survived in the conventions of early Germanic art and poetry at a time when their original function and meaning were either lost or only partly understood. (1957, 160)

Anderson proposes that *wurman* is the Old English word 'purple' meaning 'blood' in this context (1983, 207 and note 10).

3-4a Cf. *Wanderer, hu sliþen bið sorg to geferan* (30); the poet uses the traditional language of exile poetry to present Weland's plight here; see Greenfield (1955).

4b See 28-42 note.

7 Raffel cites a number of the translations offered by critics for this elusive refrain (1972, 5-6); Mitchell discusses it in his section on the use of the genitive case, and tentatively offers "It passed over from that; it can from this" as an acceptable translation, observing that "(t)he exact reference of *þæs* and *þisses* is a literary, not a syntactical, problem" (*Old English Syntax*, Oxford: Clarendon Press, 1985), 1404-05. He explains *þæs* and *þisses* as genitives 'of point of time from which'. Erickson examines the underlying syntactical structure of these genitives and concludes that "(they) are not predicate pseudo-subjects as they would be if the constructions were really impersonal, but in fact real subjects or at least what remains of the real subjects after Postal-type deletions have taken place . . . . The main NP of the subject *mæg* [*ofergan*] is the same as that for *ofereode*, with the dependent genitive again being pronominalized. The structure is exactly equivalent to the first stave of the refrain, though what the pronoun refers to depends on the interpretation of the last stanza of the poem" (1975, 81-82).

[Raffel's article is more noteworthy for showing how misguided even the most respected scholars can sometimes be in their interpretations of Anglo-Saxon poems; he refers specifically to Bloomfield (1964) which is an attempt to define the form of *Deor* in terms of a hypothetical prose introduction.]

Regardless of the minor differences among the various translations offered for the refrain (and there have been well over one hundred of them), it seems that the poet is saying that both fortune and misfortune pass in time, and that all men are thrust forward irresistibly experiencing both of these one after the other in an unending sequence.

14-17 Mæthhild's sorrow was caused by a vision she had foreshadowing her imminent death; she dreamed that she was to drown in the Vending River. Geat builds a bridge over the river, but Mæthhild cannot elude her fate, and while the rest of her party is off chasing deer she falls into the river and drowns. The two extant versions of the tale end differently: in the Norwegian version, Geat plays his harp and Mæthhild rises from the river restored to life and freed from the power of the evil spirits who caused her death; in the Icelandic version, Geat casts his harp to the ground twice in frustration and grief, breaking many of the strings, but still manages to play it and cause Mæthhild to rise from the river. However, she is dead.

He buries her and later makes new strings for his harp from some strands of her hair.

As Kiernan demonstrates, emending this passage as Malone and others have done in the past creates more problems than it resolves (1975). In order to make sense of the episode Malone emends line 14 to read *mon[e] gefrugnon* and interpreted *frige* to be an otherwise unknown genitive singular form of *freo* 'lady / wife'; it should be added that *mone*, though the etymologically correct form from which Modern English 'moan' is derived, is not recorded elsewhere in Anglo-Saxon literature. Two emendations have been incorporated here: *frugnon* for MS *gefrugnon* in line 14 and *hi[m]* [Grein] for MS *hi* in line 16 since a smooth and meaningful translation, consonant with the story as preserved in the analogues Malone cites (1977, 8-9), is otherwise impossible. Kiernan translates 16 "so that the grieving love (of his) took her from death entirely" (1978, 334), but does not account for the form of *slæp* or for *ealle* as an adverb.

him seo sorglufu is to be translated 'his grieving love'. Kiernan's point that *slæp* is the object of *binom* and that it is to be taken figuratively as 'the sleep of death' or simply 'death' is accepted here. *ealle* is understood to be the dative singular of the adjective used substantively. Thus the episode can be translated,

> Many of us learned that about Mæthhild: the sexual passions of Geat became boundless so that his grieving love cheated death in every way.

Kiernan contends that *Deor* is an Anglo-Saxon consolation of philosophy, and that, in fact, the Anglo-Saxon *scop* Deor is to be understood to be Boethius. He identifies the characters in *Deor* with equivalent figures in Boethius' work so that Mæthhild and Geat correspond to Orpheus and Eurydice, Weland to Fabricus (this substitution was made in the Alfredian version, and Kiernan suggests "it may be the prototype for the procedure of the *Deor* poet" (1978, 334)), Theodoric and Eormanric are taken as a pair as an example of ironic retribution (a theme dealt with in Boethius) since Theodoric the Goth (the persecutor of Boethius), in Germanic legend Dietrich von Bern, "was in turn cruelly persecuted by Eormanric" (338). [Theodoric and Nero are paired in the Alfredian Boethius.]

Eliason (1965) argues that the story of Mæthhild and Geat concerns a father's incestuous love of his daughter. The line of argument, by which he arrives at the identification of Geat as the son of the continental Offa, transfers the incestuous act from his mother to him, associates this story with the Offa-Thryth digression in *Beowulf*, and dates the poem to precisely 787, demands an enormous amount of credulity of the reader interested in sound argument based on verifiable data rather than unbridled speculation.

18-19 Scholars continue to debate whether the tyrant referred to here is Theodoric the Great or Wolfdietrich; the former appears the more plausible candidate when it is recalled that he was the persecutor of, among others, Boethius, and it is known from the *Hildebrandslied* that "he was an exile . . . for thirty years, and that this exile ended ultimately in his triumph" (Norman, 1965, 209); Frankis' investigations reveal that *Mæringa burg* refers to Ravenna (1962, 162-64). Malone argues the case for Wolfdietrich. His investigation shows that in traditional tales transmitted over a long period fact and fiction easily become entwined (1977, 9-13), so that even if Wolfdietrich was the historical identity intended by the poet, he probably thought that that Theodoric was the tyrant who was also responsible for the death of Boethius. [We must remember that medieval poets did not have countless reference texts available to them and that they probably would not have thought to consult them when engaged in creative activity even had they had them.]

21 Eormanric was the uncle of Theodoric the Ostrogoth mentioned in the previous stanza. He also appears in *Widsith* (1.8b-9a and 1.88-92) where he is portrayed as both an ideal king and a grim tyrant; Fry notes that the *Widsith* "poet and his fictional *scop* Widsith speak in different voices, varying in their estimates of Ermanric" (1980, 39), whereas Malone goes to great lengths to reconcile the two apparently contradictory characterizations of Eormanic in *Widsith* (1962, 29-35).

22 *wylfenne geþoht*: Kiernan, in support of his argument that the Alfredian Boethius is the likely source for *Deor*, notes the following description of Eormanric: *Gif þu þonne on hwilcum men ongitst, þæt he biþ gitsere and reafere, ne scealt þu hine na hatan man, ac wulf* (1978, 339 and note 22).

28-42 As Bloomfield notes (1986, 274-77), the observation that everyone experiences unforeseen reversals of fortune in this life is not exclusively or necessarily Boethian; see 1.51b-53 note (and compare the similar formulations in two of the Exeter Book wisdom poems, *The Fortunes of Men*, 64-71a (cited below, 28-34 note), and *The Gifts of Men*, 1-7). However, the similarity between 31-34 and the following passage from the closing of *The Consolation of Philosophy* is remarkable:

> God looks down from above, knowing all things, and the eternal present of his vision concurs with the future character of our actions, distributing rewards to the good and punishments to the evil. Our hopes and prayers are not directed to God in vain, for if they are just they cannot fail. (tr. Richard Green, New York: Bobbs-Merrill, 1962, p. 119)

28 siteð: The tense shift from preterite to present at this point in the poem suggests that the *exempla* cited thus far are to be contrasted with or used as points of reference for what follows, or perhaps, that what follows has universal significance.

Mitchell observes that conditional sentences not introduced by a conjunction are possible in Old English, but occur almost exclusively in prose (*A Guide to Old English*, Oxford, Blackwell, rev. 1982, paragraph 179.7); this passage may then begin 'If a man sits . . .'

28-34 Cf. *Wanderer* 58-62a (which may be regarded as an example of anti-heroic literature):

> Forþon ic geþencan ne mæg geond þas woruld
> for hwan modsefa min ne gesweorce,
> þonne ic eorla lif eal geondþence,
> hu hi færlice flet ofgeafon,
> modge maguþegnas

[Wherefore I cannot think for all this world why my mind does not grow dark when I ponder deeply the life of men, how they suddenly abandon the hall, proud kindred-thanes];

and *Fortunes of Men* 64-71a:

> Swa missenlice meahtig dryhten
> geond eorþan sceat eallum dæleð,
> scyreð ond scrifeð ond gesceapo healdeð,
> sumum eadwelan, sumum earfeþa dæl,
> sumum geoguþe glæd, sumum guþe blæd,
> gewealdenne wigplegan, sumum wyrp oþþe scyte,
> torhtlicne tiir, sumum tæfle cræft,
> bleobordes gebregd

[Thus the almighty Lord apportions for all variously over the expanse of the earth, allotting and ordaining, and overseeing their fates: prosperity to one, a portion of miseries to another, gladness in youth to one, glory in war to another, controlled battle-play, throwing and shooting to one, illustrious glory, skill with the die to another, deftness at the coloured-board];

cf. also *Gifts of Men* 1-7.

35 Cf. *Seafarer* 1, *Mæg ic be me sylfum soðgied wrecan*, *Wife's Lament* 1-2a, *Ic þis giedd wrece bi me ful gomorre, / minre sylfre sið* and *Resignation* 96b-97, *Ic bi me tylgust / secge þis sarspel ond ymb siþ spræce*; note also *Beowulf* 1723b-24.

37 Why does the poet say *deor wæs* (preterite) his name unless a deliberate pun on *dyre-deor* is intended?

40 *londryht*: See 1.93-96 note.

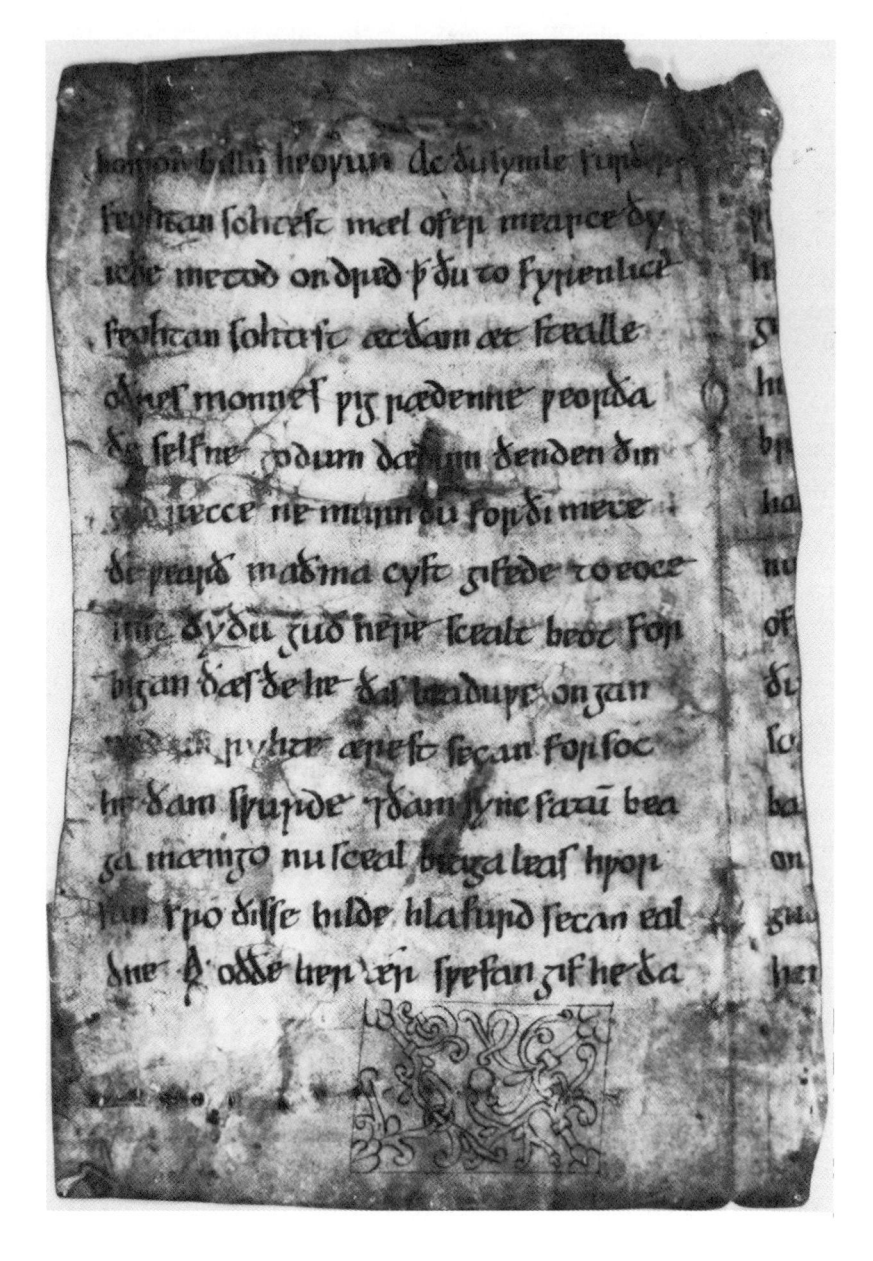

PLATE 4 Copenhagen, Royal Library, Ny Kgl. S. MS 167b, 1ᵛ. *Waldere*, lines 17-32.

THREE: WALDERE

INTRODUCTION

On 12 January 1860, Professor E.C. Werlauff, Chief Librarian of the Royal Library of Copenhagen, found the two leaves which have come down to us today as the only surviving fragments of the 'Walter' legend in Old English; these are now catalogued as MS Ny Kgl. S. 167b in that same library. It is not known how these two part sheets of an otherwise unknown Anglo-Saxon manuscript came to be in the library in Copenhagen; the most likely explanation is that they were brought back from England by G.J. Thorkelin when he returned from studying Anglo-Saxon manuscripts under royal commission in 1791.[1]

Date: Late tenth or early eleventh century.

Provenance: The place of origin of these fragments cannot be determined palaeographically or codicologically due to the paucity of evidence; the dialect of the text is predominantly West-Saxon, with a sprinkling of Northumbrian forms.[2]

History: As indicated above, once discovered the manuscript has since remained in the Royal Library in Copenhagen.

Description: The Manuscript consists of two vellum fragments (each of which has been trimmed in such a way as to preserve,

---

[1] Norman (1949, 1).
[2] See the Introduction to *Widsith*, note 20.

tantalizingly, the last letter or two of each line of its now missing conjugate folio),[3] each approximately 210 × 144 mm with a writing space of approximately 150 × 108 mm, and with 15 long lines of text. The folio numbered 2 in this edition has an original defect in the vellum (a warble fly hole?), so that no text is missing due to it. There is nothing extraordinary about the use of abbreviations, word division, punctuation, or the use of accents; ruling, however, is not visible, and in line 31 the appropriate rune is found for the word *eðel* (see Plate 4). At the bottom of folio 1^v there is some acanthus leaf ornamentation framed in a rectangle; T.D. Kendrick suggests it was probably northern, and by an English artist of limited ability working in the Danelaw in the style of the school of Winchester, but adapting this to the tastes of an Anglo-Danish population.[4] The script is an angular Anglo-Saxon minuscule lacking in grace.

Compilation: Given that there are only two leaves extant and that there are analogues for this story, it is ironic that there was in the past some disagreement over which of the folios should come first, although today most scholars accept the order found here, that is, with that beginning '*hyrde hyne* . . .' positioned first.[5]

Text

The text is generally known as *Waldere*, after the protagonist whose story it relates.

Structure, theme and genre: The story of Walter of Aquitaine and Hiltgunt (or Hildegyth) as known from the Medieval Latin epic poem *Waltharius* is summarized thus by Norman:[6]

> Attila, king of the Huns, made war on the western nations. Franks, Burgundians and Aquitanians, without fighting, submitted to the Hunnish yoke and offered hostages. Gibicho, the Frankish king, sent Hagano, Heriricus the Burgundian sent his only daughter Hiltgunt, Alphere, king of Aquitania, sent

---

[3] Zettersten reproduces facsimiles of the fragments and transcribes what survives of these conjugate folios (1979, 10-11).

[4] Norman (1949, 4-5). This description seems a bit strained, but a more sophisticated and succinct analysis has not been forthcoming.

[5] Norman thinks it not unlikely that the two fragments are from the same gathering, and examines the implications this has for the amount of text lost (1949, 1-4).

[6] It is thought that the *Waltharius* was written by Ekkehard I of St. Gall (circa 910-73); see Zettersten (1979, 3).

his only son Waltharius who had been betrothed to Hiltgunt. The hostages were well treated. When Gibicho died and his son Guntharius succeeded he refused to continue to pay the tribute, and Hagano fled. There was no pursuit. Some time later Waltharius and Hiltgunt fled. Hiltgunt collected two chests full of treasure, Waltharius plied Attila and his retinue with wine until they had all succumbed to a drunken stupor, and the two fled . . . . Attila offered rich rewards; nobody dared to take up the pursuit. The fugitives reached the Rhine, were ferried over and offered the ferry-man strange fish as a reward. These reached the table of Guntharius, and Hagano, after the ferry-man had been interrogated, guessed that Waltharius had returned. In spite of Hagano's warning Guntharius, together with eleven knights, set out to rob the Aquitanian of maiden and treasure. Hagano accompanied the king. Meanwhile, Waltharius had reached the Vosges towards morning, had camped in a defile and lay down to sleep whilst Hiltgunt kept watch. She woke him when the Franks approached. Hagano repeated his warnings, Waltharius offered a hundred, then two hundred rings. In vain, and the fight began. Only one man at a time could offer battle in the defile . . . . (Hagano) and Guntharius lay in wait and attacked him in the open when the pair continued their journey in the morning. In the fight the king lost a leg. To save the deathblow Hagano threw his body between the combatants. The sword of Waltharius broke on Hagano's helmet and, as he threw the hilt away, Hagano cut off his right hand. Thereupon, fighting with a short sword in his left hand, Waltharius took out one of Hagano's eyes and six of his teeth. That was the end of the contest and Hiltgunt attended to the wounds. Hagano and the king went back to Worms and the lovers proceeded on their way. After his marriage Waltharius reigned for thirty years. (1968, 26)

The summary is given at length since the Old English fragments are totally inscrutable without it.

The Commentary here assumes that Hildgyth is the speaker of 1-32, Hagano of 33-42, and Waldere of the remaining lines.[7] Whilst

---

[7] Other possibilities for the allocation of the speeches have been entertained; see Zettersten (1979, 4-5), and the commentary to the text here.

Waldere is for the most part an heroic poem in the native Germanic tradition, it also has a Christian philosophical substratum, evident in 22-23 and 59-61. Campbell outlines the criteria which lead him to conclude that the Old English *Waldere*, of which these fragments are the only remnants, was a poem of epic proportion comparable to *Beowulf*, and not merely a short Germanic lay (1962, 15 ff).

Language: *Waldere* is recorded primarily in the West-Saxon dialect; the few non-West-Saxon forms are:

Northumbrian
hworfan (30), *hafa* (34), and *standað* (50).[8]

---

[8] These forms, taken with Kendrick's observations on the decoration, suggest the manuscript may have been produced in the Danelaw.

WALDERE

   . . . hyrde hyne georne:
   "Huru Weland[es]   worc ne geswiceð
3 monna ænigum   ðara ðe Mimming can
   hear[d]ne gehealdan;   oft æt hilde gedreas
   swatfag ond sweordwund   sec[g] æfter oðrum;
6 Ætlan ordwyga,   ne læt ðin ellen nu gy[t]
   gedreosan to dæge,   dryhtscipe [........]
           * * *   [nu] is se dæg cumen,
9 þæt ðu scealt aninga   oðer twega
   lif forleosan   oððe lang[n]e dom
   agan mid eldum,   Ælfheres sunu;
12 nalles ic ðe, wine min,   wordum cide
   [ð]y ic ðe gesawe   æt ðam sweord[p]legan
   ðurh edwitscype   æniges monnes
15 wig forbugan oððe   on weal fleon,
   lice beorgan,   ðeah þe laðra fela
   ðinne byrn /-homon   billum heowun,
18 ac ðu symle furðor   feohtan sohtest
   mæl ofer mearce;   ðy ic ðe metod ondred,
   þæt ðu to fyrenlice   feohtan sohtest
21 æt ðam ætstealle,   oðres monnes
   wigrædenne;   weorða ðe selfne
   godum dædum   ðenden ðin God recce;
24 ne murn ðu for ði mece -   ðe wearð maðma cyst
   gifeðe to eoce   [mid] ðy ðu Guðhere scealt
   beot forbigan   ðæs ðe he ðas beaduwe ongan

---

2 MS *weland*.
4 MS *hearne*, with the *n* expuncted.
5 MS *sec*.
8 *nu*] MS now illegible.
10 MS *lange*.
11 *nu*] The *-nu* is questionable.
12 *cide*] *-e* is barely visible.
13 MS damaged.   The MS may read *-wlegan*.
25 MS *gifede*.   *mid*] Almost illegible; see *Commentary*.

44   LEOÐ

27 [mi]d unryhte   ærest secan;
   forsoc he ðam swurde   ond ðam syncfatum,
   beaga mænigo;   nu sceal beaga leas
30 hworfan from ðisse hilde,   hlafurd secan
   ealdne eðel   oððe her ær swefan
   gif he ða . . ."

                    II
33 ". . . ce bæteran   2ʳ
   buton ðam anum   ðe ic eac hafa
   on stanfate   stille gehided;
36 Ic wat þæt [h]i[t] ðohte   Ðeodric Widian
   selfum onsendon   ond eac sinc micel
   maðma mid ði mece,   monig oðres mid him
39 golde gegirwan;   iulean genam
   þæs ðe hine of nearwum   Niðhades mæg,
   Welandes bearn,   Widia ut forlet;
42 ðurh fifela geweald   forð onette."
      Waldere mað[e]lode,   wiga ellenrof,
   hæfde him on handa   hildefro[f]re
45 guðbilla gripe,   gyddode wordum:
   "Hwæt, ðu huru wendest,   wine Burgenda,
   þæt me Hagenan hand   hilde gefremede
48 ond getwæmde feðewigges;   feta, gyf ðu dyrre,   /
   æt ðus heaðuwerigan   hare byrnan;   2ᵛ
   standað me her on eaxelum   Ælfheres laf,
51 god ond geapneb   golde geweorðod,
   ealles unscende   æðelinges reaf
   to habbanne   þonne ha[n]d wereð
54 feorhhord feondum;   ne bið fah wið me

27 mid] The first two letters are only partially visible.
31 The MS has the e rune here.
36 hit] MS ic.
42 þurh] The u is expuncted.   geweald] The w has been altered from f; MS damaged.
43 maðelode] The first e is barely visible.
44 MS hildefrore.
47 hagenan] The e has been added interlinearly.
48 getwæmde] The æ has been altered from u.
50 The f has been altered from t.
53 MS had.

WALDERE 45

    þonne [w]ifl[e] unmægas eft ongynnað,
    mecum gemetað, swa ge me dydon.
57 Ðeah mæg sige syllan se ðe symle byð
    recon ond rædfæst ryhta gehwilces;
    se ðe him to ðam halgan helpe gelifeð,
60 to Gode gioce, he þær gearo findeð
    gif ða earnunga ær geðenceð.
    Þonne moten wlance welan britnian,
63 æhtum wealdan þæt is . . ."

---

54 *ne*] MS *he*.
55 MS damaged.
62 MS *mtoten*.

COMMENTARY

2 Norman points out that any discussion of *Waldere* is bound to become a discussion of comparative literature since these fragments contain the only reference to the Walter story in Old English. Although it is assumed here that Hildgyth is the speaker in the first fragment, her name does not even appear in the surviving text (1969, 265).

Compare *Beowulf* 1460b-61, where the poet is speaking about Unferth's sword Hrunting: *næfre hit æt hilde ne swac / manna ængum þara þe hit mid mundum bewand.*

welandes: [Stephens]; see 2.1-13 note.

4 *heardne*: [Bugge]; cf. *Beowulf* 2067a, *heaðobearna*, which suggests, however, that this may be a standard simplification of this consonant cluster.

4b-5 This has the form of a gnomic utterance; see 1.11-13 note, and compare also *Beowulf* 572b-73 and 2029b-31.

6-11 For the use of the framing device here (*Ætlan ordwyga... Ælfheres sunu*) see 1.38-44 note. If this is accepted as an example of such a device, as it seems to be, it argues against Pheifer's punctuation of the passage which places the fullstop after *ordwyga*, taking the verse to be in apposition to *secg*. He contends that it makes no sense to call someone fleeing from Attila's court his champion, but there is no reason why this hero could not have been a champion there until he fell in love with Hildgyth and fled to his homeland.

7 *dryhtscipe*: See 1.37 note for a discussion of the significance of this word and other terms of rank in Anglo-Saxon poetry.

8b [Bugge]; emended with reference to *Beowulf* 2646b which is identical; compare also 6.104b.

9-11 Busse and Holtei (writing about *Maldon* specifically, but concerned with heroic poetry in general) observe:

> The characteristic feature of a definition of heroism is the abstract idea of a heroic situation which is determined by a free choice between two ways of acting: the respective evaluation and consequences of these alternatives are diametrically opposed to each other. Only when a possibility is given for

this dialectic relation to choose one way or the other, tied up with one consequence or the other, does the conception of heroism then make sense. Thus the definition of what is heroic depends on the dialectic of social norm and standard. In most instances, the alternative ways of acting are on the one hand privately agreeable to the actor but socially disgraceful, whereas on the other hand they are privately disagreeable but will socially be appreciated and rewarded. (1981, 615)

This choice between two alternatives (often between achieving lasting glory or dying in battle) is found frequently in the poems under discussion here; see, for example, 4.26b-27 (unspecified), 6.207-08 (die or avenge their lord), 6.291-93, 3.29b-31 and *Beowulf* 2895a-97b (survive battle or die fighting).

10 *langne*: Although the MS reading *lange* is acceptable, Norman observes: "To be remembered 'for a long time' is not enough for a Germanic warrior; he wants 'everlasting glory'" (1949, 36); cf. 5.3b (*ealdorlangne tir*), 1.143b (*heahfæstne dom*) and *Beowulf* 953b-55a and 1384-89 (quoted in 1.140 note).

16 *lice beorgan*: See 5.36b note

18-19a The notion that one aspect of heroic behaviour is not retreating a step under any circumstances is found elsewhere in the poems under discussion here (see 6.246-47, 275-76 and *Beowulf* 2524b-26a, *Nelle ic beorges weard / oferfleon fotes trem, ac unc [furður] sceal / weorðan æt wealle*).

21 *ætstealle*: There is only one other instance of this word in the poetry (in *Guthlac* 179), and it is usually defined from context to mean 'assistance, battle, station'; other compounds with the element *-stealla* are less obscure because the meaning of their first element and its relationship to the second are clearer (for example, *lindgestealla* and *hondgesteallan* (*Beowulf* 1973a and 2169a)).

22b-23 These lines may be compared with Wiglaf's words of exhortation to Beowulf:

> 'Leofa Biowulf, læst eall tela,
> swa ðu on geoguðfeore geara gecwæde,
> þæt ðu ne alæte be ðe lifgendum
> dom gedreosan; scealt nu dædum rof,
> æðeling anhydig, ealle mægene
> feorh ealgian; ic ðe fullæstu.' (2663-68)

['Beloved Beowulf, see the whole thing through completely since you said long ago in your youth that you would not allow your reputation to fail while you were living; now, my resolute prince, brave in deeds, you must defend your life with all your strength; I shall assist you . . .]

See 57-61 note for discussion of the role of a favouring deity in heroic poetry.

23 *god*: As on many occasions in *Beowulf*, this could refer to a god other than the Christian deity; however, lines 59-61 leave little doubt concerning the Christian perspective of the fragment (Robinson (1985) discusses this point at some length with respect to the overall Christian narratory viewpoint in *Beowulf*).

25 The MS is damaged here and critics have advanced three different readings, *mid* (as here, following Holthausen), *unc* (Norman) and *mit* (Zettersten).

29 *beaga*: Some editors have emended the second occurrence of this to *bega*, but it makes perfect sense as it stands, and the antithesis of *mænigo-leas* is poetically satisfying; it also reinforces the theme of 'a choice between two alternatives' discussed in 9-11 note.

30 Pheifer takes *hlafurd* as accusative (citing *Beowulf* 267-68 and *Elene* 981-82 as supporting evidence for the "formula" *Hlaford secan*), and translates "Now is he fated either to return from this battle, seek his lord, the ancient homeland, without the treasure, or die here first" (1960, 183). The punctuation here implies that *Guðhere* (25b, and the *he* in 26b and 28a) is the unexpressed subject of *sceal*, which governs both *hworfan* and *secan*: "Now he must turn from this battle bereft of neck-rings, the lord must seek his ancient homeland or die here beforehand"; either reading can be defended and is acceptable.

33-42 Although it is assumed here that Hagano is the speaker of these lines, Norman cites analogues from *Beowulf* and other poems where a long speech is interrupted and the speaker reintroduced before the speech is continued which suggests that Waldere could be the speaker here (Norman, 1969, 269-70). Elsewhere, Norman — who has pondered this poem for longer than most other critics — offers the following translation for this troublesome and elusive passage:

. . . such a better one apart from the one in addition which I have kept quietly in its (treasure chest?) (ornamented sheath?).

I am aware that Ðeodric intended to send it to Widia himself, moreover, much treasure along with the sword, and many further things to adorn with gold: he received the reward for an earlier deed: Widia, Niðhad's grand-son, the child of Weland, released him from dire straights [sic]: he hurried forth from the domain of the giants. (1968, 25)

He subsequently reviews the alternative interpretations possible, depending on who is understood to be speaking these lines.

35 *stanfate*: This is a much-discussed crux, apparently referring to either a jewel-studded sheath or a casket in which a sword is being transported.

36 *hit*: [Rieger].

38b-39a These difficult verses are open to interpretation; possible senses are, "(intended) to outfit (/ bedeck) many another man with him with gold" or "(intended to send) many another thing along with it to adorn with gold" (but see Norman's translation cited above in 33-42 note).

41 *Widia*: A famous adventurer in Germanic legend (who appears also in *Widsith*); see 2.1-13 note.

42 Cf. *Beowulf* 808, *on feonda geweald feor siðian* and 902b-03, *He mid Eotenum wearð / on feonda geweald forð forlacen.*

43 See 33 note.

maþelode: For the significance of this word being used to introduce the first reported speech of Waldere see 1.1 note (§ 2).

44 *hildefrofre*: [Müllenhof]; in *Beowulf*, it is thought that *hildeleoman* (1143b) could be the name of the sword placed on Hengest's lap; see 4.35 note.

46b Magoun observes that the fact that the exact equivalent of this formula appears in the *Atlakviða* (18, *vin Borgunda*) does not prove a knowledge of Scandinavian literature on the part of the *Waldere* poet, but that a stock of traditional formulas for defining "a person in terms of his role of protectorship of a people or persons" was shared by "Old Germanic singers of the Migration period and after" (1958, 216 and 218).

46-49 The vaunting and bold tone of this address seems to be expected of heroes in certain situations; compare 4.24-27 (Sigeferth's speech) and 6.45-61 (Byrhtnoth's reply to the Viking messenger).

50 Magoun points out the formulaic nature of this verse, noting that it "constitutes a theme, the theme of a hero's wearing in combat or elsewhere a piece of armor . . . inherited from an ancestor (citing as corroborative evidence *Beowulf* 454b [sic — actually 546b], 2191b, 2611b and 2628b), and observes that it is not to be taken literally or historically to imply that Ælfhere is dead since it is known from Middle High German sources that he was alive to greet Waldere when he returned home from exile. He might also have noted *Beowulf* 1547b-49, 1900-03a, 2158-62 and 2190-92a.

53 Ortoleva (1979).

54 *bið*: Zettersten identifies this as an imperative, presumably translating it "Be not false to me when . . ."

ne: [Stephens].

55 *wifle*: [Schwab].

unmægas: The use of the negative form of a word may have carried more force than did merely expressing the idea with a completely different word or paraphrase; ie, to be an 'un-kinsman' is probably more treacherous than being simply an enemy. In *Beowulf*, the narrator uses *unleofe* as a term of reproach for those who deserted Beowulf in his time of greatest need (2863b). It is noteworthy that Wiglaf's speech which follows opens like a maxim or gnomic utterance ("*Þæt, la, mæg secgan se ðe wyle soð specan* . . ." (see note 1.11-13 above)) since reflections on unkinsmanlike and 'un-friendlike' behaviour occur throughout the poems, eg, *Beowulf* 2166b-69a and 2600b-01; see also 6.221-24 note.

57-61 The hero's success in the poetry often depends on his working in partnership with a favouring deity, usually the Christian God; in *Beowulf*, the narrator observes:

>   ond þone ænne heht
> golde forgyldan, þone ðe Grendel ær
> mane acwealde, swa he hyra ma wolde,
> nefne him witig God wyrd forstode
> ond ðæs mannes mod (1053b-57a)

[and he ordered compensation to be paid in gold for the one whom Grendel had earlier killed in his wickedness, as he would have more had not God in his wisdom and the courage of that man averted that fate], and,

> þær him aglæca ætgræpe wearð;
> hwæþre he gemunde mægenes strenge,
> gimfæste gife ðe him God sealde,
> ond him to Anwaldan are gelyfde,
> frofre ond fultum; ðe he þone feond ofercwom,
> gehnægde hellegast (1269-74a)

[there the terrible one grabbed him; yet he recalled the power of his strength, the ample gift God had given him, and trusted in the Almighty for comfort, solace and help; by that he overcame the enemy, laid low the hellish spirit];

see also *Beowulf* 1550-56 and 2858-59.

58 Zetterstan reads *rædfest*, but the second *ash* is quite clear.

61 "if he earlier considers how to earn it".

FOUR: THE FINNSBURH FRAGMENT

INTRODUCTION

Manuscript

The Finnsburh Fragment is known only from a transcript made by George Hickes before 1705 when it was included in his *Thesaurus* (I.192-93). He indicates there that the fragment was found in a volume of homilies written in Anglo-Saxon minuscule which was housed in the Lambeth Palace Library. Either Hickes or his printer subsequently lost the sheets, but it is thought that the volume of homilies referred to may be either MS 487 or MS 489 in the present library collection.[1] Nothing further of value can be said concerning the date, origin or later medieval provenance of the manuscript. There are a number of obvious misreadings of the original, but it cannot be ascertained if these were made by Hickes as a copyist or if they reflect carelessness on the part of his printer, who would have been unfamiliar with the script and the language of the text.

Hickes prints the text in half-lines (or verses), his only punctuation being a full stop after each of these. In addition to the first word in each line, four other words are capitalized; it is not known how

---

[1] The first of these is the likelier candidate since it is in the script usually described by Hickes as 'Semi-Sax.' whereas the second is not. Dating from the thirteenth century, the former has 67 vellum folios (approx. 7 × 5 inches in size) of 28 long lines. Hickes does not indicate whether the folios containing the Fragment were bound in the volume of homilies or merely inserted loosely somewhere within the codex.

many of these capital letters are to be attributed to Hickes. Fry reproduces the first page of the transcript as a frontispiece for his edition (1974).

Text

The poem takes its title from the location of the battle as given in line 36 of the fragment, *swylce eal Finnsburuh fyrenu wære.* Other details of the story treated here are known from the so-called 'Finnsburh Episode' in *Beowulf* (1063-1159). The Fragment and Episode have been edited together on a number of occasions, the latest and most comprehensive study being Alan Bliss' edition (1982) of J.R.R Tolkien's lecture notes.

Structure, theme and genre: In his study of the Old English epic style, Campbell compares the contrasting styles of *Beowulf* and *Waldere* — examples of the epic in Old English — with *The Finnsburh Fragment*, which he classifies as the only surviving Anglo-Saxon example of a Germanic heroic lay (1962, 16). The Fragment opens with a speech by a person identified only as a young king. Some editors — most recently Tolkien — emended the text so that the adverb *næfre*, the third word in the Fragment, reads *Hnæf*. This, however, is unwarranted, and would not have been suggested but for the similarity between *næfre* and the king's name (surely we can wait till line 40 to find out his name; after all, we are not told Beowulf's name until line 343 of the epic).

Working with the evidence available in both the Fragment and the Episode, Tolkien provides a reconstruction of the events at Finnsburh (1982, 159-62). Hnæf, the leader of the Danes, has come to visit his sister, Hildeburh, and her family in the autumn, perhaps with the intention of staying over the winter; he has a retinue of sixty men, probably not all warriors.[2] Finn is the leader of the Frisians; his marriage to Hildeburh, the daughter of Hoc, had probably been a political marriage to seal an alliance.[3] As the Fragment opens, hostile warriors are approaching the Danes who are camped within a hall. Tolkien believes that the violence might have erupted between the Jutish mercenaries — who were in the service of both parties — and then spread to envelop the Frisians and the Danes,[4] but we

---

[2] See the Commentary on *swanas* (39) below.
[3] See Tolkien (1982, 39-45, 53 and 159-62), and 1.45-48 note above.
[4] See Tolkien 100-04 and 159-62.

cannot be sure of this. The outcome of the attack is not revealed in the Fragment; the Danes resist for five days without losing a man, and the poem breaks off with a warrior giving a report on the fighting to his king. From the Episode we discover that Hildeburh lost both her son and brother in the initial encounter, and that after the death of Hnæf, Hengest, the leader of the Jutish mercenaries in Hnæf's service, became leader of the whole visiting company. A treaty was drawn up establishing a fragile peace between the Danes, Frisians and Jutes, but during the long, troubled winter that followed, Hengest and his men brooded over the unsatisfactory agreement into which they had been forced. Finally, violence is renewed. Finn is killed and Hildeburh is carried off, back to her people.

Of the surviving Anglo-Saxon secular heroic poems, this is the only one which neither makes mention of the Deity nor has a Christian philosophical substratum; but the fact that it is a fragment may account for this.

Language: The Finnsburh Fragment is recorded primarily in West-Saxon; many forms which look like Anglian, Kentish or Northumbrian may also be late West-Saxon, but the following are definitely not early West-Saxon.

Northumbrian
sword (15), *hwearflicra* (34), *heordra* (26);

Kentish
scefte (7), *cweþ* (24), *nefre* (39);

Anglian
wæg (43).

Identifiable late West-Saxon forms are: *scyneð* (7), *buruhþelu* (30), and *Finnsburuh* (36).

THE FINNSBURH FRAGMENT

    ... [hor]nas byrnað næfre?" 192
    Hleoþrode ða hearogeong cyning:
3 "Ne ðis ne dagað eastan, ne her draca ne fleogeð,
ne her ðisse healle hornas ne byrnað;
            * * *
ac her forþ berað; fugelas singað,
6 gylleð græghama, guðwudu hlynneð,
scyld scefte oncwyð; nu scyneð þes mona
waðol under wolcnum; nu arisað weadæda
9 ðe ðisne folces nið fremman willað;
ac onwacnigeað nu, wigend mine,
habbað eowre linda, hicgeaþ on ellen,
12 windað on orde, wesað onmode."
    Ða aras mænig goldhladen ðegn, gyrde hine his swurde;
ða to dura eodon drihtlice cempan,
15 Sigeferð and Eaha hyra sword getugon,
and æt oþrum durum Ordlaf and Guþlaf
and Hengest sylf hwearf him on laste.
18   Ða gyt Garulf Guðere styrode
ðæt he swa freolic feorh forman siþe
to ðære healle durum hyrsta ne bære,
21 nu hyt niþa heard anyman wolde,
ac he frægn ofer eal undearninga,
deormod hæleþ, hwa ða duru heolde:
24 "Sigeferþ is min nama <cweþ he>; ic eom Secgena leod,
wreccea wide cuð; fæla ic weana gebad,
heordra hilda; ðe is gyt her witod

---

1 Hickes' transcript begins with *-nas.*
3 Hks *eastun.*
11 Hks *landa.* Hks *Hie geaþ.*
12 Hks *on mode.*
19 Hks *for-man.*
20 Hks *bæran.*
21 Hks *any man.*
24 See *Commentary.*
25 Hks *Wrecten.* Hks *weuna.*

THE FINNSBURH FRAGMENT

27 swæþer ðu sylf to me   secean wylle."
 Ða wæs on healle   wælslihta gehlyn;
sceolde celæs bord   cenum on handa,
30 banhelm berstan;   buruhðelu dynede
oð æt ðære guðe   Garulf gecrang,
ealra ærest   eorðbuendra,
33 Guðlafes sunu,   ymbe hyne godra fæla,
hwearflicra hræw;   hræfen wandrode
sweart and sealobrun;   swurdleoma stod
36 swylce eal Finnsburuh   fyrenu wære.
 Ne gefrægn ic næfre wurþlicor   æt wera hilde
sixtig sigebeorna   sel gebæran,
39 ne nefre swanas hwitne medo   sel forgyldan
ðonne Hnæfe guldan   his hægstealdas.
 Hig fuhton fif dagas   swa hyra nan ne feol
42 drihtgesiða, /   ac hig ða duru heoldon.   193
Ða gewat him wund hæleð   on wæg gangan,
sæde þæt his byrne   abrocen wære
45 heresceorpum hror,   and eac wæs his helm ðyrl;
ða hine sona frægn   folces hyrde
hu ða wigend hyra   wunda genæson
48 oððe hwæþer ðæra hyssa . . .

---

29 Hks *borð. cenum on*] Hks *genumon*.
34 Hks *hwearflacra*.
38 Hks *gebærann*.
39 *swanas*] Hks *swa noc*.

COMMENTARY

1 *hornas*: See 3-9 note.

1-2 Tolkien (following Trautmann) ends line 1 and the opening fragmentary sentence after *byrnað* and reads line 2 as *[H]næf hleoþrode, heaþogeong cyning* (see his commentary (1982, 83)).

2 *hearogeong*: Grundtvig suggests the emendation *heaþogeong*, and many editors adopt this reading. Neither reading is recorded elsewhere.

2-12 Fry identifies in these lines the formulaic theme 'Hero on the Beach' and details its constituents: this "underlies the passage, the hero Hnæf, his Danish retainers, their journey, dawn, Beasts of Battle, flashing weapons, and impending carnage" (1974, 31). Dane points out the weaknesses in Fry's argument, which arise from a number of false assumptions (1982, 443), observing, "The search for a pre-defined theme has led only to a recasting of assumptions in the form of conclusions . . . and extensive lists suggesting the widespread occurrence of the supposed theme" (448). He concludes, "The 'fixed content' of the theme, then, is illusory. Any of its components is expendable. What appears to be a set theme is simply a particular response to a pattern established in the surrounding narrative context" (447).

3-9 Sims-Williams examines this narrative device of offering alternative explanations for a phenomenon or incident before arriving at the correct identification — in this case, trying to explain the source of bright light flashing in the distance — and cites a number of parallels for it in Irish and Welsh literature. The *Finnsburh* example departs from the usual format by having someone produce "erroneous explanations, which are all repeated in the negative by Hnæf, before Hnæf gives the correct explanation" (1976-78, 508). He later summarizes the threefold function of such a narrative device: "It would create a brief moment of suspense and awaken the audience's sense of expectation before an important development in the plot; it would provide an opportunity for vivid direct speech and a display of language; and the use of well-chosen images in the erroneous alternative explanations would evoke that sense of events being larger than life which is the essence of a heroic narrative" (513).

5a This verse is apparently corrupt, there being neither a subject nor an object for *berað*; compare 6.12b-13a, *ongan þa forð beran / gar to guðe*, where the subject is clearly Eadric of line 11a and *beran* governs the object *gar*. Some text, probably two verses, is missing before this line.

5b-7a These four self-contained paratactic principal clauses juxtapose in rapid succession some of the traditional concepts and elements associated with confrontation in Anglo-Saxon heroic poetry, creating a startling and effective impression of the frantic action of large scale hand-to-hand mortal combat.

8 *waðol*: This is related to *weallian*, 'to wander' (cf. *staðolsteall* for an equivalent phonological relationship).

11 *linda*: [Bugge].

hicgeaþ: [Kemble].

11-12 Cf. 6.4, *hicgan to handum and to hige godum* and 6.20, *and bæd þæt hyra randan rihte heoldon*.

13 Tolkien argues that there is the balance of a line missing after *mænig*, and that *goldhladen . . . swurde* once formed a discrete complete line (1982, 86).

goldhladen: Though the constituents are common, the compound appears only here. It should be noted that these are not common troops, but men of means and rank who gird themselves with gold-adorned armour and weapons; note also *drihtlice* (14b) and *drihtgesiða* (42a), and see 1.37 note on the significance of such compounds in Anglo-Saxon poetry. In 39 note, it is argued that the troops accompanying Hnæf were not regular fighting men, but a company of noblemen, household servants, and (most likely) administrators.

ðegn: In his analysis of the structure of society in late Anglo-Saxon England, Loyn notes,

> . . . there emerged in later Anglo-Saxon England a class bound by special legal bonds to the king and to his representative, ealdorman or earl, a class that may in its growth represent the territorialization of political power. The thegn was the typical member of such a class, and his function was twofold: he was a skilled fighting man; he was also a landholder substantially responsible for the maintenance of local peace in his community or communities. (1957, 98)

See 1.37 note for a discussion of other special terms of rank (and compounds formed from these) used in the poems edited here.

19b "to start with"; cf. 1.6b and note, and *Beowulf* 740b and 2286b.

20 *bære*: [Kemble].

24 *cweþ he*: This is clearly extra-metrical, probably intrusive, and should not be considered part of the text.

25 *wreccea*: [Wülker].

weana: [Kemble].

29 *celæs*: Cf. 6.283a, *cellod bord*. Both *celæs* and *cellod* are otherwise unknown. All that can be said about these is that it seems clear that there was some (perhaps archaic and thus unfamiliar) word used to describe a shield in the Anglo-Saxon poetic *wordhord* which began *cel-*. This being the case, *celæs bord* and *banhelm* are both in the nominative and in apposition: "The *celæs* shield in the hands of bold men, the skull-protector (ie, helmet) must needs be shattered (or, 'were destined by their nature to shatter')."

cenum on: [Grein]; for Hks *genumon*.

33b-34 Osborn places a full stop after *sunu* and edits line 34a to read *hwearf lacra hwær*. She offers two interpretations: i) "Around him many a good fight whirled where the raven wandered," and ii) something like, "Around him many good men fell, sacrifices (/. . . many skilled fights take place), where the raven wandered," — both of which she finds "equally attractive". If the first is accepted, then the raven overhead is "the central figure in a fiery sworddance. If *lacra* is taken in this sense, only Garulf has fallen so far, and the skilful sword-play surges around his body." If the second is accepted (with the reading "sacrifices"), then the circling raven may be identified with a psychopomp / goddess who hovers at death waiting to ferry off the souls of the dead; she cites several pagan and Christian analogues for such a notion in English and other medieval literatures (1970, 185-88). Other plausible emendations of Hickes' troublesome offering are the one offered here, translated ". . . around him many good ones, the corpses of the fleeting (/transitory)"; or, *hwearflicra, hwær* (preferred by Fry, 1969 and 1974), translated ". . . and about him many good ones, [many] active ones, where . . ." (1969, 241).

34 *hwearflicra hræw*: [Grein, 1867].

35 *sealobrun*: Though the constituents of this compound are common, the word is not recorded elsewhere.

swurdleoma: Cf. *Beowulf* 1143b (*hildeleoman* — perhaps the name of the sword itself), 1523a (*beadoleoma*) and 2583a (*hildeleoman*) for analogous formations; see 3.4 note.

35-36 Cf. *Beowulf* 2313b, *bryneleoma stod*.

36 *Finnsburuh*: It can never be known exactly where Finnsburh was located, but Fry (simply by repunctuating *Beowulf*, 1125-29a) has at least clarified the textual crux in the Episode which suggested that the Frisian king's hall was situated outside Frisia.

37-38 Cf. *Beowulf* 1011-12,

> Ne gefrægen ic þa mægþe maran weorode
> ymb hyra sincgyfan sel gebæran

[I have never heard of a nation behaving better around their treasure-giver in so great a company]; and also 2014b-16a.

and also 2014b-16a.

38 *sigebeorna*: This compound is unrecorded elsewhere though its constituents are common.

39 Tolkien makes two lines of this:

> ne nefre swanas sel forgyldan
> hwitne medo, [heardgesteallan,]

(1982, 20 and 89 commentary).

swanas: [Grein]. This word does not appear elsewhere in Anglo-Saxon verse; it is used in prose with the meaning 'herdsman' or 'peasant'. In Old Norse, *sveinn* means 'boy / page / esquire'; Old Saxon *sven* means 'swineherd' and Old High German *svein* means 'servant / herd'. Tolkien observes that *swan* is not connected with *swin*, but with the reflexive pronoun; cf. *swæs*, 'one's own, dear'. "Thus **swaina-* would mean 'belonging to one's own household, personal retainer' (1982, 89)."

All the evidence found here and in the Episode suggests that Hnæf's visit was a social event (coming as it did before Yuletide), a get-together with his sister, nephew and brother-in-law, but that something tragically went wrong with the plan (recall that Tolkien argues that the hostilities probably erupted between two groups of Jutes, some in Hnæf's company, the others in Finn's, and that the relatives were unwillingly drawn into it). Thus Hnæf's band is not made up of warriors, but noblemen and household servants (see above and 13 note). This also accounts for the amazement conveyed by the poet in stressing that (in spite of the nature of his troops) Hnæf's retainers managed to defend themselves honourably for five days without the loss of a single life. The fact that they have armour with them does not argue against this since the poet tells us that it was highly ornamented (the men are *goldhladen*), indicating that it was probably more valuable than functional.

39-40 Robinson observes,

> We know from *Maldon* and from *Beowulf* itself that the vow to serve the leader was made when the warrior drank the mead, as if accepting the drink confirmed the binding force of the oath (1985, 75-76).

He cites analogues from other Germanic literature which clearly delineate the full implications of the ritual alluded to here, and which put references to Hrothgar's worthy troops as *druncne* in the proper light; see also 6.211-15 and *Beowulf* 2633-38.

45 *heresceorpum hror*: Tolkien finds this line objectionable, but 'active in his battle equipment' is the subject of *sæde*, and makes perfect sense in this context where the defenders have been unexpectedly fighting for their lives for the past five days, and as the first casualties are sustained, a warrior reports to Hnæf that their arms are beginning to fail them. Tolkien emends the verse to read *heresceorp unhror*, even though *unhror* is unattested elsewhere; here and in many other instances, Tolkien shows himself prone to improving the text by rewriting it. [In fairness to Tolkien, it must be said it is unlikely that he expected his teaching notes to be published posthumously as if they were his final say on these matters.]

46 *folces hyrde*: Greenfield examines the other instances of this formulaic verse "to assess its use in context", and concludes that the referent here "is much more likely to be Hnæf" (1972, 98), contrary to the almost universally held view among critics that it is Finn. In the five instances in which it occurs in *Beowulf* (610a, 1832a, 1849a, 2644b, 2981a), the referent is clearly indicated (it occurs only once elsewhere, in *Metres of Boethius*, 10.49b, where its referent is identified later). Not only is Hnæf mentioned a few lines earlier (40a), but the inherent logic of the narrative's progress suggests this,

that after holding the doors for five days the Danes suffer their first casualty, and that this turn of events is what is being reported to the king in question; it should be recalled that a great number of Frisians had already fallen in the fray (31-34a).

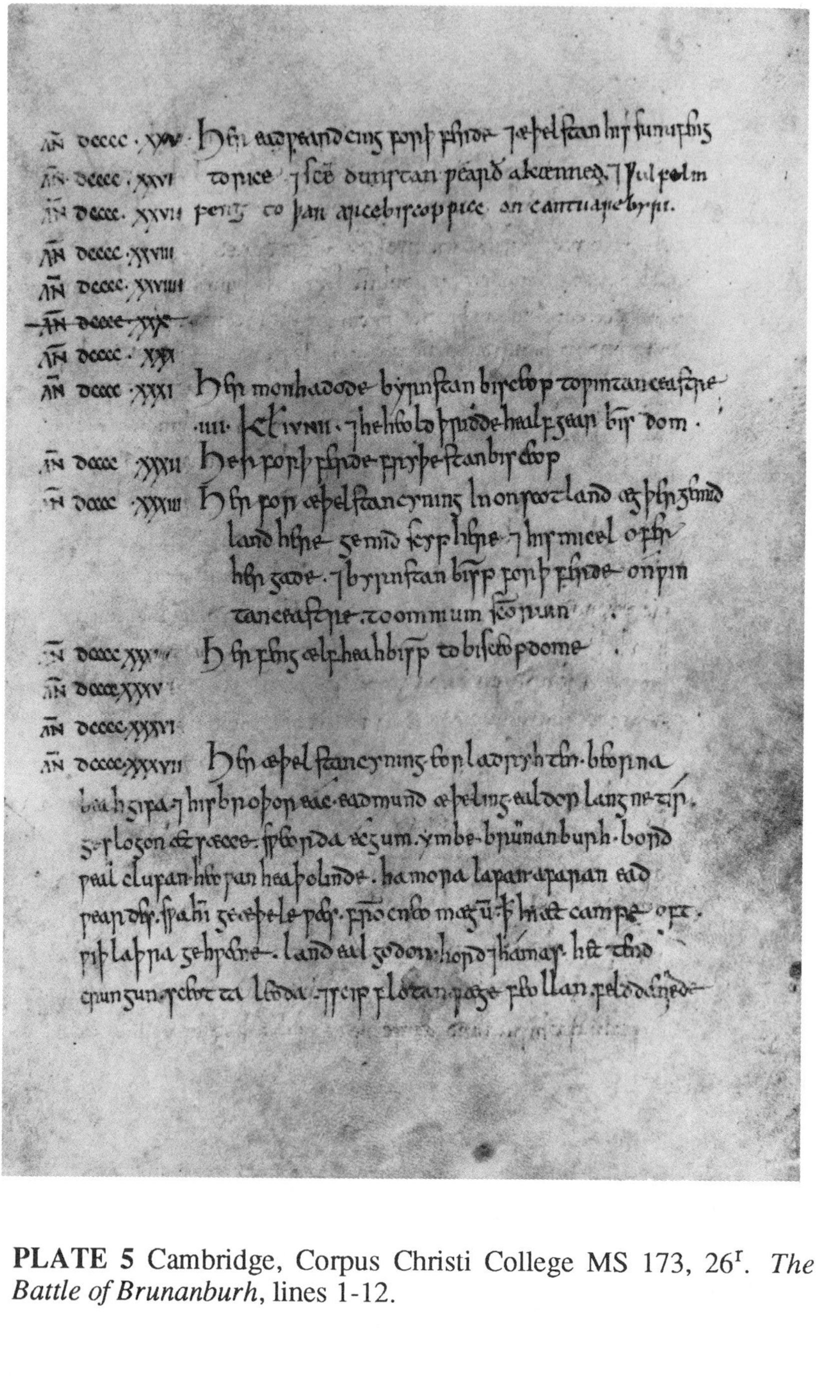

PLATE 5 Cambridge, Corpus Christi College MS 173, 26ʳ. *The Battle of Brunanburh*, lines 1-12.

FIVE: THE BATTLE OF BRUNANBURH

INTRODUCTION

Manuscript

The Battle of Brunanburh is recorded in the following witnesses for the *Anglo-Saxon Chronicle* as the entry for the year 937:

A MS Corpus Christi College Cambridge 173, 26^r-27^r
[the poem is in a tenth century hand (see Plates 5-7)];
B British Library MS Cotton Tib. A.VI, 31^r-32^r
[also in a tenth century hand];
C British Library MS Cotton Tib. B.I, 141^{r-v}
[the poem is in an eleventh century hand];
D British Library MS Cotton Tib. B.IV, 49^r-50^r
[also in an eleventh century hand].

Since the history and interrelationship of the various witnesses for the *ASC* is such a complex and contentious issue, the reader is referred to the Bibliography, where the major editions and studies of it are listed.

Text

The poem lacks a title in the *ASC*, but is generally known as *The Battle of Brunanburh*, taking its title from the location of the battle as given in line 5 of the text; there is some doubt as to the exact location of Brunanburh (but see 5.5 note).

Structure, theme and genre: The Battle of Brunanburh is one of several poems in the ASC that are either panegyrics upon royal persons or celebrations of memorable events, or a combination of these, as in this instance; the others appear as entries for the years 942, 973, 975, 1036 and 1065.[1] Brunanburh is by far the best of these, the rest generally being considered inferior (but see 6.45 note).[2]

Brunanburh is a work of high quality which consciously exploits the modes of the traditional Anglo-Saxon heroic verse. Of late, its sophisticated rhetorical style has been the subject of critical discussion.[3] Some of the traditional conventions of heroic verse it employs are: i) the battle lasts a whole day; ii) there is fierce pursuit of the enemy; iii) the victors return in triumph; and iv) the beasts of prey remain on the battlefield devouring the carrion.

The style of the poems in the ASC reflects the response to the study and imitation of traditional Anglo-Saxon alliterative verse techniques in the eleventh century, apparently a time of transition for the traditional verse form.[4] It is interesting to note that although 21 verses of the poem are identical to others in the surviving corpus of Anglo-Saxon poetry, a considerable number of words are unique to it (16 in 73 lines; see Commentary, 3). Campbell observes that the narrative advances verse by verse showing a tightness of style and good control of the verse form. Unlike *The Battle of Maldon*, it is not primarily an historical poem, and so differs in that it does not attempt to give an eyewitness account of the battle, or any

---

[1] These are edited by Elliott van Kirk Dobbie, *The Anglo-Saxon Minor Poems*, ASPR VI (New York: Columbia Univ. Press, 1942), pp. 16-26.

[2] Note, for example, the unskilled use of traditional formulae (the *ofer*-phrases in particular) in *The Death of Edgar* (in the entry for 975):
And þa wearð eac adræfed deormod hæleð,
Oslac, of earde ofer yða gewealc,
ofer ganotes bæð, gamolfeax hæleð,
wis and wordsnotor, ofer wætera geðring,
ofer hwæles eðel, hama bereafod

[And then Oslac, a brave-minded warrior, was driven from the country, over the tossing of the waves, over the gannet's bath, a grey-haired warrior, wise and eloquent, over the commotion of the waters, over the homeland of the whale, deprived of a home].

[3] See Addison (1982), Bolton (1968), Campbell (1966 and 1967), Johnson (1968), Lawler (1973) and Lipp (1969).

[4] See the Commentary for *forgrunden* (43) and *hwit* (63), and Campbell's detailed analysis of the poem's metre (1938, 16-42); also Scragg's discussion of the metre and style of *The Battle of Maldon* (1981, 28-35) and Cable's article on the dating of poems from metrical evidence (1981).

geographical details concerning the site. *Brunanburh* is a panegyric whose important features are its use of perspective, its fine structural balance and use of antithesis throughout, its highly rhetorical style, and its unabashed patriotism. Athelstan is rightly regarded as the king of all Britain by this poet who has a keen sense of historical perspective.

Language: The four extant versions of *The Battle of Brunanburh* are all recorded in late tenth century West-Saxon; further details concerning the dialectal peculiarities of these, and especially of the *A*-version, are found in Campbell (1938, 8-15).

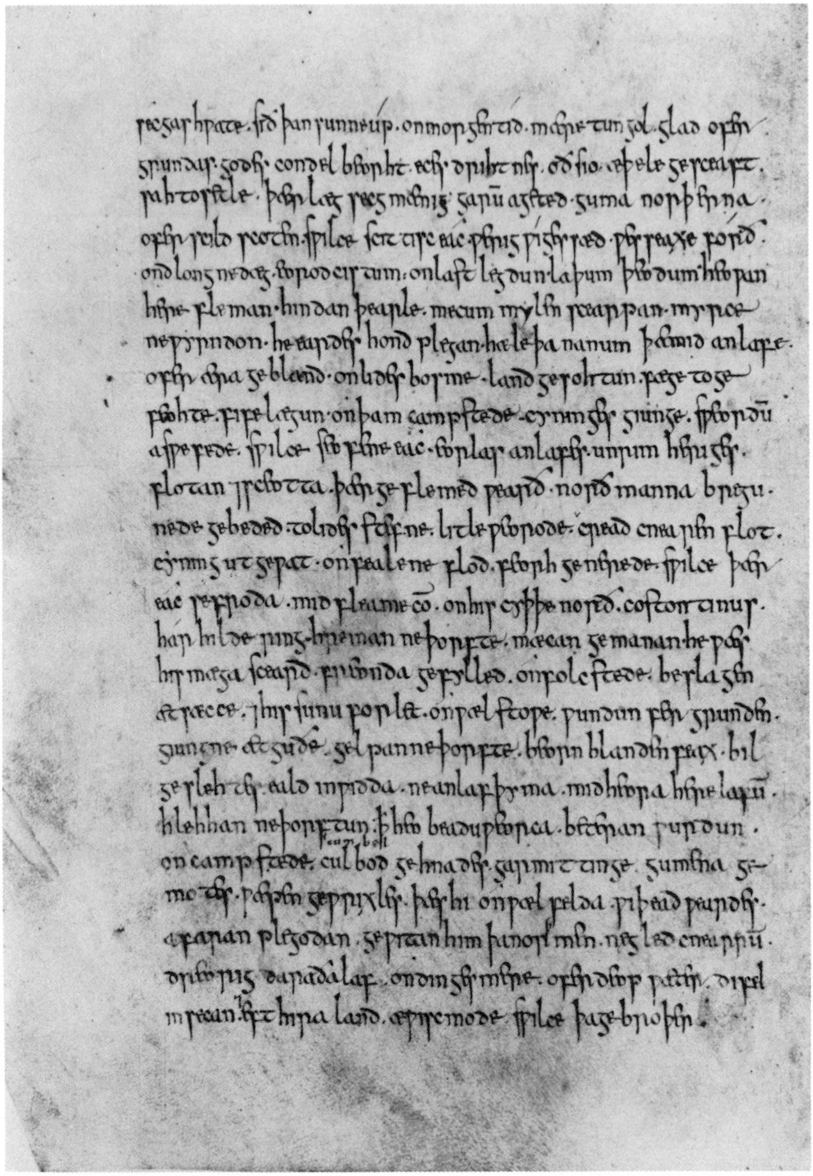

PLATE 6 Cambridge, Corpus Christi College MS 173, 26ᵛ. *The Battle of Brunanburh*, lines 13-57.

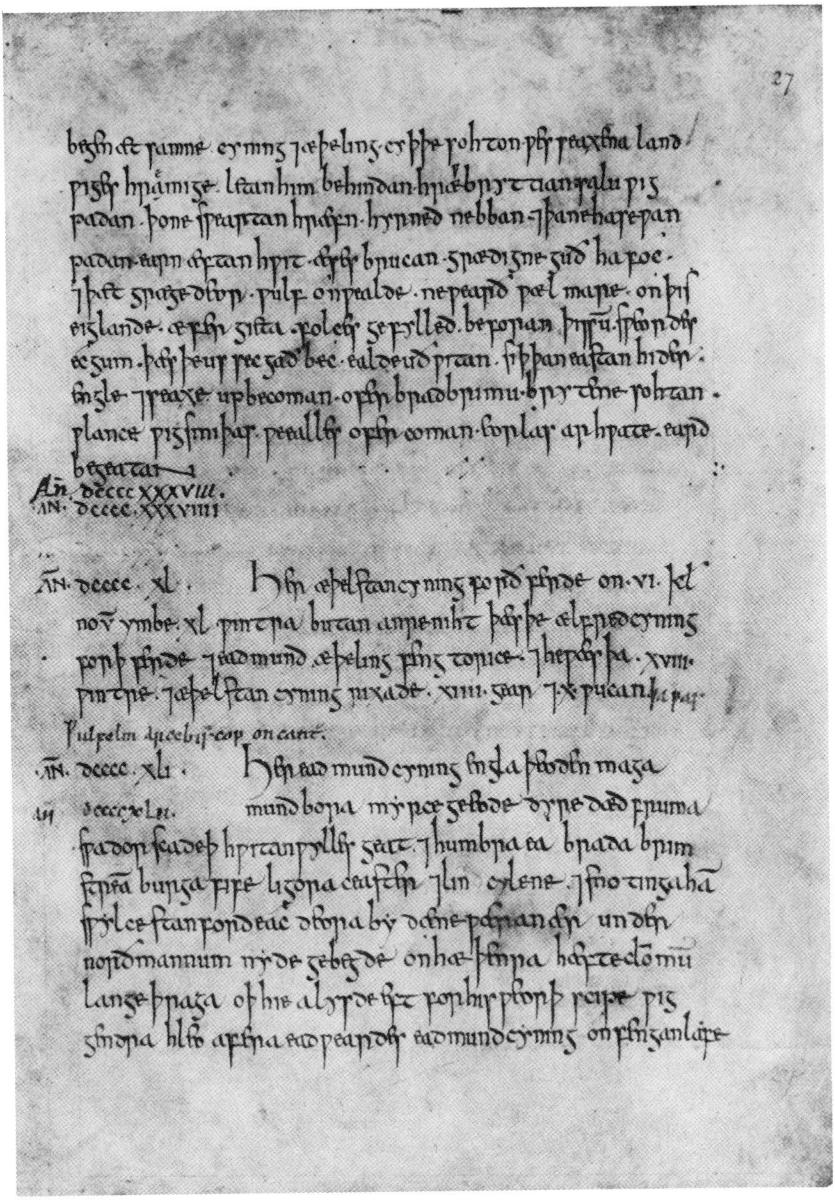

PLATE 7 Cambridge, Corpus Christi College, MS 173, 27ʳ. *The Battle of Brunanburh*, lines 58-73.

THE BATTLE OF BRUNANBURH

    Æþelstan cyning   eorla dryhten,
    beorna beahgifa   and his broþor eac
3 Eadmund æþeling,   ealdorlangne tir
    geslogon æt sæcce   sweorda ecgum
    ymbe Brunanburh;   bordweal clufan,
6 heowan heaþolinde   hamora lafan
    afaran Eadweardes;   swa him geæþele wæs
    from cneomægum   þæt hi æt campe oft
9 wiþ laþra gehwæne   land ealgodon
    hord and hamas.   Hettend crungun,
    Sceotta leoda   and scipflotan
12 fæge feollan;   feld dænnede /
    secga swate   siðþan sunne up
    on morgentid,   mære tungol
15 glad ofer grundas,   Godes condel beorht,
    eces Drihtnes   oð sio æþele gesceaft
    sah to setle.   Þær læg secg mænig
18 garum ageted,   guma norþerna
    ofer scild scoten,   swilce Scittisc eac
    werig wiges sæd.   Wesseaxe forð
21 ondlongne dæg   eorodcistum
    on last legdun   laþum þeodum,
    heowan herefleman   hindan þearle
24 mecum mylenscearpan;   Myrce ne wyrndon
    heardes hondplegan   hæleþa nanum
    þæra þe mid Anlafe   ofer eargebland
27 on lides bosme   land gesohtun,

---

5 A *brunnanburh* with first *n* interlinear.   D *heordweal*.
11 BCD *leode*.
12 *dænnede*] A second *n* added interlinearly: BCD (see spelling variants).
13 *secga swate*] BCD: A *secgas hwate*.
16 *oð*] B *þæt*.   *sio*] D *se*.
18 BCD *guman norþerna* (see spelling variants).
20 *sæd*] D *ræd*: C adds *ond*.
24 D *mycelscearpum*.
25 A *he eardes*.

fæge to gefeohte. Fife lægun
on þam campstede cyningas giunge,
30 sweordum aswefede; swilce seofene eac
eorlas Anlafes, unrim heriges
flotena and Sceotta. Þær geflemed wearð
33 Norðmanna bregu, nede gebeded
to lides stefne litle weorode;
cread cnear on flot, cyning ut gewat
36 on fealene flod, feorh generede.
Swilce þær eac se froda mid fleame com
on his cyþþe norð, Constontinus
39 har hildering; hreman ne þorfte
mecga gemanan: he wæs his mæga sceard,
freonda gefylled on folcstede,
42 beslagen æt sæcce, and his sunu forlet
on wælstowe wundun forgrunden,
giungne æt guðe; gelpan ne þorfte
45 beorn blandenfeax bilgeslehtes
eald inwidda, ne Anlaf þy ma;
mid heora herelafum hlehhan ne þorftun,
48 þæt heo beaduweorca beteran wurdun
on campstede - cumbolgehnastes,
garmittinge, gumena gemotes,
51 wæpengewrixles - þæs hi on wælfelda
wiþ Eadweardes afaran plegodan.
Gewitan him þa Norþmen nægledcnearrum,

---

26 *þære þe*] BCD (see spelling variants): A *þæ.* *eargebland*] BCD (see spelling variants): A *æra gebland*.

27 C *liþes*.

29 *cyningas*] BCD (see spelling variants): A *cyninges*.

31 *anlafes*] C adds *and*.

32 A *flotan*.

35 *cnear on*] A *cnearen*. D *flod* (see note).

38 A *costontinus*.

39 *har*] D *hal*.

40 *mecga*] A *mæcan*. *he*] BC *her*.

41 *on*] C adds *his*.

42 *beslagen*] B *forslegen*.

43 A *fergrunden*.

47 *hlehhan*] D *hlybban*.

49 A *culbodgehnades* with the interlinear gloss *vel cumbel*.

51 *þæs*] D adds *þe*.

54 dreorig daraða laf on Dingesmere
ofer deop wæter Difelin secan,
eft Ira land æwiscmode;
57 swilce þa gebroþer / begen ætsamne   27^r
cyning and æþeling cyþþe sohton,
Wesseaxena land wiges hremige.
60 Letan him behindan hræ bryttian
saluwigpadan, þone sweartan hræfn
hyrnednebban, and þane hasupadan
63 earn æftan hwit æses brucan,
grædigne guðhafoc and þæt græge deor
wulf on wealde. Ne wearð wæl mare
66 on þis eiglande æfre gieta
folces gefylled beforan þissum
sweordes ecgum, þæs þe us secgað bec,
69 ealde uðwitan, siþþan eastan hider
Engle and Seaxe up becoman,
ofer brad brimu Brytene sohtan,
72 wlance wigsmiþas, Wealas ofercoman,
eorlas arhwate, eard begeatan.

---

53 A *normen* with *þ* added interlinearly. *nægledcnearrum*] D *dæg gled on garum.*
55 D *deopne.* D *dyflig.*
56 A adds *ond* interlinearly before *eft.* a *hira.*
57 D *bege æt runne.*
59 *hremige*] an earlier *a* for the first *e* expuncted.
60 A *hræw* with *w* added interlinearly. D *bryttinga.*
62 A *hasewanpadan.*
64 D *cuðheafoc.*
66 D *þisne.* A *æfer.*
67 B *afylled.*
70 B *sexan.*
71 BCD *brade.*
72 A *weealles.*

PHONOLOGICAL AND SPELLING VARIÀNTS

(Final readings only are cited here, not earlier forms which were subsequently corrected in the various manuscripts.)

1 B *æþestan*   BC *cing*   BCD *drihten*
2 B *beaggifa* C *beahgyfa*   3 C *ealdorlagne*   D *tyr*
4 B *geslogan*   B *sake:* D *secce*   C *swurda*   B *ecggum*
5 BC *embe*   BC *brunnanburh bordweall*   C *clufon*
6 C *heowon*   B *heaðolina:* C *heaþolinda:* D *heaðolinda*   D *hamera*   BCD *lafum*
7 B *eaforan:* C *aforan:* D *eoforan*   D *eadweardæs*
8 BCD *fram*   B *cneomagum* B *hie*   B *gehwane*   B *ealgodan:* D *gealgodon*
10 D *heted*   BCD *crungon*   11 BCD *scotta*   C *scypflotan*
12 BC *dennade:* D *dennode*
13 BC *upp*   15 BCD *candel*   16 BC *seo*
17 D *sætle*   B *manig:* CD *monig*
18 B *forgrunden*   D *norþærne*
19 BCD *scyld*   BD *sceoten swylce*   BCD *scyttisc*
20 BC *wigges*   B *westsexe:* C *wessexe*
21 BCD *andlangne*   BCD *eoredcystum*
22 BC *legdon:* D *lægdon*   C *ðeodon*
23 C *heowon*   B *hereflyman:* C *hereflymon:* D *heora flyman*
24 BC *mylenscearpum*   25 BCD *handplegan*
27 B *gesohtan:* CD *gesohton*   28 D *feohte*   BCD *lagon*
29 B *ðæm*   B *ciningas:* C *cingas*   BC *geonge:* D *iunga*
30 C *aswefde*   D *swylce*   B *seofone:* C *vii*
31 BD *herges*   32 BCD *scotta*   BCD *geflymed*
33 BCD *brego*   CD *neade*   BCD *gebæded*
34 D *stæfne*   BCD *lytle*   C *werode*
35 D *creat*   B *cing:* C *cining*
36 CD *fealone*   CD *generode*
37 BD *swylce*   38 BCD *constantinus*
39 BC *hilderinc:* D *hylderinc*   D *hryman*
40 B *mecca:* C *meca:* D *mecga*   BC *maga*

42 C *beslegen:* D *beslægen*   B *sace:* D *sæcge*   D *forlæt*
43 BCD *wundum*   BCD *forgrunden*
44 BCD *geongne*   BCD *gylpan*
45 BC *blandenfex*   B *billgeslyhtes:* CD *billgeslihtes*
46 BC *inwitta:* D *inwuda*   BD *þe*
47 CD *hyra*   D *hereleafum*   BC *hlihhan*   BD *þorftan*
48 B *hie:* CD *hi*   BCD *beadoweorca*   B *wurdan:* CD *wurdon*
49 BCD *cumbolgehnastes*   50 D *garmittunge*   51 B *hie*
52 B *eaforan:* C *aforan*   CD *plegodon*
53 CD *gewiton*   C *hym*   BC *norðmenn:* D *norðmen*   C *negledcnearrum:* D *dæg gled on garum*
54 C *dreori*   B *daroða:* C *dareþa:* D *dareða*   B *dyngesmere:* D *dynigesmere*
55 B *dyflen:* C *dyflin*   B *secean*   56 CD *yra*
57 BD *swylce*   B *gebroðor:* C *broðor:* D *gebroþor*   BC *ætsomne*
58 BC *cing*   D *eaðeling*   B *sohtan*
59 BD *westseaxna:* C *wessexena*   BC *wigges*
60 C *leton:* D *læton*   C *hym behindon*   B *hraw:* CD *hra*   B *bryttigean:* C *brittigan*
61 BCD *salowigpadan*   C *hrefn*
62 D *hyrnetnebban*   BC *þone*   B *hasopadan:* C *hasupadan*
64 D *grege*
66 BC *þys*   B *eglande:* CD *iglande*   BCD *æfre*   BC *gyta:* D *gita*
67 B *afylled*   BCD *þyssum*   68 C *swurdes*   B *secggeaþ*
69 B *syþþan* 70 C *sexe*   BC *upp*   CD *becomon*
71 C *bretene sohtan:* D *britene sohton*   72 CD *ofercomon*
73 D *arhwæte*   BC *begeaton*

COMMENTARY

1 The absence of speeches in *Brunanburh* is uncharacteristic of traditional heroic poetry and indicative of its literary character and the poet's cool objectivity; Frese observes,

> ... *The Battle of Brunanburh* is an entirely soundless imagined experience; the act of human utterance has been completely subsumed here into the silence of written record. (1986, 89)

1-7 On the use of the framing device here, see 1.38-44 note.

3 *ealdorlangne*: This otherwise unrecorded form was probably formed by analogy with the common adjective *ondlongne* which appears in line 21, demonstrating the flexibility of the poetic language. Considering the poet's impressive use of rhetorical devices in *Brunanburh*, the proportionately large number of *hapax legomena* in the poem (listed in the following paragraph) is perhaps evidence of his attempt to rejuvenate the poetic vocabulary and to write in the traditional manner. (Of course, it must always be remembered that there has probably been extensive loss of material which once existed.) A number of critics of *Brunanburh* consider it "to be an entirely artificial or literary poem", but see 62b-63 note. (Robinson (1985) observes that the *Beowulf* poet deliberately attempts to rejuvenate the vocabulary for greater artistic effect; see 1.1 note on *maðolade*.)

The *hapax legomena* are: *arhwate* (73), *bilgeslehtes* (45), *cnear* (35), *cumbolgehnastes* (49), *dingesmere* (54), *ealdorlangne* (3), *garmittinge* (50), *geæpele* (7), *guðhafoc* (64), *hasupadan* (62), *heaþolinde* (6), *herefleman* (23), *mylenscearpan* (24), *nægledcnearrum* (53), *scipflotan* (11), and *wælfelda* (51).

3b-4a This seems to be traditional formulaic phraseology; cf. *Beowulf* 2996b: *syððan hie ða mærða geslogon* (referring to the achievements of Eofor and Wulf in the Swedish conflict).

5 *ymbe Brunanburh*: In the most recent article discussing the location where the battle might have been fought, Wood argues that the Domesday settlement called Brynesford on White Hill (hence the *-burh*) is probably to be identified with *Brunanburh* of the poem. Though the derivation of *-brynes* from *-brun* cannot be substantiated

phonologically, the forms are very similar; however, "it is the strategic significance of Brunanburh which forces our attention upon it" (1980, 212), lying as it does on the Viking Age route from Northumbria into the Five Boroughs.

7 *geæþele*: See 1.4b-5a note. Loyn observes concerning the office of kingship,

> From the seventh century forward no ruler who could not claim membership of one of the royal dynasties governed an English folk without earning for himself the opprobrium of some of his people. It was held even by the most restrained commentators as shameful that a man not of the royal kin should be elevated to the kingship. Ælle of Northumbria was bluntly described by the Anglo-Saxon Chronicler (under 867) as an *ungecynde cining*, a king not of proper ruling stock. Belief in the importance of the blood royal may therefore be isolated as an early and basic characteristic of English political thought. (1984, 15)

12b-13a "The field resounded with the blood of men." This example of synaesthesia (rarely found in Anglo-Saxon poetry) has disturbed a number of critics, but Berkhout points out that its sensory appeal "lies in the vividness of its combined oral-visual effect" (1974, 162). He cites a Biblical analogue (and perhaps its source) in Genesis 4:10 (*Vox sanguinis fratris tui clamat ad me de terra*), and observes that the Old English *Genesis* poet retained the figure in his rendering of the Biblical narrative (1012b-13a, *and his blod to me / cleopað and cigeð*). Editors that have not accepted the use of this figure here usually emend to *dunnade* 'to grow dark'.

Frese observes that this reading of the passage is "quite consonant with the poem's otherwise unbroken silence that mirrors the rarity of reported speech in the *Anglo-Saxon Chronicle*" (1986, 91).

13-17 This is an elaborate use of variation to express something quite straightforward, that the battle lasted all day long; such descriptions of the sun's progress are common in the poetry (compare, for example, *Phoenix* 90-99a). In addition to displaying a knowledge of rhetorical devices, however, the poet is establishing the central imagery of his poem, in which Æthelstan and, earlier, the continental Germanic tribes who came to England, are associated with the glory of the rising sun in the east (see 42 note). Compare the structure of the following from *Beowulf*:

siððan hie sunnan leoht geseon meahton,
oþ ðe nipende niht ofer ealle,
scaduhelma gesceapu scriðan cwoman
wan under wolcnum (648-51a)

[. . . from the time they could see the light of the sun until the darkness of night was advancing over everything, creatures of the covering darkness came gliding forth, obscure beneath the clouds];

and,

Siððan heofones gim
glad ofer grundas (2072b-73a)

[After the jewel of heaven had glided over the expanses . . .]

Isaacs (1963, 247), seeing some significance in the use of *setle* here, argues that there is a submerged metaphor in the passage, the sun being "personified as an ideal retainer returning to the mead bench in his lord's hall at the end of the day" (Anderson, 1973, 363). Anderson, however, demonstrates that *setle* usually appears in collocation with *sunne* in descriptions of the passing of the day, and that it is unlikely that the poet intended to invoke an association of the resting place of the sun with the *medusetl* of a Germanic lord. He further observes that "(a) special artistic effect is created by the suspension of the collocation" [*sunne . . . setle*].

19b The poet apparently found this formulaic phrase useful for the antithetical structure he intended to develop and for advancing the narrative since he used it again in variant forms at 30b and 37a.

20-28 Page notes that the poet does not say that the West-Saxon *fyrd* and the Mercians fought as allied forces at Brunanburh, but i) that the West-Saxons pursued the enemy all day long (a cliché, as noted in the Introduction here), and ii) that after the battle, as the enemy fled in disarray in two contingents, "(t)heir flight led them through English Mercia where local troops harassed them until they reached safety" (Page, 1982, 340). Note the *E*-version of the *ASC* for 937: *Her Æðelstan cyning lædde fyrde to Brunanbyrig*; no mention is made of Mercian allies. In general, critics have assumed the English army was comprised of allied forces; see, eg, Lawler (1973), 54 and 63.

24 *mylenscearpan*: 'sharpened on a grindstone'; cf. 6.108b-109, *feolhearde speru, / grimme gegrundene garas fleogan.*

28 *fife*: Note *seofene* (30b) and *unrim* (31b); this use of an incremental pattern is probably rhetorical.

32b-36 Comparing these lines with passages in *Beowulf* which describe the launching of ships, Fry observes that the phrase *to lides stefne* (34a) is used to indicate the undignified manner in which Anlaf and his little band of survivors, pressed by need (33b), work the boat loose from the shore "by applying men's weight to the outboard prow," and translates 35a, "He (Anlaf) pressed the ship onto the flood" (1981, 65-66).

35 *cnear*: This is found only here and in the compound *nægledcnearrum* in 53b. Campbell notes that its only Germanic cognate is Old Norse *knörr* which usually means 'merchant-ship' (1938, 108). It is probably an example of an Anglo-Saxon poet using a Scandinavian word to describe something Scandinavian, to create a certain atmosphere or air of authenticity in his work. It has been suggested that the *Maldon* poet uses Scandinavianisms for the purpose of literary characterization; see 6.29-41 note.

flot The scribe of the *D* version omitted lines 35b-36a when his eye jumped from *flot* to *flod* in 36a, a common scribal error known as homœoarchy.

36 Cf. 3.16a, 6.193-94 and *Beowulf* 2599a, where *ealdre burgan* may be ironic in that by saving their lives they did not save their lord (*ealdor*).

42 *sunu*: Lawler suggests that a pun may be intended here since the glory of the West-Saxon leaders is associated with the sun coming from the east in the imagery used by the poet throughout the poem (1973, 57).

43 *forgrunden*: Since this participle here modifies *sunu*, its form would normally be *forgrundenne* (as some editors have emended it), but that form is metrically undesirable; Campbell observes, "In O.E. the past participle is sometimes uninflected where an ordinary adjective would be inflected" (1938, 112; however, see 63 note below).

44 Cf. *Beowulf* 2873-74a,

    Nealles folccyning fyrdgesteallum
    gylpan þorfte

[Not at all was there need for the people's king to boast about his comrades in battle].

The *Brunanburh* poet is clearly using traditional rhetorical phrasing here (the formula occurs elsewhere in *Beowulf* in a different context; see 2995b-96a). However, the extension of the figure and the development of the poem's characteristic antithetical structure are indicative of the not inconsiderable skill of the poet.

53 *nægledcnearrum*: See *cnear* 35 note and 6.29-41 note.

54 *dreorig*: Wentersdorf argues that there is a semantic development here from the meaning 'bleeding to death' to 'ill-fated / doomed to die'; citing analogous uses of *dreorig* elsewhere in the verse and noting 28a, *fæge to gefeohte*, he translates "the ill-fated [Norsemen] who had survived battle" (1973, 237).

60-65a Campbell draws attention to "the free use of the definite article in this passage, which would have been avoided in the older poetry" (1938, 119).

It is noteworthy that three verses in this passage (61a, 62a, 65a) appear in virtually identical form in the description of the beasts of battle in *Judith* (at 211a, 212a, 206a respectively); Magoun (1955) illustrates the highly formulaic diction of all twelve instances of the theme of the 'Beasts of Battle' in Anglo-Saxon poetry, but his analysis is predictably limited to technical matters, and lacks the critical perspicacity of Greenfield's (1955) treatment of the theme of exile and its associated verbal collocations.

62b-63 Van't Hul and Mitchell argue that this unique and sharply descriptive passage shows that the *Brunanburh* poet is "capable of evoking other than purely literary responses" (1980, 390), something earlier criticism generally did not concede. The poem's highly stylized and rhetorical manner is often considered a fault when in another age it would have been held a strength.

63 *hwit*: To account for this uninflected form in a line with excellent metre Campbell observes that the half line was probably the poet's deliberate parenthesis, so that the half-line should be read "outside the grammatical flow of the passage" (1938, 119).

64 *guðhafoc*: This is a unique compound made from common words; Campbell notes that it is "the only recorded compound with *hafoc* in the second element . . . apart from names of kinds of hawks" (1938, 119).

65b-68a "Never yet within this island has there been a greater slaughter of folk felled by the sword's edges before this one" (Bradley, 1982, 518).

SIX: THE BATTLE OF MALDON

INTRODUCTION

Manuscript

The Battle of Maldon is known today only from a transcript made by David Casley, Underkeeper of the Cotton Library, some time between 1718 and 1725 (see Plate 8).[1] Originally, it was in British Library MS Cotton Otho A.XII, one of the many manuscripts mutilated or destroyed in the disastrous fire at Ashburnham House in 1731; no fragments of the manuscript survive. The transcript is now preserved in Bodleian Library MS Rawlinson 203 (pages 7-12). The poem had been the third item in the Otho manuscript, occupying folios 57^r-62^v (if the fourth item began at the top of 63^r). It is of interest that the only manuscript witness for Asser's *Life of King Alfred* occupied the first 55 folios of the same manuscript, and that it too was wholly lost and is known only from a transcript. Richards argues that, although *The Battle of Maldon* was contained in a discrete gathering in the Otho MS, a topical relationship can be demonstrated among the texts in that codex; she does not consider Asser's *Life* or the A-S Charms that precede *Maldon* since they were not bound with the other poems until early modern times (1984, 79 and 85). She demonstrates the similarities between the lives of Byrhtnoth and St. Elphege (whose *Vita* follows *Maldon* in the Otho

---

[1] Until 1986, the transcript was ascribed incorrectly to John Elphinstone, Underkeeper of the Cotton Library until his dismissal by Bentley, the Keeper, in 1716-17 (see Rogers (1985)); Plate 9 is a sample of Casley's everyday hand.

MS), in that they both refused payment of ransom to the Vikings and precipitated "their own deaths by insisting on taking a stand against the persistent Viking incursions" (1984, 82). Elphege was martyred in 1012 on Easter Sunday, and was venerated at Canterbury; Byrhtnoth was also commemorated there for having bequeathed properties in Essex to Christ Church. Continuing her analysis, she demonstrates the topical relationship of the remaining texts in the codex and suggests that successive compilers had a common purpose, "to preserve the accomplishments of local heroes for the historical record and to respond to Norman challenges regarding the authenticity of English saints" (1984, 80). The manuscript was at Barking Abbey in the twelfth century when further material was added to it, and linguistic and circumstantial evidence suggest strongly that it originated at Canterbury; see Richards (1984, 83-85 and notes 1 and 3).

History: The text is first mentioned in Thomas Smith's *Catalogue* of the Cotton Library published in 1696, where it is described as *Fragmentum quoddam Historicum de Eadrico, etc, Saxonice* ('a certain historical fragment about Eadric, etc., in Saxon'). Humphrey Wanley's analysis of a few years later is more accurate and informative:

> Fragmentum capite et calce mutilum, sex folios constans, quo Poetice et Stylo Caedmoniano celebratur virtus bellica BEORHTNOTHI Ealdormanni OFFAE et aliorum Anglo-Saxonum, in proelio cum Danis ('a fragment damaged at the beginning and the end, consisting of six folios, in which the warlike virtues of Byrhtnoth the ealdorman, of Offa, and of other Anglo-Saxons are celebrated poetically in the style of Caedmon').

In his transcript, Casley attempts to reproduce some of the orthographic features of the lost manuscript, but often his eighteenth-century letter forms intrude into the text. The poem was first printed (in prose form) from the transcript by Thomas Hearne in 1726 at the end of his edition of John of Glastonbury's *Chronicle*, and then (in verse) by Benjamin Thorpe in 1834 in his *Analecta Anglo-Saxonica*. The transcript in the Rawlinson MS remained unknown until rediscovered by Neil Ker in the early 1930s. Nothing further can be said about the original except that the poem seems to have occupied a single quire of the manuscript, and that since it consisted of 6 folios in the eighteenth century and the usual insular format for a quire was 8, not very much of the poem has been lost; indeed, the poem seems quite complete as a narrative.

Text

The poem is traditionally known as *The Battle of Maldon*, taking its title, like *Finnsburh* and *Brunanburh*, from the location of the battle. The battle is recorded in the *C*, *D* and *E* versions of the *ASC* sub anno 991 by the common entry:

> Her wæs Gypeswic gehergod, and æfter ðon swiðe raðe wæs Brihtnoð ealdorman ofslegen æt Mældune. And on ðam geare man geræ dde ðæt man geald ærest gafol Denescum mannum, for ðam miclan brogan ðe hi worhton be ðam særiman; ðæt wæs ærest X ðusend punda. Ðæne ræd geræ dde ærest Syric arcebisceop.

[The entry in the *A*-version is less reliable than usual in this matter for two reasons, namely, that it has the entry under the wrong year (993), and it includes in the same entry details known to belong properly to 994.]

Other accounts of the battle survive in two Latin historical works: the *Vita Oswaldi* written by Byrhtferth at Ramsey Abbey between 997 and 1005; and the twelfth century *Liber Eliensis*, which is not very reliable, and which conflicts with the contemporary reports on a number of details.[2]

Structure, theme and genre: *The Battle of Maldon* celebrates a battle lost by the English, and is rightly regarded as an historical poem, although it is not without literary merit.[3] Byrhtnoth was an *ealdormann* of Essex of noble birth, and by 991 was the leading man of that rank in England. As the *ASC* entry implies, his loss on the battlefield was perhaps the turning point in the conflict between the English and the Danes during the reign of Ethelred (Unræd). The poem is not overburdened with precise detail concerning the conflict, and consequently many critics have spilt a river of ink writing articles in which they try to reconstruct the battle, guess the size of each

---

[2] These are summarized by Scragg (1981, 9-14).

[3] See Anderson (1970), Blake (1976 and 1978), Campbell (1962), Clark (1968 and 1979), Doane (1978), Hillman (1985), Irving (1961), Macrae-Gibson (1970), Nolan and Bloomfield (1980), Robinson (1976), Stuart (1982), Swanton (1968), Thundyil (1975), and Woolf (1976).

force, and calculate if the English might have won had it not been for the controversial *ofermod* of Byrhtnoth.[4]

All this aside, what is of interest is the poem's literary merit and tradition (these are discussed extensively in the Commentary). It contains a series of vignettes affording glimpses of traditional Anglo-Saxon heroic society (by then an anachronism) at work: the young man turning from the leisure of hawking to the reality of war; Byrhtnoth emboldening his youthful warriors as he arrays the battle-line; the Viking messenger shouting out his insulting challenge; Byrhtnoth's sarcastic reply; the ritualistic brandishing of weapons accompanying each uttered pledge or threat; the fateful moment when the enemy host is granted a better position; the chaos caused when the fleeing coward Godric is mistaken for Byrhtnoth; the recollection of boasts made earlier in the meadhall, and how these must be fulfilled if one is to live and die honourably. The most dramatic moment comes towards the end of the fragment when the *eald geneat*, Byrhtwold, brandishing his shield and shaking his spear, utters the now immortal lines,

Hige sceal ðe heardra, heorte ðe cenre,
mod sceal ðe mare, ðe ure mægen lytlað

encapsulating his indomitable and honourable resolve either to win or lie slain on the field of slaughter with his lord.

Language: *The Battle of Maldon* is recorded in late West-Saxon, in a form which would be consonant with its probable Anglian origin. Of course, since it survives only in a sometimes unreliable transcript, it is not advisable to place too much emphasis on particular forms; Scragg's analysis shows the predictable admixture of non-West-Saxon forms.[5] What is of greater interest is that the poet seems to have used some Scandinavian expressions in the speeches of the Vikings for characterization.[6]

---

[4] This scholarship is summarized and evaluated by Gneuss (1976).
[5] See Scragg (1981, 23-28).
[6] See Robinson (1976) and the Commentary (note to lines 29-41).

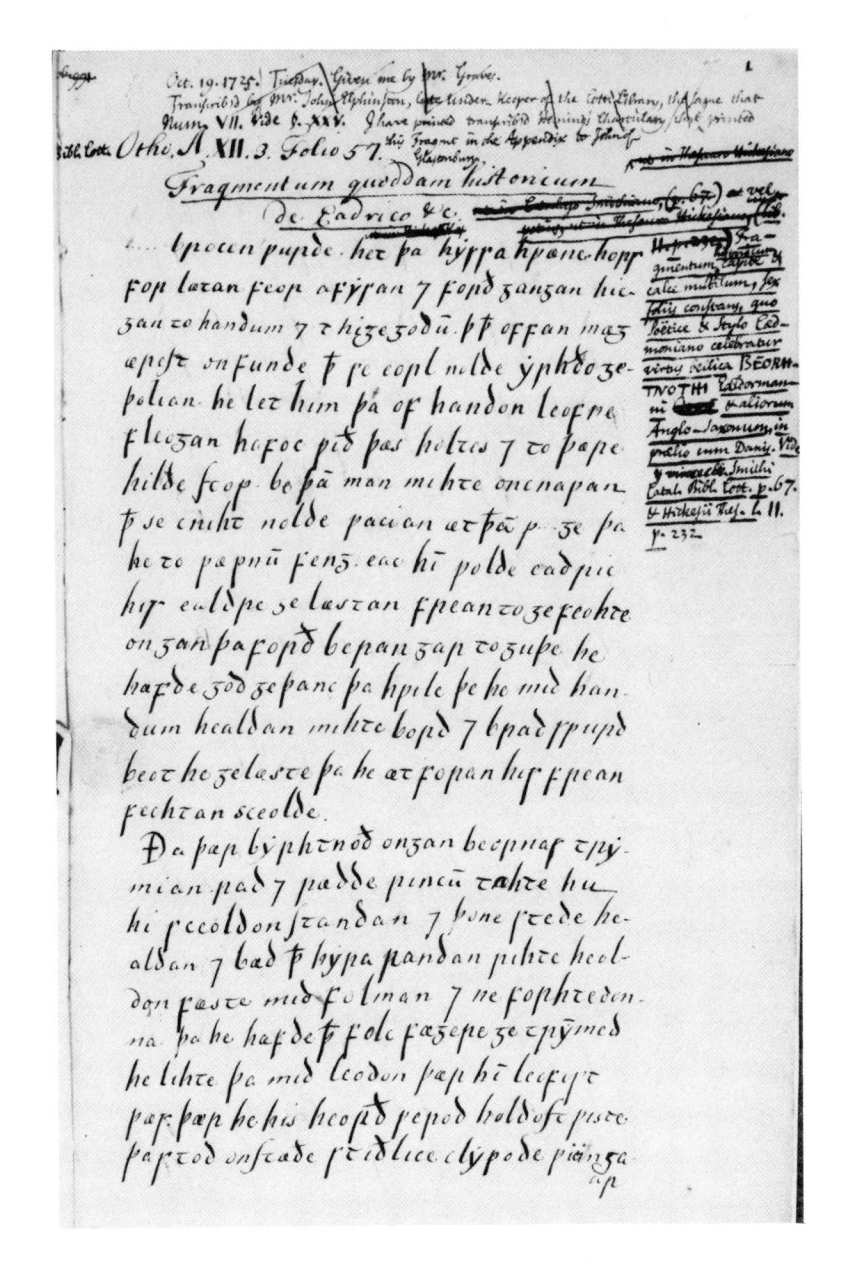

PLATE 8 Oxford, Bodleian Library, MS Rawlinson B.203, p. 7. Casley's transcript of the opening lines of *The Battle of Maldon*.

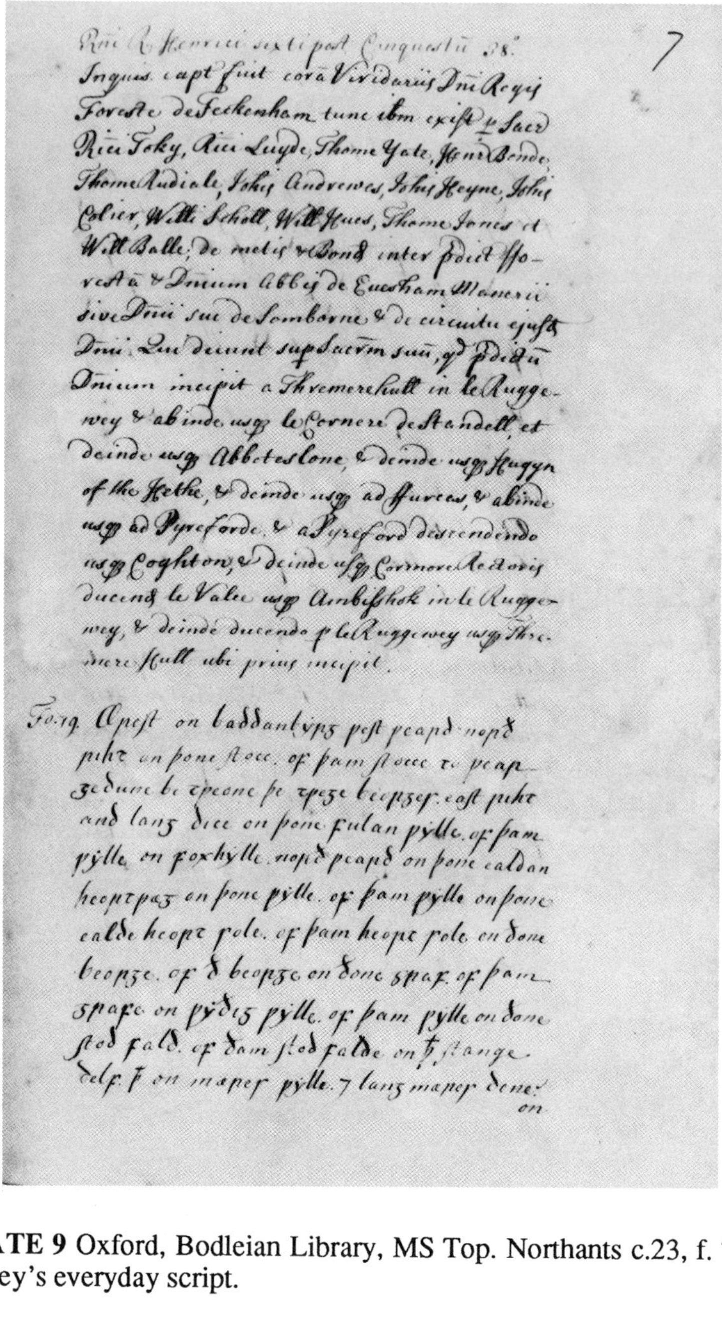

Rōi R. Henrici sexti post Conquestū 38°. 7
Inquis. capt fuit corā Viridariis Dni Regis
Foreste de Feckenham tunc ibm exist p Sacr
Rici Toky, Rici Lugde, Thome Yate, Henr Bonde,
Thome Radiale, Johis Andrewes, Johis Heyne, Johis
Colier, Willi Scholl, Will Hues, Thome Jones et
Will Balle; de metis & Bond inter pdict ffo-
restā & Dnium Abbis de Euesham Manerii
sive Dnii sui de Somborne & de circuitu ejusd
Dnii. Qui dicunt sup Sacrm suū, qd pdictū
Dnium incipit a Thremerehull in le Ruggewey & abinde usq le Cornere de Standell, et
deinde usq Abbeteslone, & deinde usq Huggyn
of the Hethe, & deinde usq ad ffurcas, & abinde
usq ad Pyreforde. & a Pyreford descendendo
usq Coghton, & deinde usq Cornore Rectoris
ducend le Valee usq Ambisshok in le Ruggewey, & deinde ducendo p le Ruggewey usq Thre-
mere Hull ubi prius incipit.

Fo. 19. Ƿest on baddanbyriᵹ ƿest ƿeard norð
riht on þone stocc. of þam stocce to ƿear
ᵹedune betƿeone þe tƿeᵹe beorᵹes. east riht
and lanᵹ dice on þone fulan ƿylle. of þam
ƿylle on foxhylle. norð ƿeard on þone caldan
heortƿaᵹ on þone ƿylle. of þam ƿylle on þone
calde heort ƿole. of þam heort ƿole on ðone
beorᵹe. of ð beorᵹe on ðone sƿar. of þam
sƿare on ƿyðiᵹ ƿylle. of þam ƿylle on ðone
stod fald. of ðam stod falde on þ̄ stange
delf. þ̄ on mares ƿylle. 7 lanᵹ mares ðene.
on

PLATE 9 Oxford, Bodleian Library, MS Top. Northants c.23, f. 7r.
Casley's everyday script.

THE BATTLE OF MALDON

        . . . brocen wurde.   7^r
Het þa hyssa hwæne   hors forlætan,
3 feor afysan   and forð gangan,
hicgan to handum   and t[o] hige godum.
Þ[a] þæt Offan mæg   ærest onfunde
6 þæt se eorl nolde   yrhðo geþolian
he let him þa of handon   leofne fleogan
hafoc wið þæs holtes   and to þære hilde stop -
9 be þam man mihte oncnawan   þæt se cniht nolde
wacian æt þam w[i]ge   þa he to wæpnum feng;
eac him wolde Eadric   his ealdre gelæstan,
12 frean to gefeohte;   ongan þa forð beran
gar to guþe;   he hæfde god geþanc
þa hwile þe he mid handum   healdan mihte
15 bord and brad swurd;   beot he gelæste
þa he ætforan his frean   feohtan sceolde.
   Ða þær Byrhtnoð ongan   beornas trymian,
18 rad and rædde,   rincum tæhte
hu hi sceoldon standan   and þone stede healdan,
and bæd þæt hyra randan   rihte heoldon,
21 fæste mid folman   and ne forhtedon na;
þa he hæfde þæt folc   fægere getrymmed,
he lihte þa mid leodon   þær him leofost wæs
24 þær he his heorðwerod   holdost wiste.
   Þa stod on stæðe,   stiðlice clypode
wicinga / ar   wordum mælde   7^v
27 se on beot abead   brimliþendra
ærænde to þam eorle   þær he on ofre stod:
"Me sendon to þe   sæmen snelle,
30 heton ðe secgan   þæt þu most sendan raðe

---

4 Cas *t hige*.
5 Cas *þ þæt*.
10 *þam*] Cas *þa* with a macron above each letter. *wige*] Cas *w....ge*, leaving room for about two letters.
18 *rædde*] *æ* corrected.

beagas wið gebeorge;   and eow betere is
þæt ge þisne garræs   mid gafole forgyldon
33 þon we swa hearde   [hi]lde dælon;
ne þurfe we us spillan;   gif ge spedaþ to þam
we willað wið þam golde   grið fæstnian;
36 gyf þu þ[æ]t gerædest   þe her ricost eart
þæt þu þine leoda   lysan wille,
syllan sæmannum   on hyra sylfra dom
39 feoh wið freode   and niman frið æt us,
we willaþ mid þam sceattum   us to scype gangan,
on flot feran,   and eow friþes healdan."
42   Byrhtnoð maþelode,   bord hafenode,
wand wacne æsc,   wordum mælde,
yrre and anræd   ageaf him andsware:
45 "Gehyrst þu, sælida,   hwæt þis folc segeð?
Hi willað eow to gafole   garas syllan,
ættrynne ord   and ealde swurd,
48 þa heregeatu   þe eow æt hilde ne deah;
brimmanna boda,   abeod eft ongean,
sege þinum leodum   miccle laþre spell
51 þæt her stynt unforcuð   eorl mid his werode
þe wile gealgean   eþel þysne,
Æþelredes eard,   ealdres mines,
54 folc and foldan;   feallan sceolon
hæþene æt hilde -   to heanlic me þinceð
þæt ge mid urum sceattum   to scype / gangon   8^r
57 unbefohtene   nu ge þus feor hider
on urne eard   in becomon;
ne sceole ge swa softe   sinc gegangan -
60 us sceal ord and ecg   ær geseman,
grim guðplega,   ær we gofol syllon."
Het þa bord beran,   beornas gangan
63 þæt hi on þam easteðe   ealle stodon;
ne mihte þær for wætere   werod to þam oðrum -
þær com flowende   flod æfter ebban,
66 lucon lagustreamas;   to lang hit him þuhte

---
33 Cas ..*ulde*.
36 Cas *þat*.
48 *heregeatu*] *t* altered from *c*.
61 *we*] Cas *þe*.

hwænne hi togædere   garas beron.
Hi þær Pantan stream   mid prasse bestodon,
69 Eastseaxena ord   and se æschere;
ne mihte hyra ænig   oþrum derian
buton hwa þurh flanes flyht   fyl genername.
72 Se flod ut gewat.
            Þa flotan stodon gearowe,
wicinga fela   wiges georne.
Het þa hæleða hleo   healdan þa bricge
75 wigan wigheardne   se wæs haten Wulfstan,
cafne mid his cynne   - þæt wæs Ceolan sunu -
þe ðone forman man   mid his francan ofsceat
78 þe þær baldlicost   on þa bricge stop.
Þær stodon mid Wulfstane   wigan unforhte,
Ælfere and Maccus   modige twegen
81 þa noldon æt þam forda /   fleam gewyrcan
ac hi fæstlice   wið ða fynd weredon
þa hwile þe hi wæpna   wealdan moston.
84   Þa hi þæt ongeaton   and georne gesawon
þæt hi þær bricgweardas   bitere fundon,
ongunnon lytegian   þa laðe gystas -
87 bædon þæt hi upgangan   agan moston,
ofer þone ford faran,   feþan lædan.
    Ða se eorl ongan   for his ofermode
90 alyfan landes to fela   laþere ðeode;
ongan ceallian þa   ofer cald wæter
Byrhtelmes bearn - beornas gehlyston:
93 "Nu eow is gerymed: gað ricene to us
guman to guþe;   God ana wat
hwa þære wælstowe   wealdan mote."
96   Wodon þa wælwulfas   - for wætere ne murnon -
wicinga werod,   west ofer Pantan,
ofer scir wæter   scyldas wegon,
99 lidmen to lande   linde bæron.
    Þær ongean gramum   gearowe stodon
Byrhtnoð mid beornum;   he mid bordum het
102 wyrcan þone wihagan   and þæt werod healdan
fæste wið feondum;   þa wæs f[e]ohte neh,
tir æt getohte: wæs seo tid cumen

---

101 *mid(second)*] *d* altered from *ð*.
103 Cas *fohte*.

105 þæt þær fæge men   feallan sceoldon.
     Þær wearð hream ahafen;   hremmas wundon,
     earn æses / georn -   wæs on eorþan cyrm;
108 hi leton þa of folman   feolhearde speru,
     [grimme] gegrundene   garas fleogan;
     bogan wæron bysige,   bord ord onfeng.
111 Biter wæs se beaduræs: beornas feollon,
     on gehwæðere hand   hyssas lagon;
     wund wearð Wulfmær,   wælræste geceas
114 Byrhtnoðes mæg -   he mid billum wearð,
     his swustersunu,   swiðe forheawen.
     Þær wærð wicingum   wiþerlean agyfen:
117 gehyrde ic þæt Eadweard   anne sloge
     swiðe mid his swurde   swenges ne wyrnde
     þæt him æt fotum feoll   fæge cempa;
120 þæs him his ðeoden   þanc gesæde,
     þam burþene,   þa he byre hæfde.
     Swa stemnetton   stiðhicgende
123 hysas æt hilde,   hogodon georne
     hwa þær mid orde   ærost mihte
     on fægean men   feorh gewinnan,
126 wigan mid wæpnum.
          Wæl feol on eorðan.
     Stodon stædefæste;   stihte hi Byrhtnoð,
     bæd þæt hyssa gehwylc   hogode to wige,
129 þe on Denon wolde   dom gefeohtan;
     wod þa wiges heard,   wæpen up ahof,
               * * *
     bord to gebeorge   and wið þæs beornes stop;
132 eode swa anræd   eorl to þam ceorle -
     ægþer hyra oðrum   yfeles hogode.
     Sende ða se særinc   suþerne gar
135 þæt gewundod wearð   wigena hlaford;
     he sceaf þa mid ðam scylde   þæt / se sceaft tobærst,
     and þæt spere sprengde   þæt hit sprang ongean;
138 gegremod wearð se guðrinc: he mid gare stang

---
109 *grimme*] Supp. ed.
113 Cas *weard*.
116 Cas *wærd*.
118 *swurde*] *r* altered.

>   wlancne wicing   þe him þa wunde forgeaf;
>   frod wæs se fyrdrinc;   he let his francan wadan
> 141 þurh ðæs hysses hals -   hand wisode
>   þæt he on þam færsceaðan   feorh geræhte.
>   Ða he oþerne   ofstlice sceat
> 144 þæt seo byrne tobærst: he wæs on breostum wund
>   þurh ða hringlocan -   him æt heortan stod
>   ætterne ord;   se eorl wæs þe bliþra:
> 147 hloh þa modi man,   sæde Metode þanc
>   ðæs dægweorces   þe him Drihten forgeaf.
>   Forlet þa drenga sum   daroð of handa,
> 150 fleogan of folman   þæt se to forð gewat
>   þurh ðone æþelan   Æþelredes þegen;
>   him be healfe stod   hyse unweaxen,
> 153 cniht on gecampe,   se full caflice
>   bræd of þam beorne   blodigne gar
>   Wulfstanes bearn,   Wulfmær se geonga;
> 156 forlet forheardne   faran eft ongean:
>   ord in gewod   þæt se on eorþan læg
>   þe his þeoden ær   þearle geræhte;
> 159 eode þa gesyrwed   secg to þam eorle -
>   he wolde þæs beornes   beagas gefecgan,
>   reaf and hringas   and gerenod swurd. /   10ʳ
> 162   Þa Byrhtnoð bræd   bill of sceðe
>   brad and brunecg   and on þa byrnan sloh;
>   to raþe hine gelette   lidmanna sum
> 165 þa he þæs eorles   earm amyrde;
>   feoll þa to foldan   fealohilte swurd:
>   ne mihte he gehealdan   heardne mece,
> 168 wæpnes wealdan.   Þa gyt þæt word gecwæð
>   har hilderinc,   hyssas bylde,
>   bæd gangan forð   gode geferan;
> 171 ne mihte þa on fotum leng   fæste gestandan
>   he to heofenum wlat: * * *
>   "Geþance þe,   ðeoda Waldend,
> 174 ealra þæra wynna   þe ic on worulde gebad;
>   nu ic ah, milde Metod,   mæste þearfe

---

138 *gegremod*] first *g* altered.
145 *þurh*] *r* altered from *wynn*.
171 Cas *gestundan*.

LEOÐ

  þæt þu minum gaste godes geunne
177 þæt min sawul to ðe siðian mote,
  on þin geweald, Þeoden engla,
  mid friþe ferian. Ic eom frymdi to þe
180 þæt hi helsceaðan hynan ne moton."
  Ða hine heowon hæðene scealcas,
  and begen þa beornas þe him big stodon -
183 Ælfnoð and Wulmær begen lagon
  ða onemn hyra frean feorh gesealdon.
  Hi bugon þa fram beaduwe þe þær beon noldon:
186 þær wurdon Oddan bearn ærest on fleame,
  Godric fram guþe, and þone godan forlet
  þe him mænigne oft mear gesealde;
189 he gehleop þone eoh þe ahte / his hlaford,   10^v
  on þam gerædum - þe riht ne wæs -
  and his broðru mid him begen ær[n]don,
192 Godwine and Godwig guþe ne gymdon
  ac wendon fram þam wige and þone wudu sohton,
  flugon on þæt fæsten and hyra feore burgon,
195 and manna ma þonne hit ænig mæð wære
  gyf hi þa geearnunga ealle gemundon
  þe he him to duguþe gedon hæfde.
198 Swa him Offa on dæg ær asæde
  on þam meþelstede þa he gemot hæfde
  þæt þær modelice manega spræcon
201 þe eft æt þear[f]e þolian noldon.
  Þa wearð afeallen þæs folces ealdor,
  Æþelredes eorl. Ealle gesawon
204 heorðgeneatas þæt hyra heorra læg;
  þa ðær wendon forð wlance þegenas,
  unearge men efston georne -
207 hi woldon þa ealle oðer twega:
  lif forlætan oððe leofne gewrecan.
  Swa hi bylde forð bearn Ælfrices,
210 wiga wintrum geong wordum mælde,

---

191 Cas *ærdon*.
192 Cas *godrine*.
196 þa] þ altered.
201 Cas *þære*.
208 Cas *for lætun*.

Ælfwine þa cwæð, he on ellen spræc:
"Gemunu þa mæla þe we oft æt meodo spræcon
213 þonne we on bence beot ahofon,
hæleð on healle, ymbe heard gewinn;
nu mæg cunnian hwa cene sy -
216 ic wylle mine æþelo eallum gecyþan, / 11^r
þæt ic wæs on Myrcon miccles cynnes;
wæs min ealda fæder Ealhelm haten,
219 wis ealdorman woruldgesælig;
ne sceolon me on þære þeode þegenas ætwitan
þæt ic of ðisse fyrde feran wille,
222 eard gesecan, nu min ealdor ligeð
forheawen æt hilde; me is þæt hearma mæst -
he wæs ægðer min mæg and min hlaford."
225 Þa he forð eode, fæhðe gemunde,
þæt he mid orde anne geræhte,
flotan on þam folce þæt se on foldan læg
228 forwegen mid his wæpne. Ongan þa winas manian,
frynd and geferan, þæt hi forð eodon;
Offa gemælde, æscholt asceoc:
231 "Hwæt þu, Ælfwine, hafast ealle gemanode
þegenas to þearfe; nu ure þeoden lið,
eorl on eorðan, us is eallum þearf
234 þæt ure æghwylc oþerne bylde,
wigan to wige, þa hwile þe he wæpen mæge
habban and healdan, heardne mece,
237 gar and god swurd; us Godric hæfð,
earh Oddan bearn, ealle beswicene:
wende þæs formoni man þa he on meare rad,
240 on wlancan þam wicge, þæt wære hit ure hlaford;
forþan wearð her on felda folc totwæmed,
scyldburh tobrocen; abreoðe his angin
243 þæt he her / swa manigne man aflymde." 11^v
    Leofsunu gemælde, and his linde ahof,
bord to gebeorge; he þam beorne oncwæð:
246 "Ic þæt gehate þæt ic heonon nelle
fleon fotes trym ac wille furðor gan,
wrecan on gewinne minne winedrihten;
249 ne þurfon me embe Sturmere stedefæste hælæð

---
224 Cas *ægder.*

            wordum ætwitan,   nu min wine gecranc
            þæt ic hlafordleas   ham siðie,
252   wende fram wige;   ac me sceal wæpen niman,
            ord and iren."   He ful yrre wod,
            feaht fæstlice,   fleam he forhogode.
255   Dunnere þa cwæð,   daroð acwehte,
            unorne ceorl,   ofer eall clypode,
            bæd þæt beorna gehwylc   Byrhtnoð wrece:
258   "Ne mæg na wandian   se þe wrecan þenceð
            frean on folce,   ne for feore murnan."
            Þa hi forð eodon,   feores hi ne rohton;
261   ongunnon þa hiredmen   heardlice feohtan,
            grame garberend,   and God bædon
            þæt hi moston gewrecan   hyra winedrihten
264   and on hyra feondum   fyl gewyrcan.
            Him se gysel ongan   geornlice fylstan;
            he wæs on Norðhymbron   heardes cynnes,
267   Ecglafes bearn,   him wæs Æscferð nama;
            he ne wandode na   æt þam wigplegan
            ac he / fysde forð   flan genehe -   12ʳ
270   hwilon he on bord sceat   hwilon beorn tæsde;
            æfre embe stunde   he sealde sume wunde
            þa hwile ðe he wæpna   wealdan moste.
273   Þa gyt on orde stod   Eadweard se langa
            gearo and geornful;   gylpwordum spræc,
            þæt he nolde fleon   fotmæl landes,
276   ofer bæc bugan   þa his betera leg;
            he bræc þone bordweall   and wið þa beornas feaht
            oðþæt he his sincgyfan   on þam sæmannum
279   wurðlice wrec   ær he on wæle lege.
               Swa dyde Æþeric   æþele gefera,
            fus and forðgeorn,   feaht eornoste,
282   Sibryhtes broðor   and swiðe mænig oþer
            clufon cellod bord,   cene hi weredon;
                              * * *
            bærst bordes lærig   and seo byrne sang
285   gryreleoða sum;   þa æt guðe sloh
            Offa þone sælidan   þæt he on eorðan feoll,

---

270 *beorn*] *o* altered.
275 Cas *fleogan*.

and ðær Gaddes mæg   grund gesohte.
288 Raðe wearð æt hilde   Offa forheawen;
     he hæfde ðeah geforþod   þæt he his frean gehet,
     swa he beotode ær   wið his beahgifan -
291 þæt hi sceoldon begen   on burh ridan,
     hale to hame,   oððe on here crincgan,
     on wælstowe   wundum sweltan -
294 he læg ðegenlice   ðeodne gehende.
     Ða wearð borda gebræc;   brimmen / wodon
     guðe gegremode;   gar oft þurhwod
297 fæges feorhhus.   For[ð] ða eode Wistan,
     Þurstanes suna,   wið þas secgas feaht;
     he wæs on geþrang   hyra þreora bana,
300 ær him Wigelmes bearn   on þam wæle læge.
     Þær wæs stið gemot -   stodon fæste
     wigan on gewinne;   wigend cruncon
303 wundum werige.
              Wæl feol on eorþan.
     Oswold and Eadwold   ealle hwile,
     begen þa gebroþru,   beornas trymedon,
306 hyra winemagas   wordon bædon
     þæt hi þær æt ðearfe   þolian sceoldon,
     unwaclice   wæpna neotan.
309 Byrhtwold maþelode,   bord hafenode,
     se wæs eald geneat,   æsc acwehte;
     he ful baldlice   beornas lærde:
312 "Hige sceal þe heardra,   heorte þe cenre,
     mod sceal þe mare,   þe ure mægen lytlað;
     her lið ure ealdor   eall forheawen,
315 god on greote;   a mæg gnornian
     se ðe nu fram þis wigplegan   wendan þenceð;
     ic eom frod feores;   fram ic ne wille,
318 ac ic me be healfe   minum hlaforde,
     be swa leofan men   licgan þence."
     Swa hi Æþelgares   bearn ealle bylde,
321 Godric to guþe;   oft he gar forlet,

---
292 Cas *crintgan*.
297 Cas *forða*.
300 Cas *wigelines*.
314 *forheawen*] *a* added interlinearly.

wælspere windan   on þa wicingas;
swa he on þam folce   fyrmest eode,
324 heow and hynde   oðþæt he on hilde gecranc;
næs þæt na se Godric   þe ða guðe forbeah . . .

---

324 Cas *od þæt.*
325 Cas *gude.*

COMMENTARY

1-184 Parks observes (with reference to both Classical and Germanic literature) that the ritual known as the flyting has four constituents; with respect to *Maldon*, these are: i) engagement (1-28); ii) the verbal exchange / flyting itself (29-61, 84-95); iii) martial combat (96-184); and iv) ritual resolution (168-80). He compares this passage with *Iliad* XX.158-352 to illustrate similarities between the English and Greek use of the convention. For further discussion of the flyting, see Anderson (1970), Blake (1976) and Clover (1980), which have extensive annotations.

2-4 Cf. 4.10-12.

4 As Rogers notes, Casley seems prone to omitting letters, although no particular pattern or recurrent cause can be detected; this is more odd because similar omissions do not seem to occur in his transcript of Vespasian B.xxiv (1986, 153).

14-15a In the poetry, there are many instances of extended circumlocution (always modified to suit the context) to express simple, common notions; cf. *Beowulf* 29b-30, *swa he selfa bæd / þenden wordum weold wine Scyldinga* ('as he himself had commanded, the friend of the Scyldings, while he still ruled with words').

17 *Byrhtnoð*: Irving's statement that *Maldon* is about "an old man named Byrhtnoth and his retainers, petty noblemen of Essex, fighting and dying in a local battle which the disdainful historian might call a scuffle of no great importance in the long run" (1961, 458) belies the fact that Byrhtnoth was one of the most important and influential political figures not just in Essex, but in all England, and that his death, regardless of the ultimate significance of the lost battle, was considered a great loss; it was, after all, recorded in several versions of the *Chronicle*, something which should not be taken lightly. (See Scragg (1981, 14-20) for a comprehensive biographical sketch.)

Irving further observes that the *Maldon* poet exhibited great skill in creating "a heroic poem out of brute fact", being disadvantaged by having "to forgo the great resources of epic poets" (1961, 467). In general, critics regard *Maldon* more highly than Irving does; see, for example, Sklar (1975; discussed below in 45 note), who is able to discern that *Maldon* represents a different poetic tradition, the popular rather than the classical, and who in her investigation proceeds with sensitivity and insight rather than with "brute" force.

18 *rincum tæhte*: Stuart argues that the *Maldon* poet is primarily concerned with examining "man's ability to deceive himself" — in this instance particularized in Byrhtnoth who is a leader of inexperienced troops (whom he has to instruct on the spot in how to prepare for a battle), but who almost from the outset acts like an impetuous young Germanic hero instead of the thoughtful, mature *ealdormann* he should be; it is he who "takes the first step towards loosing the lord-retainer bonds" (1982, 130-31). She contends that "*Maldon* has an underlying ironic structure and that its meaning, like that of some other heroic pieces, is ultimately antiheroic" (126). That an antiheroic interpretation may have been possible for or acceptable to some Anglo-Saxons is argued by Cross (1971). A very different understanding of the poem's major theme is represented by Robinson and Johnson; see 181-82 note.

24 *heorðwerod*: Byrhtnoth's instincts and strategy are sound in alighting here; later in the narrative, it is the members of this group, the *heroðgeneatas* (204a), whose instinctive and immediate reaction is to remain on the battlefield and to avenge their lord.

29-41 Robinson (1976, 26-28) proposes that these lines probably represent the first literary use of dialect in English, although the use of *cnearr* and *nægledcnearr* in *Brunanburh* (5.35, 5.53) to describe Scandinavian ships may be an earlier example of the same thing in a more rudimentary form. The words and syntactical units singled out by Robinson are: *grið* (35), *garræs* (32), *þon* (33), *most* (30), *hilde dælan* (33), *sylfra dom* (38), *gif ge spedaþ to þam* (34) and *eow friþes healdan* (41); a number of these were noted by others in the past. See Scragg's note on line 33 (1981, 69-70), and Robinson's response to it (1986, 103-04).

In her re-examination of the evidence concerning the geographical and historical milieu in which *Maldon* might have been written, Clark notes (for those who would date the poem with respect to the degree of Scandinavian influence on the Old English vocabulary and syntax) that,

> The point is not, however, that Scandinavian evidence is especially strong here; rather that, once a Southern-Danelaw provenance is accepted for the poem and its implications understood, such influence loses all chronological bearing.

(1983, 18)

See also 51 note on *eorl*.

Noting the abundance of pronouns in this speech and in Byrhtnoth's reply, Blake proposes "that the frequency of the pronouns here was a deliberate contrivance used to create a contrast between the Danes and the English" (1976, 242). Thus, in the messenger's speech, *we / us* should be understood to refer only to the Vikings; likewise, in Byrhtnoth's speech they refer only to the English. Translations in the past have often been ambiguous in their treatment of this passage. A similar tactful or strategic use of pronouns may be observed in Beowulf's reply to Unferth's charge that he was reckless as a youth and in the dialogue between Adam and the satanic messenger in *Genesis B*. For further discussion of the structural nature of the flyting, see 45-61 note.

32 *garræs*: A *hapax legomenon*; others occurring in *Maldon*: *beaduræs* (111), *bricgweardas* (85), *ceallian* (91), *cellod* (283), *easteð* (63), *færsceaða* (142), *feolheard* (108), *feorhhus* (297), *forheardne* (156), *forðgeorn* (281), *forwegen* (228), *hringlocan* (145), *lytegian* (86), *stemnettan*, *unbefohtene* (57), *unorne* (256)*wihagan* (102), and *woruldgesælig* (219). Many of these are simply compounds comprised of common constituents; a number of the others are discussed in the Commentary as they occur.

38 *on hyra sylfra dom*: Cf. *Beowulf* 895a, *selfes dom*; and, with reference to Heremod's behaviour, Garmonsway is right to translate *æfter dome* as 'as the standard of kingly honour requires' (1965, 141), that is, according to his proper judgement as king. Cf. also *Beowulf* 2179a, *dreah æfter dome*, which Garmonsway translates 'lived honorably'.

42 The use of *maþelode* to introduce the first reported speech of Byrhtnoth is most likely significant (see note 1.1 paragraph 2); the use of a virtually identical set of formulae in 309 to introduce the famous utterance of Byrhtwold should also be noted.

45,75,288 In these three lines the second stress in the off-verse bears the alliteration; lines 29, 32, 84, 192, 204, 230 and 254 have double alliteration in the off-verse; and there is triple alliteration in the on-verse of lines 2, 74, 96, and 113. The use of sporadic rhyme to supplement the alliteration is also noteworthy (eg, in lines 271 and 282); it is also found in the *Chronicle* poems for the years 1036 and 1086, and in the *Proverbs of Alfred, Worcester Fragments* and La3amon's *Brut*. Sklar argues that the departures from classical Old English verse techniques do not indicate "a lack of skill on the part of the poet, but stem, rather, from the encroachment of the popular poetic tradition upon the classical" (Sklar, 1975, 410). She concludes,

> Janus-like, *Maldon* looks to past and future, providing a forum for the confrontation between two native traditions, the new poetic, crude, even churlish perhaps, but vital, ready to assume command when the hero dies. (1974,417)

Further to her argument, it should be noted that these verses (characterized by monosyllables, lack of variation, the absence of functional poetic compounds and compressed metaphors) read much like prose in many ways; they depend on something different to give them life. This tendency towards prosaic verse in *Maldon* has often been regarded as simply a defect, indicating that Old English verse was in a state of decline in the eleventh century, and not examined for what it might contribute towards our understanding of the development of later English verse form; that is, it was regarded as a disjunction of form and content. See 230 note for further discussion.

45-61 Anderson illustrates the craft and skill of the *Maldon* poet by examining his use of verbal echoes in Byrhtnoth's reply to the Viking messenger; these involve word-play on *gafol* and the ideas associated with it; the echoing observable in *swa hearde* (33a) *swa softe* (59a); the play on the intensifying *for-* in 32b and 51a; and the echoing in *þam sceattum* (40a) and *urum sceattum* (56a), among others (1970, 197). This seems to have been a common technique in the poetry since it is observable elsewhere in Beowulf's reply to Unferth concerning the swimming contest with Breca and in Adam's reply to the satanic messenger in *Genesis B* (522-46). In each of these instances, the person replying addresses the points of the previous speaker one at a time in an orderly fashion, almost in the manner one would expect to find in a legal forum (such as the *witenagemot*); this is appropriate since in this instance the terms of a treaty are being proposed, in *Beowulf* a charge is being refuted, and in *Genesis* a reinterpretation of a divine covenant is being considered.

48 *heregeatu*: Irving notes that the use of this term is ironic here as it technically refers to 'a feudal payment in weapons to a lord on the death of his tenant' (1961, 461). The poet's intention here may or may not be ironic, but Irving's use of the term 'feudal' is surely anachronistic.

51 *eorl*: Critics argue that this use of *eorl* in the technical sense 'ealdormann', involving a semantic borrowing from Scandinavian *jarl*, must necessarily post-date Cnut's accession; see, for example, McKinnell (1975) and Blake (1978). However, in her reconsideration of the linguistic and historical data relevant to the dating of the poem, Clark concludes that "its appearance in *Maldon*, far from seeming to imply post-Cnutian composition, begins to look simply like a piece of Southern-Danelaw dialect" (1983, 18). Noting that by 1066 *eorl* was firmly enough "established as a term of rank . . . to become at once the English equivalent of Old-French *quens/conte*", this would mean, if the view that *eorl* only acquired the sense of 'our own English commander' after the accession of Cnut was accepted, that it took but one generation for the meaning "to spread from Anglo-Danish official usage into general currency" (1983, 19), which is highly improbable.

53 Robinson suggests that these and other references to Ethelred the Unready in the poem (151 and 202-03) may be ironic "if we can assume that the poem was composed long enough after the battle for the audience to know that the king had proved unworthy of the sacrifices that were made in his name." At virtually the same moment that Byrhtnoth and his followers were laying their lives down on the field of slaughter, Ethelred was arranging to begin annual payment of tribute to the Scandinavians; the *BCD Chronicle* entries for 991 "make the essential connections" (1976, 28-32). Arguing in the same vein, Clark observes that "Byrhtnoth's reference to Æþelred explicitly sets the poem in an unheroic, indeed debased age . . ." (1968, 59).

57 *unbefohtene*: This and *unorne* (256) are examples of the poet expressing negative ideas by adding the prefix *un-* to the positive form of the word, which must have been a common practice. However, it is suggested at 3.55 note that these words (which are directly antithetical to the positive form) might sometimes have been laden with increased significance.

74 *þa bricge*: This is the much-discussed causeway:

> In 1926 E.D. Laborde put the final piece of reality into the puzzle [concerning the historical accuracy of *Maldon*] by showing that the Northey Island causeway just south of Maldon on the Blackwater fits exactly the complicated combination of geography and tide required by the scenes and events of the poem. (Petty and Petty, 1976, 435)

Petty and Petty present the results of a geological survey of the proposed site of the battle and list seven observations concerning its topography, the most relevant being that in 991 the distance across the channel was 120 yards, the land sloped gently down to the river bank, the channel was unfordable except at a manmade hard, and that at high tide the causeway was covered to a depth of six feet (1976, 444-45).

77 *franca*: Literally, 'something Frankish', this came to be used as a generic term for a spear or lance. A weapon referred to by the medieval Latin word *francisca* was found buried with the Merovingian king Childeric who died in 482.

86 *lytegian*: Though this verb does not appear elsewhere, the related adjective *lytig* 'crafty / cunning / astute' and the preterite form *belytegade* 'allure / seduce' suggest Bosworth-Toller's 'act cunningly' is one possible meaning. However, as Clark points out, "no trickery appears in our text"; 'to act cunningly' has no referent (1968, 53). Clark further observes,

> ... if our poet, or perhaps historian, saw Byrhtnoth's gullibility as crucial to the action and a key to the significance of the event, the poem should have been more explicit about the hero's failure. (1968, 54)

As noted above, *lytig* also means 'astute', and the context here better supports a meaning similar to this: since they could not get past the *bricgweardas*, the Vikings made a better plan (ie, began to act astutely) and asked for fairer terms under which to conduct the battle. For whatever reason (and a suggestion is made in 89-90 note), Byrhtnoth agreed to this and, in retrospect, the Vikings can be seen to have acted cunningly.

89-90 Robinson concedes that Byrhtnoth made a strategical error in allowing the Scandinavians easier passage to the mainland, but suggests that he did so because he was probably concerned for the welfare of English civilians trapped on the island at the time of the landing of the invading force; the island was "apparently under cultivation and may even have been under permanent settlement" (1976, 32-33). Johnson notes that if the poet's primary concern had been the *ofermod* of Byrhtnoth, he would have mentioned it more than once, and then almost as if in passing. She notes that the poet spends nearly half the poem detailing the consequences of Godric's flight on Byrhtnoth's horse that led to the desertion of a great number of troops, the turning point in the battle; "the poet leaves no room for doubt about the ethical nature of that behavior, asserting 'þe hit riht ne wæs' (190)" (1985, 41). See also 181-82 note.

91, 98 A number of critics have noted the figurative connotations of the metaphorical use of *cald* here, but regarded *scir* as adding a touch of naturalistic detail. Fletcher suggests that *scir* may also have been used metaphorically at times, and perhaps has an antithetical function here. *Scir* is associated with hope of victory elsewhere in the poetry; here *cald* is associated with the English, *scir* with the Vikings. Fletcher observes,

> Perhaps the play between water from the one side *cald* and from the other side *scir* may be regarded as a further device in the *Maldon* poet's repertoire of foreshadowing. (1984, 437)

91 *ceallian*: This "lexical survivor from the heroic age" is rightly regarded by Stanley as a native, not a Scandinavian, word (1969, 98-99); this observation arises from his reconsideration of the forms *-calla* and *ceallian* as possible evidence for Scandinavian influence on Old English vocabulary, and hence for the dating of certain Anglo-Saxon poems.

96 *wælwulfas*: This is not necessarily depreciative or pejorative, and may merely be a metaphorical term for warrior; *heorowulfas* is used to describe the Israelites in *Exodus* (181a) and *hildewulfas* for Abraham in *Genesis* 2052a (as noted by Cross, 1965, 108).

102 *wihagan*: As Scragg notes, this is literally 'battle-hedge', a "defensive wall of overlapping shields shown clearly in the Bayeux Tapestry and other contemporary illustrations" (1981, 75).

109 *grimme*: [Holthausen 1910]; *grimme* is supplied on the strength of *Ruin* 14a.

115 *swustersunu*: Much has been written about this relationship, especially since it was singled out by Tacitus in the *Germania*; however, see 221-24 note. In the poem, the fall of Wulfmær (the nephew) is not so important as Edward the *burþegn*'s reaction to it, which is singled out as exemplary.

122 *stemnetton*: Harris, from a consideration of the context here, its etymological probability (it is related to *stefnan* 'fix / institute'), and its single appearance in Middle English (*steuentið* in *The Life of Saint Katherine* where it translates Latin *ommutescitis* 'fall silent'), argues convincingly that 'stop (talking)' is the meaning of this

obscure word. With the example of Edward before them, the young cadets (*hys(s)as*) stop, and (silently) think (*hogodon*) about how they ought to bear themselves during the balance of the contest (1976, 113-14).

127-31 There has probably been a scribal omission between lines 130 and 131, accounting for disagreement among critics about the exact meaning of this passage; *wiges heard* refers to Byrhtnoth, and *þæs beornes* probably to the Viking warrior; see Robinson (1976, 34-35). Other scribal omissions occur at lines 172 and 284.

129 *dom gefeohtan*: cf. *Beowulf* 953b-55a (quoted at 1.140 note).

134 *suþerne gar*: See Swanton's discussion of the possible significance of this adjective in this particular context (1968, 447 and note 23). The most attractive and least troubling proposal is that it is a poetic allocation rather than a particularized or generic usage: Swanton cites a number of examples to illustrate that, "Anglo-Saxon thinking not uncommonly ascribed antipathetic abstract qualities to the regions of the south."

149 *drenga*: from Old Norse *drengr* 'young man'; see 6.29-41 note.

172 It is generally recognized that there is a scribal omission here.

173 *geþance*: Most editors, including Scragg, supply the personal pronoun *Ic* before the verb, but see note 211-15.

173-80 Compare *Beowulf* 928-29a and 953b-56, where a speech by Hrothgar is framed by two brief addresses to a deity, giving thanks to him for a day / night's work well done (by Beowulf, who has just defeated Grendel in Heorot). Robinson demonstrates that care must be taken to distinguish the different narrative voices in *Beowulf* so that the structures set up so diligently by the poet are not destroyed by an insensitive reading. There is no need to capitalize words referring to a deity here (in *Beowulf*); indeed, to do so deprives the text of much of its thematic and narrative texture (1985, 32-34).

Cross admonishes critics (such as Huppé and Bloomfield) who interpret Anglo-Saxon poems from a firmly entrenched Christian doctrinal position, often forcing a reading upon a text to make it conform to their expectations. In this instance, Byrhtnoth is seen to embody the major virtues conventionally discernible in the character of a Christian martyr (1965, 93-94 et passim). Cross argues that he may embody *fortitudo* and *justitia*, but he is decidedly lacking in *prudentia/sapientia* and *temperantia* (1965, 100-03).

180 In his detailed examination of the nature and function of prayer in Old English narratives, Bzdyl notes that this alludes "to the traditional belief that the good and bad angels fight over a man's soul when he dies" (1982, 149). Arguing in the same vein as Cross (see previous note), he warns against interpreting all prayers "solely as a mode of *implicit self-characterization*", noting that modern critics "acknowledge the literal meaning of the prayer but focus only on how the prayer's nuances should affect the reader's view of the character praying" (1982, 145).

scealcas: Given the poet's use of Scandinavianisms (see 29-41 note and 149 note), it is possible that this word, rather than having its normal Old English meaning of 'man / servant', is used in the sense of its Old Norse cognate *skalkr* 'rogue' (see Cross, 1965, 106), but such depreciatory characterization is not applied consistently throughout the poem, and is not necessary for the development of its major theme (see the next note).

181-82 Here and in lines 223 and 314-15, the poet uses the verb *heawan* or its intensified form *forheawan* to describe the attack on Byrhtnoth. It is known from other sources that Byrhtnoth was beheaded in the onslaught, and Robinson suggests that the poet describes this atrocity in this reserved and suggestive fashion so as not to misdirect "readers into viewing the narrative as primarily a conflict between virtuous Englishmen and evil Vikings" (as Norman does (1969, 3)); in his opinion, the poem is about a more important conflict, "the tensions within the English ranks" (1976, 38). Johnson, though stating her argument differently, agrees with this view, noting that it is the behaviour of the cowards within the English ranks, deserting their lord in his time of greatest need (Byrhtnoth himself says, "*nu ic ah, milde Metod, mæste þearfe / þæt þu minum gaste godes geunne. . .*" (175-76)) that the poet has chosen to emphasize (1985, 414-15). [The *Beowulf* poet also tells us that Beowulf's cowardly retainers fled to the woods deserting him in his time of great need (*miclan þearfe*, 2849b)]. The poet contrasts their action with that of the loyal retainers through the repetition of the word *þearf* in 201, 232, 233 and 307. Failure to recognize the poet's major concern continues to lead critics to strained and fanciful allegorical interpretations of the poem; see, for example, Hillman (1985).

183 *noldon*: (also at 201b and *woldon* 207a) Busse and Holtei note that the poet is emphasizing repeatedly the free choice that the heroes are making in this critical situation (1981, 616); see 3.9-11

for further discussion of the seminal notion in heroic poetry of there being two antithetical alternatives which repeatedly confront the protagonists and antagonists.

188 *mear*: Campbell observes that 'h' remained finally (*Old English Grammar*, Oxford: Clarendon Press, 1959, paragraph 464); Scragg suggests that the MS may have read *mearg gesealde*, and that this unique form may be due to the transcriber, noting his *forða* for *forð ða* in 297 (1981, 279), and also that *mear* falls at the end of a line.

190 *þe*: Robinson points out that although it is possible that the faltering of the syntax here might be a deliberate anacoluthon by an artful poet, it should also be noted that *þe* is the first word on the top of a new folio (60^v) according to Hearne's edition, and it is equally likely that two or more letters have been lost here; thus the original reading might have been *þeah (þe)* (1976, 35). However, Roberts cites two examples from *Andreas* of the use of *þe* for *þe(a)h* (at 507 and 630), sometimes emended by editors, and further suggests that another instance of this may be found in *Maldon* itself, in its most celebrated lines, 312-13, where *þe* for *þe(a)h* makes perfect sense and leads to a better translation ('. . . though our might diminishes') (1982, 106).

191-97 The mention of Godric's two brothers fleeing ignominiously invites comparison with the honourable behaviour of the brothers Oswold and Eadwold who remained on the field of slaughter to avenge their fallen lord (304-08).

192 *godwine*: [Rieger].

196-97 The shameful behaviour of those who fail to recall their allegiance to their lord in time of crisis is contrasted with the proper behaviour of Ælfwine (211-24); see 212 note.

207-08 See the discussion concerning the choice between two antithetical alternatives in heroic poetry at 3.9-11 note.

211-15 Robinson observes, "We know from *The Fight at Finnsburg* that warriors who drink from the king's cup in the meadhall were expected, when war broke out, to repay his generosity with valor" (1985, 75); see 4.37-40 and note. Elsewhere, both Beowulf (*gemunde þa se goda* . . ., 758a) and Wiglaf (*Ic þæt mæl geman* . . ., 2633a) call to mind in ideal heroic fashion the obligation they have undertaken to their respective lords.

Citing Wiglaf's speech of similar tone and content which begins in the first person singular and quickly changes to the first person plural

(*Beowulf* 2633ff) as an analogue, Robinson points out that there is no need to emend the transcript here since *gemunu* is an attested first person singular present indicative form in the *Vespasian Psalter*" (1976, 36-37); for an identical omission of the personal pronoun, see *Geþance þe*, 172a.

Macrae-Gibson observes further, that an

> ... important structural principle in the sequence of heroisms from Ælfwine to Byrhtwold ... is related clearly to the choice of a young man to open and an old man to close the sequence: there is a steady change of emphasis as the poem proceeds from loyalty expressed by vengeance to loyalty expressed by death" (1970, 195).

In an examination of the complicated political manœuvring in the decade leading up to Æthelred's accession, in which many of the major figures involved in Anglo-Saxon politics were pitted against each other in either of two camps, Locherbie-Cameron suggests that the poet does not have Ælfwine mention his father in his *beot* because he was disgraced and living in exile at the time; his silence suggests "the poet's awareness of the tension between the great earls which, on the death of King Edgar, led to virtual civil war" (1978, 487).

221-24 The similarity between these and Tacitus' words in Chapter 14 of the *Germania* has often been noted: "As for leaving a battle alive after your chief has fallen, that means lifelong infamy and disgrace" (H. Mattingly, *Tacitus On Britain and Germany*, Harmondsworth: Penguin, 1948, rep. 1967, 112); note also *Beowulf* 2890b-91, *Deað bið sella / eorla gehwylcum þonne edwitlif* ('Death is better for each man than a life of disgrace'), and see 1.140 note. Woolf argues that there is no evidence for the direct influence of the *Germania* on *Maldon*, noting that elsewhere in the surviving heroic poetry "what is required of a lord's retainer after his death is not that he should die with him as an end in itself but that he should effectively avenge his lord" (1976, 69). Since it was impossible for the *Maldon* poet to describe how Byrhtnoth's retainers (or the *fyrd*) avenged him (though in 207-08 the poet tells us they wanted to), Woolf suggests the poet perhaps collapsed this familiar concept with the more alien idea of dying on the battlefield with one's lord (1976, 76 and 81).

Woolf suggests that the poet may have found the ideal of suicidal fighting in the *Bjarkamál*, but Anderson argues that the literary source for this ideal is the *Encomium Emmae* (composed at either St. Bertin's or St. Omer's, Flanders, "during the reign of Harthaknútr (1940-42)[sic]" (1986, 254). He notes that *Maldon* and the *Encomium* "have in common five clusters of detail": i) a battle flyting; ii) crossing from an island to the mainland; iii) the beasts of battle; iv) the flight of traitors; and v) the pattern of heroic speeches and warriors advancing to battle (1986, 256-60). If, however, the *Encomium* influenced *Maldon* (and this cannot be proved, although the similarities between them are striking, and it is unlikely that *Maldon* influenced the *Encomium*), then this implies a date of 1040 or later for its composition. It is not impossible that the *Maldon* poet could have been familiar with the details of the battle of Ashingdon (fought between Edmund Ironside and Cnut in 1016) from some other source, oral or literary, and have written his poem under that influence before the *Encomium* was composed, thus allowing for an earlier date of composition.

230 *æscholt*: This compound and many others from the traditional heroic poetic wordhoard (such as *wælspere* (320a), *beahgifan* (290b), *wælstowe* (293a) and *wælrest* (113b)) found here have lost their earlier efficacy; "the kennings which formerly produced brilliant imaginative compounds had now for the most part faded into prose usage as simply unrecognized metaphors. [The verse lacks] involved parallelism, parenthetic remarks, or poetic allusions which lent the older battle descriptions the dignity of formal utterance" (Swanton, 1968, 449).

Swanton concludes,

> Heroic material in the absence of heroic style inevitably falls flat, and the poem leaves one with the impression of striking all the old heroic attitudes without the traditional vocabulary which made the early heroic verse emotionally valid. *Maldon* has all the appearance of a subject executed in the wrong material: a poem composed in an heroic vein in an age that was no longer heroic. (1968, 449-50)

Swanton is right in noting that *Maldon* represents a different kind of poetry from earlier classical Old English verse, but wrong to regard it as representative of Old English verse in a state of decline; he fails to realize it is different because it represents a completely different poetic tradition; see 45 note.

246-47 See 3.18-19 note and compare 275-76.

256 *unorne*: See 57 note.

271,282 For a discussion of internal rhyme as characteristic of Old English verse in the popular tradition, see 45 note.

275 *fleon*: The confusion of this verb and *fleogan* continues into modern times; see 3.18-19a note and compare 246-47.

283 *cellod*: See 4.29 note for a discussion of this form and *celæs*.

284 Pope rightly observes that at least a line is missing before this one, which would have described the Viking's initial assault on Offa; see *Seven Old English Poems* (Indianapolis, 1966), p. 78.

294 *ðegenlice*: See 1.37 note for a discussion of this and other special terms denoting rank in Old English poetry.

309 Concerning the use of *maþelode* to introduce this important speech see 1.1 note (§ 2) and compare 42 above.

309-10 Robinson cites a close parallel in a tenth century Latin source (Widukind of Corvey's *Rerum Gestarum Saxonicarum Libri Tres*) for this speech by an old, tried warrior, and notes that, although the *Maldon* poet intended his poem to be regarded as 'true history', "the ordering of details, the portrayal of characters, and the phrasing of speeches are all shaped according to the demands of aesthetic conventions, not of literal reportage" (1976, 38-40). See Busse and Holtei for further discussion of the "artistic combination of fiction and history" in *Maldon* (1981, 620).

313 Engberg examines the collocation of *mægen* and *mod* in several poems where they seem to denote proportionate quantities of physical ability and mental ability, and how Anglo-Saxon poets exploit this collocation. She observes, concerning *Maldon*, that "Byrhtwold's words express an inverse relationship: as *mægen* decreases, *mod* increases; this is indicative of the poem as a whole". Using the analogy of an hourglass, she notes that at the beginning, the top section, *mægen* is full; by the end, the bottom section, *mod* is full (*mægen* now being empty) (1984, 218).

Roberts suggests that the *þe* in the off-verse may be for *þe(a)h*; see 190 note.

GLOSSARY

INTRODUCTION

In the Glossary the headwords follow those of *A Concise Anglo-Saxon Dictionary* by J.R. Clark Hall (revised by H.D. Meritt) with few exceptions. Variant forms of the headword that appear in the texts have been indicated in brackets. Every form of each headword that appears in the poetic texts has been recorded in the Glossary with a text and line reference, except in the case of extremely common words such as the conjunction *and*; these entries are given in the form of text number, point, line number, so that 2.14 refers to *Deor* line 14.

The organization of each type of entry (e.g. for a verb or an adjective) will become apparent as soon as the reader begins to use the Glossary. Unless otherwise indicated, all verb forms are indicative, and the first entry after the headword will be the infinitive. When a word has the same form for different cases or tenses that are being parsed in succession, that form has not been repeated; rather the two analyses are joined by the conjunction *and*. Vowel length has been indicated on each form. Cross references within the Glossary have been limited to the irregular verbs and a small number of other words which the editor thought might prove troublesome for some readers. The annotation 'see note' indicates that the word has been discussed in the 'Commentary'.

Each entry ends with etymological information that is enclosed in square brackets: uppercase forms in **bold** typeface refer to the headword in the *OED* (*/NED*) where complete etymological information will be found; lowercase forms in **bold** typeface preceded by *see* refer the reader to another entry in the Glossary. For words which do not appear in the *OED* references have been given to F. Holthausen's *Altenglisches etymologisches Wörterbuch*; if Holthausen's headword is the same as that of the Glossary entry, it has not been repeated within the square brackets. For compound words or words with one or more prefixes or suffixes etymological information has been given for each element. In addition, the first meaning given for each compound headword is usually a literal translation of its components. Forms *followed* by an asterisk are either emended or appear in the critical apparatus for another reason; those *preceded* by an asterisk are hypothetical.

ABBREVIATIONS

acc	accusative	m	masc
adj	adjective	n	neuter
adv	adverb(ial)	neg	negative
aux	auxiliary	nom	nominative
av	anomalous verb	num	number
c	circa	p	participle
comp	comparative	pers	personal
conj	conjunction	pl	plural
corr	correlative	poss	possessive
dat	dative	pp	past participle
def	definite	ppv	preterite-present verb
dem	demonstrative	prep	preposition
etc	and others	pres	present
f	feminine	pret	preterite
fl	flourished	pron	pronoun
gen	genitive	refl	reflexive
Holt	Holthausen	rel	relative
imp	imperative	sb	substantive
indecl	indeclinable	sg	singular
indef	indefinite	subj	subjunctive
inf	infinitive	sup	superlative
infl	inflected	sv	strong verb
instr	instrumental	w	with
interj	interjection	wk	weak
interrog	interrogative	wv	weak verb

A

ā *adv* always, ever; 1.110, 1.126, 6.315. [AY]

ābēodan *sv* 2 to announce, declare; *imp sg* **ābēod** 6.49; *3 sg pret* **ābēad** 6.27. [ABEDE]

ābrecan *sv* 4 to destroy; *pp f nom sg* **ābrocen** 4.44. [BREAK]

ābrēoðan *sv* 2 to fail; *3 sg pres subj* **ābrēoðe** 6.242 (ā. his angin 'may his enterprise fail'). [A-*prefix*, BRETHE]

ac *conj* but; 1.38, *etc*. [*see Holt*]

acweccan *wv* 1 to shake, brandish; *3 sg pret* **acwehte** 6.255, 6.310. [AQUETCH]

æfnan *wv* 1 to practise, perform, endure; 1.141. [*see Holt* **efnan**]

ǣfre *adv* ever; 2.11, 5.66*, 6.271 (ǣ. embe stunde 'repeatedly'). [EVER]

æftan *adv* from behind, behind; 5.63. [AFT]

æfter *prep w dat* after; 3.5, *etc*. [AFTER]

ǣghwæðer *indef pron* each (of two); *m nom sg* **ǣgþer** 6.133; *conj* **ǣgðer...and** both...and; 6.224*. [EITHER]

ǣghwilc (y) *indef pron* each; *m nom sg* 6.234. [EACH]

æht *f* possessions, wealth (*usually in pl*); *acc sg* 1.93; *dat pl* **æhtum** 3.63. [AUGHT]

ǣnig *pron* any; *m nom sg* 6.70; *m gen sg* **ǣniges** 3.14; *m dat sg* **ǣnigum** 3.3; *adj f nom sg* **ǣnig** 6.195. [ANY]

ǣr *adv* first, before; 2.41, 3.31, 3.61, 6.60, 6.158, 6.198 (on dæg ǣr 'earlier in the day'), 6.290; *conj* before, rather than; 6.61, 6.279, 6.300; *sup adj* **ǣrest**(-ost) first; *m nom sg* 1.38; *and sup adv* 3.27, 4.32, 6.124, 6.186; **þa...ǣrest** as soon as; 6.5. [ERE]

ǣrende (-ænde) *n* message; *acc sg* 6.28. [ERRAND]

ærnan *wv* 1 to run; *pl pret* **ærndon** 6.191*. [RUN]

ǣs *n* food, carrion; *gen sg* **ǣses** 5.63, 6.107. [*see Holt*]

æsc *m* spear (of ash); *acc sg* 6.43, 6.310. [ASH]

æschere *m* ash-army, (Viking) army; *nom sg* 6.69. [ASH, HERE]

æscholt *n* ash-wood, spear (of ash); *acc sg* 6.230. [ASH, HOLT]

æt *prep* at, in, by; *w dat* 1.49, 3.4, 3.13, 3.21, *etc*; (**æt us** 'at our hands') 6.39. [AT]

ætforan *prep w dat* before, in front of; 6.16. [AT, FORNE]

ǣtren (y) *adj* fatal, deadly (because poisoned); *m nom sg* **ǣtterne** 6.146; *m acc sg* **ǣttrynne** 6.47. [ATTERN]

ætsamne (o) *adv* together; 1.46, 5.57*. [AT, SAM]

ætsteall *m* assistance, battle, station; *dat sg* **ætstealle** 3.21. [*see note*; *etymology uncertain*]

ætwītan *sv* 1 (*w dat*) to reproach; 6.220, 6.250. [ATWITE]

æþele *adj* noble, generous; *m nom sg* 6.280; *m acc sg* 6.151 **æþelan**; *f nom sg* **æþele** 5.16. [ATHEL]

geæþele *adj hapax legomenon (see note)* inborn, natural; *n nom sg* 5.7. [ATHEL]
æþeling *m* nobleman, prince, chief; *nom sg* 5.3, 5.58*; *gen sg* **æðelinges** 3.52. [ATHELING]
æþelu *f/n pl* noble lineage; *nom pl* **æþele** 1.5; *acc pl* **æþelo** 6.216. [ATHEL]
ǣwiscmōd *adj* ashamed in spirit; *m nom pl* **ǣwiscmōde** 5.56. [*see Holt*; MOOD]
afaran *see* **eafora**.
āfeallan *sv* 7 to fall, be felled; *pp m nom sg* **āfeallen** 6.202. [AFALLE]
āflīeman (ȳ) *wv* 1 to put to flight, cause to flee; *3 sg pret* **āflȳmde** 6.243. [AFLEME]
āfȳsan *wv* 1 to drive away; 6.3. [A- *prefix, see* FOUS]
āgan *ppv* to have, possess, obtain; 3.11, 6.87; *1 sg pres* **āh** 6.175; *1 sg pret* **āhte** 2.38; *and 3 sg pret* 1.77, 2.18, 2.22, 6.189. [OWE]
āgiefan *sv* 5 to give; *3 sg pret* **āgeaf** 6.44; *pp n nom sg* **āgyfen** 6.116. [AGIVE]
āgītan *wv* 1 to destroy; *pp m nom sg* **āgēted** 5.18. [AGET]
āhebban *sv* 6 (*weak pres*) to raise, lift up; *3 sg pret* **āhōf** 6.130, 6.244; *1 pl pret* **āhōfon** (-an) 1.104, 6.213; *pp m nom sg* **āhafen** 6.106. [AHEAVE]
ālicgan *sv* 5 (*weak pres*) to rest; *3 sg pret* **ālæg** 1.119. [A- *prefix*, LIE]
ālīefan (ȳ) *wv* 1 to allow, grant; 6.90. [A- *prefix*; *see* LEVE]

āmierran *wv* 1 to wound, disable; *3 sg pret* **āmyrde** 6.165. [AMAR]
ān *pron* one, a certain one; *m acc sg* **ānne** 6.117, 6.226; *adj m nom sg* **āna** 6.94; *numeral m dat sg* **ānum** 3.34; *n instr sg* **āne** 1.41. [ONE]
and (o) *conj* and; 1.15, *etc*. [AND]
andlang (o) *adj* entire (space of time); *m acc sg* **ondlongne** 5.21*. [ALONG]
andswaru *f* answer; *acc sg* **andsware** 6.44. [ANSWER]
anginn (/-n) *n* action, enterprise; *nom sg* 6.242. [ANGIN]
ānhȳdig *adj* single-minded, strong-minded, resolute; *m nom sg* 2.2. [ONE; *probably* HYGD; *see Holt*]
āniman (y) *sv* 4 to take away, deprive of; 4.21*. [ANIM]
ānmōd (ōn-) *adj* one-minded, steadfast, resolute, bold, proud; *m nom pl* **ōnmōde** 4.12. [ANMOD]
ānrǣd *adj* of one mind, resolute, constant; *m nom sg* 6.44, 6.132. [ANRED]
ānunga (i) *adv* quickly, entirely, certainly; 3.9. [*see Holt* **āninga**]
ār *m* messenger; *nom sg* 6.26. [*see Holt*]
ār *f* honour; *acc sg* **āre** 2.33. [ARE, ORE]
ārǣran *wv* 1 to heighten, build; 1.140. [AREAR]
ārhwæt (a) *adj* glorious, eager for glory; *m nom pl* **ārhwate** 5.73*. [ARE; WHAT]

GLOSSARY

ārīsan *sv* **1** to arise, rise; *3 pl pres* ārīsað 4.8; *3 sg pret* ārās 4.13. [ARISE]

āsceacan *sv* **6** to shake; *3 sg pret* āscēoc 6.230. [ASHAKE]

geascian *wv* **2** to learn (by asking); *1 pl pret* geascodan 2.21. [ASK]

āsecgan *wv* **3** to say; *3 sg pret* āsǣde 6.198. [ASEEK]

āswebban *wv* **2** to put to sleep, kill; *pp m nom pl* āswefede 5.30*. [ASWEVE]

B

bæc *n* back; *acc sg* 6.276 (*in adv phrase* ofer bæc 'away'). [BACK]

bǣdan *wv* **1** to compel; *pp m nom sg* gebēded 5.33. [*see Holt*]

gebǣran *wv* **1** to behave, conduct oneself; 4.38*. [I-BERE]

bana *m* slayer; *nom sg* 6.299. [BANE]

bānhelm *m* bone-helmet, helmet or shield; *nom sg* 4.30. [BONE, HELM]

be (-i/ig) *prep w dat* by, with, among, about; 1.43, 1.100, 1.105, etc. [BY]

beadu *f* fighting, strife; *dat sg* beaduwe 6.185; *and acc pl* 3.26. [*see Holt*]

beadurǣs *m hapax legomenon* battle-rush, onslaught; *nom sg* 6.111. [*see* beadu; RESE]

beaduweorc *n* battle-work, fighting, warlike deed; *gen pl* beaduweorca 5.48*. [*see* beadu; WORK]

bēag *m* neck-ring, torque; *acc sg* 1.65, 1.90; *acc pl* bēagas 6.31, 6.160; *gen pl* bēaga 1.74, 3.29 (*twice*). [BEE]

bēaggifa (bēah-) *m* ring-giver; *nom sg* 5.2*; *dat sg* bēahgifan 6.290. [BEC, GIVE]

bealdlīce (a) *adv* boldly; 6.311; *sup* baldlīcost 6.78. [BOLD]

bearn *n* child; *nom sg* 1.74, 3.41, 6.92, 6.155, 6.209, 6.238, 6.267, 6.300, 6.320; *and nom pl* 6.186. [BAIRN]

becuman (bi-) *sv* **4** to come; *1 sg pret* bicwōm 1.94; *3 pl pret* becōman(-on) 5.70*, 6.58. [BECOME]

bedǣlan (bi-) *wv* **1** to part, deprive; *pp m nom sg* bidǣled 1.52, 2.28. [BEDEAL]

beforan *prep w dat* before; 5.67. [BEFORE]

bēgen *numeral* both; *m nom* 5.57*, 6.183, 6.191, 6.291, 6.305; *m acc* 6.182; [*perhaps m gen* bēaga 3.29; *see* bēag, *and note*]. [BO]

begietan *sv* **5** to get, obtain; *3 pl pret* begēatan 5.73*. [*Osee Holt* gietan]

behindan *prep w dat* behind; 5.60*. [BEHIND]

benc *f* bench; *dat sg* bence 6.213. [BENCH]

beniman (bi-) *sv* **4** to deprive, take; *3 sg pret* binōm 2.16. [BENIM]

bēon *av* be; 6.185; *1 sg pres* eom 4.24, 6.179, 6.317; *2 sg pret* eart 6.36; *3 sg pres* biþ (y) 1.132, 3.54, 3.57 *and* is 3.8, 3.63, 4.24, 4.26, 6.31, 6.93, 6.223, 6.233; *3 sg pres subj* sȳ 2.30, 6.215. (*see* wesan) [BE]

gebeorg *n* defence; *dat sg*
gebeorge 6.31, 6.131, 6.245.
[BERGH]
beorgan *sv* 3 to save; 3.16; *3 pl pret* **burgon** 6.194. [BERGH]
beorht *adj* bright, shining; *m gen pl* **beorhtra** 1.74; *f nom sg* 5.15.
[BRIGHT]
beorn *m* man, warrior; *nom sg* 5.45; *and acc sg* 6.270; *gen sg* **beornes** 6.131, 6.160; *dat sg* **beorne** 6.154, 6.245; *nom pl* **beornas** 6.92, 6.111; *and acc pl* 6.17, 6.62, 6.182, 6.277, 6.305, 6.311; *gen pl* **beorna** 5.2, 6.257; *dat pl* **beornum** 6.101.
[BERNE]
bēot *n* boast; *acc sg* 3.26, 6.15, 6.27(on bēot 'threateningly'), 6.213. [BEOT, I-BEOT]
bēotian *wv* 2 to vow, make a boast; *3 sg pret* **bēotode** 6.290.
[BEOTEN]
beran *sv* 4 to bear, carry; 6.12, 6.62; *3 pl pres* **berað** 4.5; *3 sg pres subj* **bære** 4.20*; *3 pl pret* **bǣron** 6.99; *3 pl pret subj* **bēron** 6.67. [BEAR]
berstan *sv* 3 to burst; 4.30; *3 sg pret* **bærst** 6.284. [BURST]
beslēan *sv* 6 to strike; *pp m nom sg* (*w gen*) **beslagen** 5.42*. [BE-*prefix*, SLAY]
bestandan *sv* 6 to stand alongside, stand either side of; *3 pl pret* **bestōdon** 6.68. [BESTAND]
beswīcan *sv* 1 to betray; *pp m acc pl* **beswicene** 6.238.
[BESWIKE]
betera *see* **gōd**.

gebīdan *sv* 1 to experience, endure; *1 sg pret* **gebād** 4.25, 6.174. [BIDE]
biddan *sv* 5 (*weak pres*) to ask; *3 sg pret* **bæd** 6.20, 6.128, 6.170, 6.257; *3 pl pret* **bǣdon** 6.87, 6.262, 6.306. [BID]
bieldan *wv* 1 to encourage, embolden; *3 sg pret* **bylde** 6.169, 6.209, 6.320; *and 3 sg pret subj* 6.234.
[BIELD]
biernan *sv* 3 to burn; *3 pl pres* **byrnað** 4.1*, 4.4. [BURN]
bill *n* sword; *acc sg* 6.162; *dat pl* **billum** 3.17, 6.114. [BILL]
billgesliht *n* sword-clash, battle; *gen sg* **bilgeslehtes** 5.45*.
[BILL, SLEIGHT]
gebindan *sv* 3 to bind; *pp m nom sg* **gebunden** 2.24. [BIND]
bisig (y) *adj* busy; *m nom pl* **bysige** 6.110. [BUSY]
biter *adj* bitter, grim, fierce; *m nom sg* 6.111; *m acc pl* **bitere** 6.85. [BITTER]
blǣd *m* fame, blowing, prosperity; *acc sg* 2.34. [BLEAD]
blandenfeax *adj* blended-hair, hair streaked w grey; *m nom sg* 5.45*.
[BLAND, FAX]
blīðe *adj* joyous; *comp m nom sg* **blīþra** 6.146. [BLITHE]
blōdig *adj* bloody; *m acc sg* **blōdigne** 6.154. [BLOODY]
bōc *f* book; *nom pl* **bēc** 5.68.
[BOOK]
boda *m* messenger; *nom sg* 6.49.
[BODE]
boga *m* bow; *nom pl* **bogan** 6.110.
[BOW]

bord *n* shield; *nom sg* 4.29*,
6.110; *and acc sg* 6.15, 6.42,
6.131, 6.245, 6.270, 6.309; *and
acc sg or pl* 6.62, 6.283; *gen sg*
bordes 6.284; *gen pl* **borda**
6.295; *dat pl* **bordum** 6.101.
[BOARD]

bordweall (/-l) *m* shield-wall; *acc
sg* 5.5*, 6.277. [BOARD,
WALL]

bōsm *m* bosom; *dat sg* **bōsme**
5.27. [BOSOM]

brād *adj* broad; *n acc sg* 6.15,
6.163; *and n acc pl* 5.71*.
[BROAD]

gebrǣc *n* crashing; *nom sg* 6.295.
[BREAK]

brecan *sv* 4 to break; *3 sg pret*
bræc 6.277; *pp* **brocen** 6.1.
[BREAK]

bregdan *sv* 3 to pull, draw; *3 sg
pret* **brǣd** 6.154, 6.162.
[BRAID]

brego (u) *m* ruler, prince; *nom sg*
5.33. [*see Holt*]

brēost *n* breast; *dat sg* **brēostum**
6.144. [BREAST]

brim *n* sea; *acc pl* **brimu** 5.71.
[BRIM]

brimlið̄end *m* seafarer, Viking;
gen pl **brimliþendra** 6.27.
[BRIM, LITHE]

brimmann (/-n) *m* seafarer, Viking; *nom pl* **brimmen** 6.295; *gen
pl* **brimmanna** 6.49. [BRIM,
MAN]

brōþor *m* brother; *nom sg* 5.2,
6.282; *nom pl* (ge)**brōðru** 6.191,
6.305 *and collective* **gebrōþer**
5.57*; *gen pl* **brōþra** 2.8.
[BROTHER]

brūcan *sv* 2 (*w gen*) to enjoy; 5.63.
[BROOK]

brūnecg (-eccg) *adj* brown-edged,
with shining edge/blade; *n acc sg*
6.163. [BROWN, EDGE]

brycg (i) *f* causeway, bridge; *acc
sg* **bricge** 6.74, 6.78. [BRIDGE]

brycgweard (i) *m hapax
legomenon* bridge-guard,
defender of a causeway/bridge;
acc pl **bricgweardas** 6.85.
[BRIDGEWARD]

brytnian (i) *wv* 2 to distribute;
3.62. [BRITTEN]

bryttian *wv* 2 to distribute, enjoy
the use of; 1.102, 5.60*. [*see
Holt*]

būgan *sv* 2 to bow down, bend,
turn (away); 6.276 (**ofer bæc b.**
'to run away, retreat'); *3 pl pret*
bugon 6.185. [BOW]

burg (-h) *f* stronghold, fortified
place; *acc sg* 2.19, 6.291. [BOROUGH]

burgðelu (**buruh-**) *f* fortress floor;
nom sg 4.30. [BOROUGH,
THEAL]

burgwaran *f pl* inhabitants of a
burg, citizens; *gen pl*
burgwarena 1.90. [BOROUGH, WERE]

būrþegn *m* bower-servant, household servant; *dat sg* **būrþēne**
6.121. [BOWER, THANE]

būtan (**-on**) *prep* except, unless;
3.34, 6.71. [BOUT, BUT]

byre *m* opportunity; *acc sg* 6.121.
[BEAR; *see Holt*]

byrne *f* coat of mail; *nom sg* 4.44,
6.144, 6.284; *acc sg* **byrnan**
3.49, 6.163. [BURNE]

byrnhama (-homa) *m* corslet-covering, coat of mail; *acc sg* **byrnhomon** 3.17. [BURNE, HAME]

C

cāf *adj* quick, strong, brave; *m acc sg* **cāfne** 6.76. [COFE]
cāflīce *adv* bravely, promptly; 6.153. [COFLY]
(ge)camp *m* battle, struggle; *dat sg* **(ge)campe** 5.8, 6.153. [CAMP]
campstede *m* battle-place; *dat sg* **campstede** 5.29, 5.49. [CAMP, STEAD]
candel (o) *f/n* candel; *nom sg* 5.15*. [CANDLE]
ceald (a) *adj* cold, cool; *n acc sg* 6.91. [COLD]
ceallian *wv* 2 to call, shout; 6.91. [CALL]
celæs *adj hapax legomenon* (*see note*); 4.29.
cellod *adj hapax legomenon* (*see note*); 6.283.
cempa *m* warrior, champion; *nom sg* 6.119; *nom pl* **cempan** 4.14. [KEMP]
cēne *adj* bold, brave, keen; *m nom sg* 6.215; *and m nom pl* 6.283; *m dat sg/pl* **cēnum** 4.29*; *comp f nom sg* **cēnre** 6.312. [KEEN]
ceorl *m* freeman, peasant; *nom sg* 6.256; *dat sg* **ceorle** 6.132. [CHURL]
gecēosan *sv* 2 to choose; *3 sg pret* **gecēas** 6.113. [CHOOSE]
cīdan *wv* 1 to quarrel, contend, blame; *1 sg pres* **cīde** 3.12*. [CHIDE]

cirm (y) *m* cry, shout, uproar; *nom sg* 6.107. [CHIRM]
clēofan *sv* 2 to cleave, separate; *3 pl pret* **clufan(-on)** 5.5*, 6.283. [CLEAVE]
clipian (y) *wv* 2 to call out; *3 sg pret* **clypode** 6.25, 6.256. [CLEPE, YCLEPT]
cnearr (/-r) *m hapax legomenon* (*see note*) small ship, a Viking vessel; *nom sg* 5.35*. [*see Holt*]
cnēowmæg (cnēo-) *m* kinsman, ancestor; *dat pl* **cnēowmægum** 5.8*. [KNEE, MAY]
cniht *m* boy, servant, retainer; *nom sg* 6.9, 6.153. [KNIGHT]
cnihtwesende *adj* as/being a youth; *nom sg* 1.39. [KNIGHT, BE]
cnōsl *n* kin, progeny; *dat sg* **cnōsle** 1.52. [*see Holt*]
(ge)crin(c)gan *sv* 3 to fall (in battle), yield, die; 6.292*; *3 sg pret* **gecrang(-c)** 4.31, 6.250, 6.324; *3 pl pret* **crungun(-con)** 5.10*, 6.302. [CRINGE]
crūdan *sv* 2 to crowd, press; *3 sg pret* **crēad** 5.35. [CROWD]
cuman *sv* 4 to come; *3 sg pret* **cōm** 5.37, 6.65; *pp m nom sg* **cumen** 3.8; *and f nom sg* 6.104. [COME]
cumbolgehnast *n hapax legomenon* clash of banners, battle; *gen sg* **cumbolgehnastes** 5.49*.
cunnan *ppv* to know how, to be able; *3 sg pres* **can** 3.3; *3 pl pret* **cuþan** 1.107. [CAN, CON]
cunnian *wv* 2 (*w gen*) to experience, find out; 6.215; *1 sg pret*

GLOSSARY

cunnade 1.52; *and 3 sg pret* 2.1. [CUN]
cūþ *adj* known; *m nom sg* 4.25; *and n nom sg* 2.19. [COUTH]
cwēn *f* queen; *acc sg* 1.102. [QUEEN]
(ge)cweðan *sv* 5 to say, speak; *3 sg pret* **cweþ** (**gecwæð**) 4.24 (*see note*), 6.168, 6.211, 6.255. [QUETHE]
cynegōd *adj* well-born; *sb m nom pl* **cynegōde** 1.56. [KIN, GOOD]
cynerīce *n* kingdom, sovereignty; *gen sg* **cynerīces** 2.26; *gen pl* **cynerīca** 1.39. [KINRICK, KINGRICK]
cyning *m* king; *nom sg* 1.34, 1.67, 1.89, 2.23, 4.2, 5.1*, 5.35, 5.58*; *nom pl* **cyningas** 5.29*. [KING]
cynn *n* tribe, family, offspring, kind; *acc sg* 1.47; *gen sg* **cynnes** 1.16, 6.217, 6.266; *dat sg* **cynne** 6.76; *and instr sg* 1.27. [KIN]
cyst *f/m* something choice, election, gift; *nom sg* 3.24; *instr pl* **cystum** 1.56. [*see* CHOOSE]
gecȳþan *wv* 1 to proclaim, make known; 6.216. [KITHE, Y-KID]
cȳþþ *f* kinship, native land; *acc sg* **cȳþþe** 5.38, 5.58. [KITH]

D

dǣd *f* deed, event; *dat pl* **dǣdum** 3.23. [DEED]
dæg *m* day; *nom sg* 3.8; *and acc sg* 5.21, 6.198; *dat sg* **dæge** 3.7; *acc pl* **dagas** 4.41. [DAY]
dægweorc *n* day's work, fixed service; *gen sg* **dægweorces** 6.148. [DAYWORK]

dǣl *m* portion, quantity, region; *nom sg* 2.30; *and acc sg* 2.34. [DEAL]
dǣlan *wv* 1 to share, divide, bestow; *1 pl pret subj* **dǣlon** 6.33. [DEAL]
dagian *wv* 2 to dawn, be day; *3 sg pres* **dagað** 4.3. [DAW]
gedāl *n* distribution; *gen sg* **gedāles** 1.73. [*see Holt*]
daroþ (**-að**) *m* spear, dart; *acc sg* 6.149, 6.255; *gen pl* **daraða** 5.54*. [DART]
dēaþ *m* death, dying; *nom sg* 2.8. [DEATH]
dēop *adj* deep, profound, serious; *n acc sg* 5.55*. [DEEP]
dēor *n* animal, beast; *acc sg* 5.64. [DEER]
dēormōd *adj* animal-spirited, bold, courageous; *m nom sg* 4.23. [DEER, MOOD]
derian *wv* 1 to harm, injure, damage; 6.70. [DERE]
dīere (ȳ) *adj* dear, precious, excellent; *m nom sg* **dȳre** 2.37. [DEAR]
dohtor *f* daughter; *nom sg* 1.98. [DAUGHTER]
dōm *m* judgement, fame, assessment, court; *acc sg* 1.140, 1.143, 3.10, 6.38, 6.129. [DOOM]
dōn *av* to do, perform, cause; *3 sg pret* **dyde** 6.280; *2 pl pret* **dydon** 3.56; *pp f acc pl* **gedōn** 6.197. [DO]
draca *m* dragon, serpent; *nom sg* 4.3. [DRAKE]
dreng *m* youth, freeman, warrior; *gen pl* **drenga** 6.149. [DRENG]

drēogan *sv* **2** to perform, take part in, endure; *3 sg pret* **drēag** 2.2. [DREE, I-DREE]

drēorig *adj* dreary, sad, ill-fated; *f nom sg* 5.54*. [DREARY]

gedrēosan *sv* **2** to fall, perish, fail; 3.7; *3 sg pret* **gedrēas** 3.4. [*see Holt* drēosan]

gedryht *f* company, host; *acc sg* 1.118. [DRIGHT]

dryhtcwēn (i) *f* army-queen, queen of the comitatus; *nom sg* 1.98. [DRIGHT, QUEEN]

dryhten (i) *m* lord, prince, ruler; *nom sg* 2.32, 5.1*, 6.148; *gen sg* **drihtnes** 5.16; *dat sg* **dryhtne** 2.37. [DRIGHTIN]

dryhtgesīð (i) *m* army-companion, warrior; *gen pl* **drihtgesīða** 4.42. [DRIGHT; *see Holt* sīð]

dryhtlic (i) *adj* lordly, noble (*see note at 1.37*); *m nom pl* **drihtlice** 4.14. [DRIGHT]

dryhtscipe *m* lordship, virtue, valour (*see note at 1.37*); *nom sg* 3.7. [DRIGHT, -SHIP *suffix and* SHAPE]

dugan *ppv* to avail, be (of) worth, thrive; *3 sg pres* **dēah** 6.48; *3 sg pret* **dohte** 1.89; *3 pl pret subj* **dohten** 1.56. [DOW]

duguð *f* body of tried retainers, nobles, glory, prosperity; *gen sg* **duguþe** 1.98; *and dat sg* 1.140, 6.197. [DOUTH]

duru *f* door, gate; *acc sg* 4.23; *dat sg* **dura** 4.14; *acc pl* **duru** 4.42; *dat pl* **durum** 4.16, 4.20. [DOOR]

durran *ppv* to dare, presume; *2 sg pres subj* **dyrre** 3.48. [DARE]

dynian (**dænn-**) *wv* **2** to sound, resound; *3 sg pret* **dynede** 4.30, 5.12*. [DIN]

E

ēac *adv* also, likewise, moreover; 3.34, 3.37, 4.45, 5.2, 5.19, 5.30, 5.37, 6.11. [EKE]

ēacen *adj* increased, vast, pregnant; *f nom sg* 2.11. [*see* EKE]

eafora (a-) *m* child, offspring; *nom pl* **afaran** 5.7*; *and acc pl* 5.52. [*see Holt*]

eald *adj* old, ancient; *m nom sg* 5.46, 6.310; *m acc sg* **ealdne** 1.122, 3.31; *m nom pl* **ealde** 5.69; *and n acc pl* 6.47; *wk m nom sg* **ealda fæder** grandfather 6.218. [OLD]

ealdor *m* elder, leader, prince, life; *nom sg* 6.202, 6.222, 6.314; *gen sg* **ealdres** 6.53; *dat sg* **ealdre** 6.11. [ALDER]

ealdorlang *adj hapax legomenon* (*see note*) eternal, life-long; *m acc sg* **ealdorlangne** 5.3*. [ALDOR, LONG]

ealdormann (/-n) *m* elder-man, chief, chief officer of a shire, alderman; *nom sg* 6.219. [ALDERMAN]

ealgian *wv* **2** to defend, protect; **gealgean** 6.52; *3 pl pret* **ealgodon** 5.9*. [*see Holt*]

eall (/-l) *adj* all, whole, every; *m acc sg* **ealne** 1.109; *m gen pl* **ealra** 1.15, 1.36, 4.32; *f nom sg* **eal** 4.36; *f acc sg* **ealle** 1.88, 6.304; *f gen pl* **ealra** 6.174; *n nom sg* **eal** 1.141; *and n acc sg* 4.22, 6.256; *pron m nom pl* **ealle**

GLOSSARY 121

6.63, 6.196, 6.203, 6.207; *and m acc pl* 6.231, 6.238, 6.320; *m dat pl* **eallum** 6.216, 6.233; *sb m dat sg* **ealle** 2.16; *and adv* **eall** completely; 6.314. [ALL]

ealles *adv* entirely, quite; 3.52. [ALL]

eard *m* native place, country, earth; *acc sg* 5.73, 6.53, 6.58, 6.222. [ERD]

earfoðe *n* hardship, trouble, torment; *gen pl* **earfoða** 2.2, 2.30*. [ARVETH]

earg (-h) *adj* cowardly, sluggish, wretched; *n nom sg* 6.238. [ARGH]

eargebland *n* wave-blend, surge (of the sea); *acc sg* 5.26*. [OAR, BLEND]

earm *m* arm; *acc sg* 6.165. [ARM]

earn *m* eagle; *nom sg* 6.107; *and acc sg* 5.63. [ERNE]

(ge)earnung *f* reward, merit, consideration; *acc pl* **earnunga** 3.61, 6.196. [EARNING]

eart *see* **bēon**.

ēaststæð (-eð) *n hapax legomenon* east bank of a river/stream, seashore; *dat sg* **ēasteðe** 6.63. [EAST, STAITH]

ēastan *adv* from the east; 1.8, 4.3*, 5.69. [EAST]

eaxl *f* shoulder; *dat pl* **eaxelum** 3.50. [AXLE]

ebba *m* ebb, low tide; *dat sg* **ebban** 6.65. [EBB]

ēce *adj* eternal, perpetual; *m gen sg* **ēces** 5.16. [ECHE]

ecg *f* edge, point, sword; *nom sg* 6.60; *dat pl* **ecgum** 5.4*, 5.68*. [EDGE]

edwītscipe (y) *m* disgrace, shame; *acc sg* **edwītscype** 3.14. [EDWIT, -SHIP suffix]

efeneald *adj* of equal age, contemporary, coaeval; *m nom sg* 1.40. [EVENOLD]

efestan (efs-) *wv* 1 to hasten, hurry; *3 pl pret* **efston** 6.206. [OFT]

eft *adv* again, afterwards, likewise; 3.55, 5.56, 6.49, 6.156 (**e. ongean** 'in reply'), 6.201, *etc.* [EFT]

elde *see* **ielde**.

ellen *n* courage, zeal, strife; *acc sg* 3.6, 4.11; *and* 6.211 (**on ellen** 'bravely'). [ELNE]

ellenrōf *adj* courageous, powerful; *m nom sg* 3.43. [ELNE; *see* Holt]

endelēas *adj* endless, eternal; *m nom sg* 2.30. [ENDLESS]

engel *m* angel, messenger; *gen pl* **engla** 6.178. [ANGEL]

ēoc *see* **gēoc**.

ēode, ēodon *see* **gān**.

eoh *m* horse; *acc sg* 6.189. [*see* Holt **eoh**]

eom *see* **bēon**.

ēoredcist (ēorod-) *f* troop, company; *dat pl* **ēorodcistum** 5.21*. [*see* **eoh**; ROAD, CHEST]

eorl *m* (brave) man, leader, nobleman, warrior (*see note at 1.37*); *nom sg* 1.12 (*see note*), 2.2, 6.6, 6.51, 6.89, 6.132, 6.146, 6.203, 6.233; *gen sg* **eorles** 6.165; *dat sg* **eorle** 2.33, 6.28, 6.159; *nom pl* **eorlas** 5.31, 5.73; *gen pl* **eorla** 2.41, 5.1. [EARL]

eorlscipe (y) *m* conduct proper to an *eorl*, courage (*see notes at 1.37 and 4.13*); *acc sg* 1.37, 1.40, 1.141. [EARL, -SHIP *suffix*]
eornoste *adv* determinedly, courageously; 6.281. [EARNEST]
eorðbūend *m* earth-dweller, man; *gen pl* **eorðbūendra** 4.32. [EARTH, BE]
eorþe *f* earth, ground, country; *acc sg* **eorþan** 1.2, 6.126, 6.286, 6.303; *and dat sg* 6.107, 6.157, 6.233. [EARTH]
ēower *poss pron* your(s); *f acc pl* **ēowre** 4.11.
ēþel *m* country, native land, ancestral estate; *acc sg* 1.96, 1.109, 3.31*, 6.52; *dat sg* **ēðle** 1.12. [ETHEL]
ēþelstol *m* ancestral seat, homeland, royal city; *acc sg* 1.122. [ETHEL, STOOL]

F

fæder *m* father, male ancestor; *nom sg* 6.218; *and acc sg* 1.114; *and gen sg* 1.96. [FATHER]
fǣge *adj* fated (to die), destined; *m nom sg* 6.119; *m gen sg* **fǣges** 6.297; *m dat sg* **fǣgean** 6.125; *m nom pl* **fǣge** 5.12, 5.28, 6.105. [FEY]
fǣgre (-ere) *adv* fairly, properly, with care; 6.22. [FAIR]
fǣhð (-o/u) *f* feud, battle, hostility; *acc sg* **fǣhðe** 6.225. [FOE]
fǣle *adj* faithful, beloved, gracious; *f dat sg* **fǣlre** 1.6. [FELE]
fǣring (ē) *f* journeying, wandering; *dat sg* **fēringe** 1.131. [*see* FARE]

fǣrsceaða *m hapax legomenon* sudden attacker, enemy; *dat sg* **fǣrsceaðan** 6.142. [FEAR, SCATHE]
fæste *adv* fast, firmly, steadily; 6.21, 6.103, 6.171, 6.301. [FAST]
fæsten *n* fortress, stronghold, fastness; *acc sg* 6.194. [FASTEN]
fæstlīce *adv* steadily, bravely, resolutely; 6.82, 6.254. [FAST]
fæstnian *wv 2* to fasten, confirm, establish; 6.35. [FASTEN]
fāh *adj* hostile, stained, guilty; *n nom sg* 3.54. [FOE]
faran *sv 6* to go, travel, exist; 6.88, 6.156. [FARE]
feallan *sv 7* to fall, die, fail; 6.54, 6.105; *3 sg pret* **fēol(l)** 4.41, 6.119, 6.126, 6.166, 6.286, 6.303; *3 pl pret* **fēollan(-on)** 5.12, 6.111. [FALL]
fealohilte *adj* yellow/golden hilted; *n nom sg* 6.166. [FALLOW, HILT]
fealu *adj* fallow, yellow, dusky, dark; *m acc sg* **fealene** 5.36. [FALLOW]
gefeccan (-cg-) *wv 2* to fetch, bring, draw; 6.160; (=**fetian**). [FETCH]
fela (æ) (*indecl*) *adj* (*w gen*) many; 1.10, 1.50, 1.99, 1.136, 2.38, 3.16, 4.25, 4.33, 6.73, 6.90. [FELE]
feld *m* field, plain; *nom sg* 5.12; *dat sg* **felda** 6.241. [FIELD]
feng *see* **fōn**.
feoh *n* cattle, money, wealth; *acc sg* 6.39. [FEE]

(ge)feoht *n* fight, battle; *acc sg* **feohtan** 3.18, 3.20; *dat sg* **gefeohte** 5.28*, 6.12 (=**feohte**). [FIGHT]
feohtan *sv* 3 to fight, strive; 6.16, 6.261; *3 sg pret* **feaht** 6.254, 6.277, 6.281, 6.298; *3 pl pret* **fuhton** 4.41. [FIGHT]
gefeohtan *sv* 3 to win (by fighting); 6.129. [FIGHT]
feohte *f* fight, battle; *nom sg* 6.103; (=**feoht**). [FIGHT]
fēolheard *adj hapax legomenon* file-hardened, hard as a file; *n acc pl* **fēolhearde** 6.108. [FILE, HARD]
fēond *m* adversary, fiend, foe; *acc pl* **fȳnd** 6.82; *dat pl* **fēondum** 3.54, 6.103, 6.264. [FIEND]
feorh *m/n* life, spirit, body; *acc sg* 4.19, 5.36, 6.125, 6.142, 6.184; *gen sg* **fēores** 6.260, 6.317; *dat sg* **fēore** 6.194, 6.259. [*see Holt*]
feorhhord *n* life-hoard, breast, soul; *acc sg* 3.54. [*see* **feorh**; HORD]
feorhhūs *n hapax legomenon* life/soul-house, body; *acc sg* 6.297. [*see* **feorh**; HOUSE]
feorr (/-r) *adj* far, far away; 1.53, 6.3, 6.57. [FAR]
gefēra *m* comrade (in arms), associate; *nom sg* 6.280; *acc pl* **gefēran** 6.170, 6.229. [FERE, Y-FERE]
fēran *wv* 1 to go, depart; 6.41, 6.221. [FERE]
ferian *wv* 1 to go, travel; 6.179. [FERRY]
fetian *wv* 2 to fetch, obtain; *imp sg* **feta** 3.48; (=**feccan**). [FET, Y-FET]
fēða *m* foot-soldier; *acc pl* **fēþan** 6.88. [FOOT]
fēðewig(g) *m* battle on foot; *gen sg* **fēðewigges** 3.48. [FOOT, WYE]
fiell (y) *m* fall, death, slaughter; *acc sg* 6.71, 6.264. [FALL]
fierd (y) *f* army, national levy, campaign; *dat sg* **fyrde** 6.221. [FERD]
fīf *num* (*usually indecl*) five; *m nom* **fīfe** 5.28; *m acc* 4.41. [FIVE]
fīfel *n* giant, sea-monster; *gen pl* **fīfela** 3.42. [*see Holt*]
findan *sv* 3 to find, meet with; *3 sg pres* **findeð** 3.60; *3 pl pret* **fundon** 6.85. [FIND]
firenlīce (y) *adv* fiercely, rashly; 3.20. [*see Holt* **firen**; -LY *suffix*]
flān *m* arrow, javelin, barb; *acc sg* 6.269; *gen sg* **flānes** 6.71. [FLANE]
flēam *m* flight; *acc sg* 6.81, 6.254; *dat sg* **flēame** 5.37, 6.186. [FLEME]
flēogan *sv* 2 to fly, take to flight; 6.7, 6.109, 6.150; *3 sg pres* **flēogeð** 4.3; *3 sg pret* **flēag** 1.127. [FLY]
flēon *sv* 2 to flee, fly from; 3.15, 6.247, 6.275* (*see note*); *3 pl pret* **flugon** 6.194. [FLEE]
flett *n* floor, hall; *dat sg* **flette** 1.3. [FLETT]
geflīeman *wv* 1 to put to flight; *pp m nom sg* **geflēmed** 5.32. [FLEME]
flōd *m/n* flood, wave, tide, sea, current; *nom sg* 6.65, 6.72; *and*

acc sg 5.36. [FLOOD]
flot *n* deep water, sea; *acc sg* 5.35*, 6.41. [FLOAT]
flota *m* boat, fleet, sailor; *acc sg* **flotan** 6.227, *and nom pl* 6.72; *gen pl* **flotena** 5.32*. [FLOTE]
flōwan *sv* 7 to flow, stream, melt; *pres p m nom sg* **flōwende** 6.65. [FLOW]
flugon *see* **flēon**.
flyht *m* flight, flying; *acc sg* 6.71. [FLIGHT]
folc *n* folk, nation, tribe; *nom sg* 6.45, 6.241; *and acc sg* 2.22, 6.22, 6.54; *gen sg* **folces** 4.9, 4.46, 5.67, 6.202; *dat sg* **folce** 6.227, 6.259, 6.323; *gen pl* **folca** 1.3. [FOLK]
folcstede *m* folk-place, battlefield; *dat sg* 5.41. [FOLK, STEAD]
folde *f* ground, earth, country; *acc sg* **foldan** 1.17, 6.54; *and dat sg* 6.166, 6.227. [FOLD]
folgian *wv* 2 to follow, serve; *1 sg pret* **folgade** 1.53. [FOLLOW]
folgoð (-að) *m* body of retainers, following, office; *acc sg* 2.38. [FOLLOW]
folme *f* hand, palm; *dat sg* **folman** 6.21, 6.108, 6.150. [FEEL]
fōn *sv* 7 to take, seize; *3 sg pret* **feng** 6.10. [FANG]
for *prep* before, on account of, in place of; (*w dat*) 1.104, 3.24, 6.64, 6.89, 6.96, 6.259. [FOR]
forbīgan *wv* 1 to bend down, humiliate, cause to retreat, diminish; 3.26; *3 pl pret* **forbīgdan** 1.48. [FOR- *prefix*, BEY]
forbūgan *sv* 2 to avoid, bend from, flee from; 3.15; *3 sg pret* **forbēah** 6.325. [FORBOW]
ford *m* ford; *acc sg* 6.88; *dat sg* **forda** 6.81. [FORD]
fore *prep* before, for the sake of, in the presence of; (*w dat*) 1.55, 1.140. [FORE]
forgiefan *sv* 5 to give, forgive, give up; *3 sg pret* **forgeaf** 1.66, 1.90, 1.95, 1.97, 6.139, 6.148. [FORGIVE]
forgieldan (y) *sv* 3 to requite, pay, forfeit; 4.39; *2 pl pret* **forgyldon** 6.32. [FORYIELD]
forgrindan *sv* 3 to grind down, destroy, kill; *pp m acc sg* **forgrunden** 5.43*. [FORGRIND]
forheard *adj hapax legomenon* very hard; *m acc sg* **forheardne** 6.156. [FOR- *prefix*, HARD]
forhēawan *sv* 7 to hack to pieces; *3 pl pret* **forhēowan** 1.49; *pp m nom sg* **forhēawen** 6.115, 6.223, 6.288, 6.314. [FOR- *prefix*, HEW]
forhtian *wv* 2 to be afraid, fear; *3 pl pret subj* **forhtedon** 6.21. [*see Holt* **fyrhtan** *and* FRIGHT]
forhycgan *wv* 2 (*earlier* 3) to disdain, despise; *3 sg pret* **forhogode** 6.254. [FOR- *prefix, see* HOW, HOWE]
forlǣtan *sv* 7 to leave, abandon, excuse; 6.2, 6.208*; *3 sg pret* **forlēt** 3.41, 5.42*, 6.149, 6.156, 6.187, 6.321. [FORLET]
forlēosan *sv* 2 to abandon, lose; 3.10. [FORLESE]
forma *adj* first; *m acc sg* **forman** 6.77; *and m dat sg* 4.19*; *and m instr sg* 1.6; *sup m nom sg* **fyrmest** 6.323 ('foremost').

[FORME, FOREMOST]
formanig (-moni) *adj* very many; *m nom sg* 6.239. **[FOR-** *prefix*, **MANY]**
forsacan *sv* **6** to refuse, reject, renounce; *3 sg pret* **forsōc** 3.28. **[FORSAKE]**
forð *adv* forth, away, forwards; 1.43, 3.42, 4.5, 5.20, 6.3, 6.12, 6.150-51 (**tō forð...þurh** 'right through'), 6.170, 6.205, 6.209, 6.225, 6.229, 6.260, 6.269, 6.297*. **[FORTH]**
forðæm (forþon/-an) *conj* therefore, on that account; 1.54, 6.241.
forðgeorn *adj hapax legomenon* eager to advance; *m nom sg* 6.281. **[FORTH, YERN]**
forðian *wv* **2** to accomplish, put forth, carry out; *pp n nom sg* **geforþod** 6.289. **[FORTH]**
forwegan *sv* **5** *hapax legomenon* to kill, carry off; *pp m nom sg* **forwegen** 6.228. **[FOR-** *prefix*, **WEIGH]**
forwrecan *sv* **5** to drive forth, banish; *3 pl pret* **forwræcon** 1.47. **[FOR-** *prefix*, **WREAK]**
fōt *m* foot (limb/measure); *gen sg* **fōtes** 6.247; *dat pl* **fōtum** 6.119, 6.171. **[FOOT]**
fōtmǣl *n* foot-measure, foot's length; *acc sg* 6.275. **[FOOT, MEAL]**
gefrǣge *n* information got by enquiry; *instr sg* 1.71. [*see Holt*]
fram (o) *prep w dat* from; 1.4, 3.30, 5.8*, 6.185, 6.187, 6.193, 6.252; *w instr* 6.316; *and adv* 6.317. **[FROM]**

franca *m* javelin; *acc sg* **francan** 6.140; *and dat sg* 6.77. [*see Holt*]
frēa *m* ruler, lord, king; *nom sg* 1.96; *acc sg* **frēan** 6.259; *and dat sg* 6.12, 6.16 6.184, 6.289. [*see Holt*]
fremde *adj* foreign, unfriendly, remote from; *n gen pl* **fremdra** 1.50. **[FREMD]**
(ge)fremman *wv* **1** to do, perform, achieve; 4.9; *3 sg pret* **(ge)fremede** 1.37, 3.47. **[FREME]**
frēod *f* friendship, peace; *acc sg* **frēode** 6.39. **[FREE** *and* **I-FREE]**
frēolic *adj* free, noble, glorious, excellent; *n acc sg*. 4.19. **[FREE]**
frēomǣg *m* free kinsman, generous kinsman; *dat pl* **frēomǣgum** 1.53. **[FREE, MAY]**
frēond *m* friend, relative; *acc pl* **frȳnd** 6.229; *gen pl* **frēonda** 5.41. **[FRIEND]**
gefricgan *sv* **5** to learn by asking; *pp* **gefrægen** 1.17 (*see* **gefrignan**)
frige *fpl* sexual love; *nom* 2.15. [*see Holt*]
(ge)frignan *sv* **3** to learn (by asking), inquire; *1 sg pret* **gefrægn** 1.10, 4.37; *3 sg pret* **frægn** 4.22, 4.46; *1 pl pret* **frugnon** 2.14*; **[FRAYNE]**
frið *m* peace, security; *acc sg* 6.39; *dat sg* **friþe** 6.179; *gen sg* (*adverbially*) **friþes** 6.41. **[FRITH]**
friðowebbe (eo) *f* peace-weaver, queen; *dat sg* **freoþuwebban** 1.6.

[FRITH, WEBBE]
frōd *adj* wise, old; *m nom sg* frōd(/-a) 5.37, 6.140, 6.317; *m acc sg* frōdne 1.114. [*see Holt*]
fruma *m* beginning, creator, firstborn; *nom sg* 1.90. [FRUME]
frymdig (-i) *adj* inquisitive, requesting; *m nom sg* 6.179 (f. bēon 'to entreat'). [*see Holt*]
fugel (-ol) *m* fowl, bird; *nom pl* fugelas 4.5. [FOWL]
full (/-l) *adv* full, very, completely; 1.119, 1.127, 6.153, 6.253, 6.311. [FULL]
furðor *adv* further, later; 3.18, 6.247. [FURTHER]
fullæstan (fylstan) *wv* 1 to help, protect, support; 6.265. [FILST]
fūs *adj* eager for, ready for; *m nom sg* 6.281. [FOUS]
gefyllan (ie) *wv* 1 to fell, slay; *pp m nom sg* gefylled 5.41; *and n nom sg* 5.67*. [FELL]
fyrdrinc *m* army-man, soldier; *nom sg* 6.140. [FERD, RINK]
fȳren *adj* fiery, afire; *f nom sg* fȳrenu 4.36. [FIREN]
fyrmest *see* forma.
fȳsan *wv* 1 to impel, shoot, send forth; *3 sg pret* fȳsde 6.269. [FUSE]

G

gafol *n* tribute; *acc sg* gofol 6.61; *dat sg* gafole 6.32, 6.46. [GAVEL]
gān *av* to go, advance; 6.247; *imp pl* gāð 6.93; *3 sg pret* ēode 6.132, 6.159, 6.225, 6.297, 6.323; *3 pl pret* ēodon 4.14, 6.260; *and 3 pl pret subj* 6.229. [GO]
(ge)gangan *sv* 7 to go, walk, advance; 4.43, 6.3, 6.40, 6.59, 6.62, 6.170; *3 pl pret subj* 6.56 gangon (tō scype g. 'embark'). [GAN, GO]
gār *m* spear; *nom sg* 1.128, 6.296; *and acc sg* 6.13, 6.134, 6.154, 6.237, 6.321; *dat sg* gāre 6.138; *acc pl* gāras 6.46, 6.67, 6.109; *dat pl* gārum 5.18. [GARE]
gārberend *m* spear-bearer, warrior; *nom pl* 6.262. [GARE, BEAR]
gārmitting *f hapax legomenon* spear-meeting, battle; *gen sg* gārmittinge 5.50*. [GARE, MEET]
gārræs *m hapax legomenon* spear-rush, battle; *acc sg* 6.32. [GARE, RESE]
gāst *m* breath, soul; *dat sg* gāste 6.176. [GHOST]
gealgean *see* ealgian.
gēapneb *adj* crooked-nibbed; *f nom sg* 3.51. [YEPE, NEB]
gearo *adj* ready; *m nom sg* 6.274; *m nom pl* gearowe 6.72, 6.100. [YARE]
gearolīce *adv* clearly; 2.10. [YARELY]
gearwe (-ro) *adv* readily; 3.60. [YARE]
gegearw(i)an (i) *wv* 1/2 to adorn; 3.39. [YARE]
(g)ēoc (īo) *f* help, support; *dat sg* ēoce 3.25, 3.60. [*see Holt*]
gēolēan (īu-) *n* reward for past deed; *acc sg* 3.39. [*see Holt; see* lēan]
geond *prep w acc* through(out), about, over; 1.51, 1.99, 1.136,

GLOSSARY

2.31. [YOND]
geondfēran *wv* 1 to travel through, traverse; *1 sg pret* **geondfērde** 1.50. [YOND, FERE]
geondhweorfan *sv* 3 to wander about, traverse; *1 sg pret* **geondhwearf** 1.109. [YOND, WHARVE]
geong (iu) *adj* (*w instr*) young; *m nom sg* 6.210; *and wk* **geonga** 6.155; *m acc sg* **giungne** 5.44*; *m nom pl* **giunge** 5.29*. [YOUNG]
georn *adj* (*w gen*) eager; *m nom sg* 6.107; *m nom pl* **georne** 6.73. [YERN]
georne *adv* eagerly, readily, clearly; 3.1, 6.84, 6.123, 6.206. [YERNE]
geornful *adj* eager; *m nom sg* 6.274. [YEARNFULL]
geornlīce *adv* eagerly, willingly; 6.265. [YERNLY]
giedd *n* poem; *gen pl* **gydda** 1.139. [YED]
gieddian *wv* 2 to speak; *3 sg pret* **gyddode** 3.45. [YED]
giefu *f* gift; *acc pl* **giefe** 1.102; *instr pl* **geofum** 1.139. [GIVE]
gieldan *sv* 3 to yield, pay, render; *3 pl pret* **guldan** 4.40. [YIELD]
giellan *sv* 3 to yell; *3 sg pres* **gylleð** 4.6; *pres p m nom sg* **giellende** 1.128. [YELL]
gielpan (e) *sv* 3 to boast; 5.44* (*w gen*). [YELP]
gielpword (y) *n* boasting-word, boast; *dat pl* (*as adv*) **gylpwordum** 'vauntingly' 6.274. [YELP, WORD]

gīeman *wv* 1 (*w gen*) to care for or about; *3 pl pret* **gȳmdon** 6.192. [YEME]
giest *m* stranger; *nom pl* **gystas** 6.86. [GUEST]
gīet (ȳ)(-a) *adv* still, yet; 4.26, 5.66*; **þā gīet** still, further; 4.18, 6.168, 6.273; **nū gīet** formerly, until now; 3.6. [YET]
gif (y) *conj* if; 3.32, 3.48, 3.61, 6.34, 6.36, 6.196. [IF]
gifeðe *adj* granted; 3.25. [GIVE; *see Holt*]
ginn *adj* wide; *m acc sg* **ginne** 1.51. [*see* YAWN]
gegirwan *see* **gegearwian**.
gīsel (ȳ) *m* hostage; *nom sg* 6.265. [YISEL]
glædlic *adj* goodly; *m acc sg* **glædlicne** 1.66. [GLAD, -LY *suffix*]
glēaw *adj* (*w gen*) prudent, wise; *m acc sg* **glēawne** 1.139. [GLEW]
glīwman (ēo) *m* gleeman, minstrel; *nom pl* **glēomen** 1.136. [GLEEMAN]
glīdan *sv* 1 to glide; *3 sg pret* **glād** 5.15. [GLIDE]
gnornian *wv* 2 to mourn, feel sorrow; 6.315. [*see Holt*]
god *m* deity, God; *nom sg* 1.133, 3.23 (*see note*), 6.94; *and acc sg* 6.262; *gen sg* **godes** 5.15; *dat sg* **gode** 3.60. [GOD]
gōd *adj* good, loyal, brave, noble; *m acc sg* **gōdne** 1.114; *m dat sg* **gōdum** 6.4; *m acc pl* **gōde** 6.170; *f nom sg* **gōd** 3.51; *f dat pl* **gōdum** 3.23; *n acc sg* **gōd** 6.13, 6.237; *and sb m nom sg* 6.315; *m acc sg wk* **gōdan** 6.187; *m gen pl*

gōdra 4.33; *comp n nom sg* **betere** 6.31; *dat/acc sg* **bæteran** 3.33; *sb m nom sg* **betera** 6.276; *m nom pl* **beteran** 5.48. [GOOD, BETTER]

gōd *n* that which is good, benefit, well-being, prosperity; *gen sg* **gōdes** 1.51, 6.176; *instr sg* **gōde** 1.89. [GOOD]

gold *n* gold; *gen sg* **goldes** 1.91; *dat sg* **golde** 3.39, 3.51, 6.35; *and instr sg* 1.129. [GOLD]

goldhladen *adj hapax legomenon* (*see note*) gold-adorned; *m nom sg* 4.13. [GOLD, LADE]

goldhroden *adj* gold-adorned; *f acc sg* **goldhrodene** 1.102. [GOLD; *see Holt* **hreodan**]

grǣdig *adj* greedy; *m acc sg* **grǣdigne** 5.64. [GREEDY]

grǣg *adj* grey; *n acc sg* **grǣge** 5.64*. [GREY]

grǣghama *adj hapax legomenon* grey-coated; *sb m nom sg* 4.6. [GREY, HAME]

gram (o) *adj* fierce, hostile; *m nom pl* **grame** 6.262; *and f acc sg* 1.128; *sb m dat pl* **gramum** 6.100. [GRAME]

gremian *wv* 2 to enrage; *pp m nom sg* **gegremod** 6.138; *pp m nom pl* **gegremode** 6.296. [GREME]

grēot *n* dirt, dust; *dat sg* **grēote** 6.315. [GRIT]

grimm (/-m) *adj* grim; *m nom sg* 2.23, 6.61. [GRIM]

grimme *adv* grimly, cruelly; 6.109*. [GRIM]

grindan *sv* 3 to grind, sharpen; *pp m acc pl* **gegrundene** 6.109. [GRIND]

gripe *m* grip, cut; *acc/dat sg* 3.45. [GRIP]

grið *n* truce, peace; *acc sg* 6.35. [GRITH]

grund *m* land, region; *acc sg* 1.51, 6.287; *acc pl* **grundas** 5.15; *gen pl* **grunda** 1.136. [GROUND]

grundlēas *adj* bottomless, numberless; *f nom pl* **grundlēase** 2.15. [GROUNDLESS]

gryrelēoð *n* song of terror; *gen pl* **gryrelēoða** 6.285. [*see Holt* **gryre, lēoð**]

guma *m* man; *nom sg* 5.18*; *nom pl* **guman** 6.94; *gen pl* **gumena** 1.133, 1.136, 5.50. [GOME]

gūð *f* fight, battle, war; *acc sg* **gūðe** 6.325*; *and gen sg* 6.192; *and dat sg* 4.31, 5.44, 6.13, 6.94, 6.187, 6.285, 6.296, 6.321. [*see Holt*]

gūðbill *n* battle-bill, sword; *gen pl* **gūðbilla** 3.45. [*see* **gūð**; BILL]

gūðhafoc *m hapax legomenon* (*see note*) battle-hawk; *acc sg* 5.64*. [*see* **gūð**; HAWK]

gūðplega *m* battle-play, conflict; *nom sg* 6.61. [*see* **gūð**; PLAY]

gūðrinc *m* battle-man, soldier; *nom sg* 6.138. [*see* **gūð**; RINK]

gūðwudu *m* battle-wood (i.e. spear, or possibly shield); *nom sg* 4.6. [*see* **gūð**; WOOD]

gyrdan *wv* 1 to gird on, belt on, encircle; *3 sg pres* **gyrde** 4.13. [GIRD]

H

habban *wv* 3 to have, hold, keep, look after, get; 6.236; *infl inf* **habbanne** 3.53; *imp pl* **habbað**

4.11; *1 sg pres* **hæbbe** (*aux*) 1.17,
hafa 3.34; *2 sg pres* **hafast**
6.231; *3 sg pres* **hafað** (**hæfð**)
1.143, 6.237; *3 sg pret* **hæfde**
1.71, 2.3, 2.10, 3.44, 6.22, 6.197,
6.289. [HAVE]
hæleð (-**æð**) *m* man, warrior, hero;
nom sg 4.23, 4.43; *and nom pl*
6.214, 6.249; *gen pl* **hæleþa** 5.25,
6.74. [HELETH]
hæðen *adj* heathen; *m nom pl*
hæðene 6.181; *and sb* 6.55.
[HEATHEN]
hafenian *wv 2* to raise aloft; *3 sg
pret* **hafenode** 6.42, 6.309.
[HEAVE]
hafoc *m* hawk; *acc sg* 6.8.
[HAWK]
hag(o)steald (**hæg**-) *adj* unmarried, independent, military (of a young man); *m nom pl*
hægstealdas 4.40. [*see Holt*
hagusteald]
hāl *adj* whole, unhurt, safe and sound; *m nom pl* **hāle** 6.292.
[HALE, WHOLE]
hālga *adj* holy; *sb m dat sg* **hālgan**
3.59. [HALLOW]
hals *see* **heals**.
hām *m* home; *acc sg* 1.7, 6.251;
dat sg **hām(e)** 1.94, 6.292; *acc pl*
hāmas 5.10. [HOME]
hamor *m* hammer; *gen pl* **hamora**
5.6*. [HAMMER]
hand (o) *f* hand; *nom sg* 3.47,
6.141, 3.53*; *and acc sg* 1.72,
6.112; *dat sg* **handa** 3.44, 4.29,
6.149; *dat pl* **handum** (-on) 6.4,
6.7, 6.14. [HAND]
handplega *m* hand-play, fighting;
gen sg **hondplegan** 5.25*. [*see*
hand; PLAY]
hār *adj* hoary, grey, grey-haired; *m
nom sg* 5.39*, 6.169; *f acc sg*
hāre 3.49. [HOAR]
hasupāda *m hapax legomenon*
dun-coated one; *acc sg*
hasupādan 5.62*. [*see Holt*
hasu *and* **pād**]
(ge)hātan *sv 7* to be called, be named, command, order, call, name, vow, promise; *1 sg pret*
gehāte 6.246; *3 sg pret* **(ge)hēt**
6.2, 6.62, 6.74, 6.101, 6.289; *3 pl
pret* **hēton** 6.30; *pp m nom sg*
hāten 1.34, 6.75, 6.218.
[HIGHT]
hē *3 pers pron* he; *m nom sg* 1.3,
1.5, 1.16, 1.37, 3.1, 3.26, 5.40*,
etc; *m acc sg* **hine** (y) 1.4, 2.5,
3.1, 3.40, *etc*; *m gen sg* **his** 1.13,
etc; *m dat sg* **him** 1.40, 1.133,
2.1, 2.3, *etc*; *nom pl* **hī** (**hȳ**) (**hīg**)
(**hēo**) 1.47, 1.108, 4.41, 4.42,
5.48*, 5.51*, *etc*; *and acc pl*
1.126, 2.16, *etc*; *gen pl* **heora**
(y/i/io) 5.47*, *etc*; *dat pl* **him** 5.7,
5.53*, 5.60*, *etc*; *f nom sg* **hēo**
2.10, 2.11, *etc*; *f acc sg/pl* **hī**
6.180; *f gen sg* **hyre** (i) 1.99, 2.8,
2.9, *etc*; *n acc sg* **hit** 1.44, 3.36,
etc. [HE]
hēahfæst *adj* lofty and secure, lasting; *m acc sg* **hēahfæstne** 1.143.
[HIGH, FAST]
(ge)healdan *sv 7* to hold, keep, grip, guard, occupy, possess, regard, rule, treat, grasp, maintain, stand (firm); 3.4, 6.14, 6.19,
6.41 (**ēow friðes h.** 'leave you in peace'), 6.74, 6.102, 6.167,
6.236; *3 sg pres subj* **hēolde** 4.23;

3 pl pret **hēoldon** 1.43, 1.45, 4.42; *and 3 pl pret subj* 6.20; *infl inf dat sg* **gehealdenne** 1.134. [HOLD]

healf *f* side (*w dat of person*); *dat sg* **healfe** 6.152, 6.318. [HALF]

heall *f* hall, dwelling, mead-hall; *gen sg* **healle** 4.4, 4.20; *and dat sg* 4.28, 6.214. [HALL]

heals (a) *m* neck; *acc sg* 6.141. [HALSE]

hēanlic *adj* humiliating, shameful; *n nom sg* 6.55. [HEAN, -LY *suffix*]

hēap *m* heap, company; *dat sg* **hēape** 1.127. [HEAP]

heard (eo) *adj* hard, bold, cruel, strong, brave; *m nom sg* 4.21, *and sb* 6.130; *m acc sg* **heardne** (**hearne**) 3.4*, 6.167, 6.236; *m gen sg* **heardes** 5.25*; *f acc sg* **hearde** 6.33; *f gen pl* **heordra** 4.26; *n acc sg* **heard** 6.214; *n gen sg* **heardes** 6.266; *n instr pl* **heardum** 1.120; *comp m nom sg* **heardra** 6.312. [HARD]

heardlīce *adv* fiercely; 6.261. [HARD, -LY *suffix*]

hearm *m* grief, sorrow; *gen pl* **hearma** 6.223. [HARM]

hearogeong (**heoro-**) *adj hapax legomenon* (*see note*) sword-young, battle-young; *m nom sg* 4.2. [*see Holt* **heoru** *and* YOUNG]

hearpe *f* harp; *dat sg* **hearpan** 1.105. [HARP]

hearra (eo) *m* lord; *nom sg* 6.204. [HER]

heaðulind (**heaðo-**) *f hapax legomenon* battle linden-wood, linden-wood shield; *acc pl* **heaþolinde** 5.6*. [*see Holt* **heaðu-**; LIND]

heaðuwerig *adj* battle-weary; *m dat sg* **heaðuwerigan** 3.49. [*see* **heaðulind**; WEARY]

hēawan *sv 7* to hew, cut down, kill; *3 sg pret* **hēow** 6.324; *3 pl pret* **hēowon** (**-an/-un**) 3.17, 5.6*, 5.23*, 6.181. [HEW]

hel(l)sceaða *m* hell-injurer or -assailant, devil; *nom pl* **helsceaðan** 6.180. [HELL, SCATHE]

helm *m* helmet, protection, cover, lord; *nom sg* 4.45. [HELM]

help *f/m* help; *gen sg* **helpe** 3.59. [HELP]

gehende *prep* (*w dat*) near to; 6.294. [HEND]

heofon *m* heaven; *dat pl* **heofonum** (**-enum**) 1.143, 6.172. [HEAVEN]

hēolde, **hēoldon** *see* **healdan**.

heonan *adv* hence, from here; 6.246. [HEN]

heorte *f* heart; *nom sg* 6.312; *acc sg* **heortan** 1.73; *and dat sg* 6.145. [HEART]

heorðgenēat *m* hearth-companion, retainer; *nom pl* **heorðgenēatas** 6.204. [HEARTH; *see Holt*]

heorðwerod *n* the body of hearth-companions, members of a comitatus; *acc sg* 6.24. [*see* **heorð-**; *see Holt* **weorod**]

hēow, **hēowon** *see* **hēawan**

hēr *adv* here, hither; 1.134, 3.31, 3.50, 4.3, 4.4, 4.5, *etc*. [HERE]

here *m* army (*used of the invading army in the ASC*); *nom sg* 1.120;

gen sg **heriges** 5.31; *dat sg* **here** 6.292. [HERE]
hereflȳma (ē) *m hapax legomenon* battle-fleer, fugitive soldier, deserter; *acc pl* **herefléman** 5.23*. [HERE, FLEE]
heregeatu *f pl* armour; *acc* 6.48. [HERE; *see Holt* **geatwe**]
herelāf *f* army-remnant, survivors of battle, booty; *dat pl* **herelāfum** 5.47*. [HERE, LAVE]
heresceorp *n hapax legomenon* (*see note*) army-clothing, battle-equipment, armour; *dat pl* **heresceorpum** 4.45. [HERE; *see Holt*]
hēt, hēton *see* **hātan**
hettend *m* enemy, adversary; *nom pl* 5.10*. [HATE]
hider *adv* hither, to this place; 5.69, 6.57. [HITHER]
hīenan (ȳ) *wv* 1 to humble, injure, afflict; 6.180; *3 sg pret* **hȳnde** 6.324. [HEAN]
gehīeran *wv* 1 to hear; *2 sg pres* **gehȳrst** 6.45; *1 sg pret* **(ge)hȳrde** 6.117; *and 3 sg pret* 3.1; *3 pl pret* **hȳrdon** 1.108. [HEAR]
hierde *m* herder, shepherd, keeper, leader; *nom sg* 4.46. [HERD]
hild *f* fight, war, battle, combat; *acc sg* **hilde** 3.47, 6.33*; *and dat sg* 3.4, 3.30, 4.37, 6.8, 6.48, 6.55, *etc*; *gen pl* **hilda** 4.26. [*see Holt*]
hildefrofre *f* consolation in battle; *acc sg* 3.44*. [*see* **hild**; FROVER]
hilderinc (-g) *m* battle-man, warrior; *nom sg* 5.39*, 6.169. [*see* **hild**; RINK]

hindan *adv* from behind; 5.23. [BEHIND]
hiredman *m* household man, retainer, warrior; *nom pl* **hiredmen** 6.261. [HIRDMAN]
hlāford (-urd) *m* lord; *nom sg* 3.30, 6.135, 6.189, 6.224, 6.240; *and acc sg* 2.39; *dat sg* **hlāforde** 6.318. [LORD]
hlāfordlēas *adj* lordless, without a lord; *m nom sg* 6.251. [LORD, -LESS *suffix*]
(ge)hlēapan *sv* 7 to leap upon, mount; *3 sg pret* **gehlēop** 6.189. [LEAP]
hlēo *m* protector; *nom sg* 2.41, 6.74. [LEE]
hlēodryhten *m* lord, protector; *dat sg* **hlēodryhtne** 1.94. [LEE, DRIGHTIN]
hlēoþor *n* song; *nom sg* 1.105. [*see Holt*]
hlēoðrian *wv* 2 to speak, cry aloud, exclaim, sing; *3 sg pret* **hlēoðrode** 4.2. [*see* **hlēoþor**]
hliehhan (e) *sv* 6 (*weak pres*) to laugh, exult; 5.47*; *3 sg pret* **hlōh** 6.147. [LAUGH]
hlūde *adv* loud; 1.105. [LOUD]
gehlyn(n) *n* sound, din; *nom sg* 4.28. [LINN]
hlynnan *wv* 1 to make noise, shout, resound; *3 sg pres* **hlynneð** 4.6. [LINN]
gehlystan *wv* 1 to listen; *3 pl pret* **gehlyston** 6.92. [LIST]
hogode, hogodon *see* **hycgan**.
hold *adj* gracious, kind, loyal; *m acc sg* **holdne** 2.39; *sup n acc sg* **holdost** 6.24. [HOLD]

holt *n/m* wood, copse: *gen sg* **holtes** 6.8. [HOLT]
hord *n/m* hoard, treasure; *acc sg/pl* 5.10. [HOARD]
horn *m* horn, projection, pinnacle, gable; *nom pl* **hornas** 4.1*, 4.4. [HORN]
hors *n* horse; *acc sg* 6.2. [HORSE]
hræfn (/-en) (**hremm**) *m* raven; *nom sg* 4.34; *and acc sg* 5.61; *nom pl* **hremmas** 6.106. [RAVEN]
hrǣw *n/m* body, corpse, carrion; *acc pl* **hrǣ** 4.34*, 5.60*. [*see Holt*]
hrēam *m* outcry, uproar; *nom sg* 6.106. [REAM]
hrēman *wv* 1 to exult; 5.39*. [*see Holt* **hrēmig**]
hrēmig *adj* exultant; *m nom pl* (*w gen*) **hrēmige** 5.59*. [*see* **hrēman**]
hremm *see* **hræfn**.
hring *m* ring; *acc pl* **hringas** 6.161; *gen pl* **hringa** 1.73. [RING]
hringloca *m hapax legomenon* enclosure made of rings (i.e. ringmail vest); *acc pl* **hringlocan** 6.145. [RING, LOUK]
hrōr *adj* active, strong, brave; *m/f nom sg* 4.45 (*see note*). [*see Holt*]
hū *adv* how; 1.56, 2.12, 4.47, 6.19. [HOW]
hund *num* hundred; 1.91. [HUND]
hūru *interj* indeed; 3.2, 3.46. [HURE]

hwā *pron* who; *m nom sg* 4.23; *interrog pron* who, what 6.95, 6.124, 6.215; *n nom sg* **hwæt** 6.45; *indef pron* anyone, someone, each; *m nom sg* 6.71; *m acc sg* **hwæne** 6.2. [WHO]
gehwā *indef pron* each; *m acc sg* **gehwæne** 5.9*. [WHO]
hwænne *conj* until the time when; 6.67. [WHEN]
hwǣr *adv, conj* where; 1.101. [WHERE]
hwæt *interj* lo, indeed; 3.46, 6.231. [WHAT]
hwæðer *indef pron* each (of two), either; *m nom sg* 4.48; *f acc sg* **gehwæðere** 6.112. [WHETHER]
hwæðere (/-ðre) *adv* however, nevertheless; 1.37. [WHETHER]
hwearflic *adj* transitory, changing; *sb gen pl* **hwearflicra** 4.34*. [WHARVE, -LY *suffix*]
hweorfan (o) *sv* 3 to move, turn, change; 3.30; *3 sg pret* **hwearf** 4.17; *3 pl pres* **hweorfað** 1.135. [WHARVE]
hwīl *f* while, time; *acc sg* **hwīle** 1.14, 2.36, 6.304; *dat pl* 6.270 (**hwīlon...hwīlon** 'at times...at times'); *conj* **þā hwīle þe** as long as; 6.14, 6.83, 6.235, 6.272. [WHILE]
gehwilc (y) *indef pron* each, any, every; *m nom sg* 6.128, 6.257; *f gen pl* 1.11; *n gen sg* **gehwilces** 3.58. [WHICH]
hwīnan *sv* 1 to whine; *pres p m dat sg* **hwīnende** 1.127. [WHINE]

hwīt *adj* white, shining, bright, clear; *m acc sg* **hwītne** 4.39, (**hwīt**) 5.63* *(see note)*. [WHITE]
hycgan (i) *wv* 2/3 to think, resolve, remember; 6.4*; *imp pl* **hicgeaþ** 4.11*; *3 sg pret* **hogode** 6.133; *and 3 sg pret subj* 6.128; *3 pl pret* **hogodon** 6.123. [HIGH]
hȳdan *wv* 1 to hide; *pp dat sg* **gehīded** 3.35. [HIDE]
hyge (i) *m* mind, heart, courage; *nom sg* 6.312; *and dat sg* 6.4. [HIGH]
hyrnednebba *m* horny-beaked one; *acc sg* **hyrnednebban** 5.62*. [HORN, NEB]
hyrst *f* ornament, jewel, treasure, trappings, armour; *acc pl* **hyrsta** 4.20. [*see Holt*]
hys(s)e *m* youth, young warrior; *nom sg* 6.152; *gen sg* **hysses** 6.141; *nom pl* **hyssas** 6.112, 6.123; *and acc pl* 6.169; *gen pl* **hyssa** 4.48, 6.2, 6.128. [*see Holt*]

I

ic *1 pers pron* I; *nom sg* 1.10, 2.35, *etc*; *acc sg* **mē** 1.56, 1.66, *etc*; *gen sg* **mīn** *(only as poss adj; see separate entry)*; *nom pl* **wē** 2.14, 2.21, *etc*; *acc pl* **ūs** 5.68, 6.60, 6.237, *etc*; *and reciprocal pron* each other 6.34; *(refl)* 6.40; *gen pl* **ūre** 6.234. *(see* **ūre***)* [I]
īegland (ēi-) *n* island; *dat sg* **ēiglande** 5.66*. [ISLAND]
ielde (e) *m* men; *dat pl* **eldum** 3.11. [*see Holt and* ELD]
iergðu (y) *f* cowardice; *acc sg* **yrhðo** 6.6. [ARGH]

ierre (y) *adj* angry; *m nom sg* 6.44, 6.253. [IRRE]
in *prep (w dat/acc)* in, into, inside; 1.55, 6.58, *etc*. [IN]
innweorud *n hapax legomenon* native tribe or people; *nom sg* 1.111. [INN, WERED]
inwidda *m* evil or deceitful one; *nom sg* 5.46*. [*see Holt* **inwitt**]
is *see* **bēon**.
īsen (**īren**) *n* iron, sword; *nom sg* 6.253. [IRON]
iūlēan *see* **gēolēan**.

L

lǣdan *wv* 1 to lead; 6.88. [LEAD]
lǣran *wv* 1 to teach, exhort; *3 sg pret* **lǣrde** 6.311. [LERE]
lǣrig *m* rim (of shield); *nom sg* 6.284. [*see Holt*]
gelǣstan *wv* 1 to serve, help, accompany, accomplish, carry out; 6.11; *3 sg pret* **gelǣste** 6.15. [LAST]
lǣtan *sv* 7 to let; *sg imp* **lǣt** 3.6; *3 sg pret* **lēt** 6.7, 6.140; *3 pl pret* **lēton** (-an) 6.108, 5.60*. [LET]
lāf *f* heirloom, remnant, thing left, survivor; *nom sg* 3.50, 5.54; *dat pl* **lāfan** 5.6*. [LAVE]
lagustrēam *m* water-current, water, river, tidal current; *nom pl* **lagustrēamas** 6.66. [LAY, STREAM]
land (o) *n* land, earth; *acc sg* 1.95, 5.9, 5.27, 5.56, 5.59; *gen sg* **landes** 6.90, 6.275; *dat sg* **lande** 6.99; *gen pl* **londa** 1.50, 1.99. [LAND]
landbūend *m* land-dweller, inhabitant; *dat pl* **londbūendum** 1.132.

[LAND, BE]
landryht (o) *n* land-right, estate; *acc sg* 2.40. [LAND, RIGHT]
lang (o) *adj* long, lasting, tall; *m nom sg* **langa** 6.273; *m acc sg* **langne** 3.10*; *n nom sg* 6.66 (**tō lang** 'too long a time'); *comp (as adv)* **leng** 6.171; *sup* **lengest** 1.28, 1.45. [LONG]
langoð (longaþ) *m* longing; *acc sg* 2.3. [LONG]
lāst *m* footprint, step; *acc sg* 5.22; *dat sg* **lāste** 4.17. [LAST]
lāð *adj* hated, hostile, hateful; *f dat sg* **lāþere** 6.90; *m nom pl* **lāðe** 6.86; *dat pl* **lāþum** 5.22; *comp n acc sg* **lāþre** 6.50; *sb gen pl* **lāðra** 3.16, 5.9. [LOATH]
lēan *n* reward; *dat sg* **lēane** 1.67, 1.95. [LEAN]
lēas *adj* devoid of; *m nom sg* 3.29. [LESS]
lecgan *wv* 1 to lay; *3 sg pret* **legde** 2.5; *3 pl pret* **legdun** 5.22*. [LAY]
lengan *wv* 1 to stretch, extend; *3 sg pret* **lengde** 1.99. [LENG]
lēod *m* man, prince, king; *nom sg* 4.24. [LEDE]
lēode *f pl* men, people, country; *nom* **lēoda** 5.11*; *acc* **lēoda** 6.37; *dat pl* **lēodum (-on)** 1.122, 6.23, 6.50. [LEDE]
lēof *adj* dear; *m dat sg* **lēofum (-an)** 1.95, 6.319; *sup m nom sg* **lēofast** 1.132, 6.23 (**þær him lēofost wæs** 'where it was most pleasing to him to be'); *sb m acc sg* **lēofne** 6.7, 6.208. [YLEOF]
lēoht *n* light; *nom sg* 1.142. [LIGHT]

lēoht *adj* light, quick; *sup f acc sg* **lēohteste** 1.72. [LIGHT]
lēoðcræftig *adj* skilled in song; *m nom sg* 2.40. [LEOTH, CRAFT]
gelettan *wv* 1 to hinder, prevent; *3 sg pret* **gelette** 6.164. [LET]
līc *n* body; *dat sg* **līce** 3.16. [LICH]
licgan *sv* 5 (*weak pres*) to lie, lie slain; 6.319; *3 sg pres* **lið (ligeð)** 6.222, 6.232, 6.314; *3 sg pret* **læg (leg)** 5.17, 6.157, 6.204, 6.227, 6.276, 6.294; *3 sg pret subj* **læge (ē)** 6.279, 6.300; *3 pl pret* **lægun (lāgon)** 5.28*, 6.112, 6.183. [LIE]
lid *n* ship; *gen sg* **lides** 5.27*, 5.34. [LITHE]
lidmann (/-n) *m* ship-man, sailor, Viking; *nom pl* **lidmen** 6.99; *gen pl* **lidmanna** 6.164. [LITHE, MAN]
geliefan *sv* 5 to trust; *3 sg pres* **gelifeð** 3.59. [LEVE, YLEVE]
liesan (y) *wv* 1 to release, ransom; 6.37. [LEESE]
līf *n* life; *nom sg* 1.142; *and acc sg* 3.10, 6.208. [LIFE]
lifgan *wv* 3 to live; 1.11; *3 sg pres* **leofað** 1.134. [LIVE]
lihtan *wv* 1 to alight, dismount; *3 sg pret* **lihte** 6.23. [LIGHT, ALIGHT]
lind *f* linden, lindenwood-shield; *acc sg* **linde** 6.244; *and acc pl* 6.99, (**linda**) 4.11*. [LIND]
lið *see* **licgan**.
lof *m* praise; *nom sg* 1.99; *and acc sg* 1.142; *gen sg* **lofes** 1.72. [LOF]

lūcan *sv* 2 to lock, join, enclose (the land); *3 pl pret* **lucon** 6.66. [LOUK]
lytegian *wv* 2 *hapax legomenon (see note)* to use guile; 6.86.
lȳtel (i) *adj* little; *n instr sg* **lītle** 5.34. [LITTLE]
lȳtlian *wv* 2 to diminish; *3 sg pres* **lȳtlað** 6.313. [LITTLE]

M

mā *see* **micle**.
mæcg (e) *m* man; *gen pl* **mecga** 5.40*. [*see Holt* **mago**]
mǣg *m* kinsman; *nom sg* 3.40, 6.5, 6.114, 6.224, 6.287; *gen pl* **mǣga** 5.40. [MAY]
mægen *n* strength; *nom sg* 6.313. [MAIN]
mǣgþ *f* tribe, country; *gen pl* **mǣgþa** 1.2*; *instr pl* **mǣgþum** 1.10. [MAY]
mǣl *n* measure, fight, mark, occasion; *acc sg* 3.19; *acc pl* **mǣla** 6.212. [MEAL]
gemǣlan *wv* 1 to speak; *3 sg pret* **(ge)mǣlde** 6.26, 6.43, 6.210, 6.230, 6.244. [MELE, I-MELE]
mǣnan *wv* 1 to say, mean, make known; 1.55. [MEAN]
gemǣran *wv* 1 to make known, honour; *3 sg pret* **gemǣrde** 1.42. [MERE]
mǣre *adj* famous, glorious; *m/n nom sg* 5.14. [MERE]
mǣst *adj see* **micel**; *and adv see* **micle**.
mǣð *f* measure, propriety, fitness; *nom sg* 6.195. [METHE]
mæðelstede (meþel-) *m* meeting-place, assembly; *dat sg* 6.199.
[*see Holt* **mæðel**; STEAD]
magan *ppv* can, will, might, may, be strong, be able; *1 sg pres* **mæg** 1.54; *and 3 sg pres* 2.7, 2.13, 2.17, 2.20, 2.27, 2.42, 3.57; *3 sg pret subj* **mǣge** 6.235; *3 sg pret* **meaht (-e)(i)** 2.11, 6.9, 6.14, 6.64, 6.70, 6.124, 6.167, 6.171. [MAY]
man *indef pron* one, people; *m nom sg* 6.9. [MAN]
gemāna *m* fellowship; *gen/dat sg* **gemānan** 5.40. [MONE, YMONE]
manian *wv* 2 to exhort, remind, advise; 6.228; *pp m acc pl* **gemanode** 6.231. [*see Holt*]
manig (æ/o) *indef pron, adj* many; *pron m acc sg* 3.38; *m nom pl* **manega** 6.200; *m dat pl* **monegum** 2.19; *adj m nom sg* **manig** 2.24, 4.13, 5.17*, 6.282; *m acc sg* **manigne** 6.188, 6.243; *m dat sg* **monegum** 2.33; *m nom pl* **mon(i)ge** 1.106, 2.14. [MANY]
mancynn (o) *n* mankind; *gen sg* **moncynnes** 1.71. [MANKIN]
mann (/-n)(o) *m* man; *nom sg* 6.147, 6.239; *and acc sg* 2.6, 2.40, 6.77, 6.243; *gen sg* **monnes** 3.14, 3.21; *dat sg* **men** 6.125, 6.319; *nom pl* **men** 1.106, 6.105, 6.206; *gen pl* **manna** 1.2*, 1.10, 1.16, 1.38, 3.3, 6.195. [MAN]
māra *see* **micel**.
maðelian *wv* 2 to speak before an assembly; *3 sg pret* **maðolade** 1.1 *(see note)*, 3.43, 6.42, 6.309. [MELL, MATHELE]
māþ(þ)um *m* treasure, valuable object; *acc sg* 1.4, 1.66; *gen pl*

māðma 3.24, 3.38. [MADME]
mearc (e) *f* mark, boundary, line; *acc sg* **merce** 1.42; *dat sg* **mearce** 3.19. [MARK]
mearh *m* horse; *acc sg* **mēar** 6.188 (*see note*); *dat sg* **mēare** 6.239. [MARE]
mēce *m* sword; *acc sg* 3.24. 6.167, 6.236; *and dat sg* 3.38; *dat pl* **mēcum** 3.56, 5.24. [*see Holt* **mǣce**]
medu (eo) *m/n* mead; *acc sg* **medo** 4.39; *dat sg* **meodo** 6.212. [MEAD]
meduheall (eo) *f* mead-hall, palace; *dat sg* **meoduhealle** 1.55. [MEAD, HALL]
men(i)gu (mænigo) *f* group, company, multitude; *dat sg* 1.55, 3.29. [MANY]
gemētan *wv* 1 to meet, find, beset; *3 pl pres* **gemētað** 1.138, 3.56. [METE]
metod *m* fate, creator, measurer; *nom sg* 6.175; *and acc sg* 3.19; *dat sg* **metode** 6.147. [METE]
micel *adj* great, intense, much, many, large, important; *n acc sg* 3.37; *n gen sg* **miccles** 6.217; *comp* **māra** more, greater; *m acc sg* **māran** 1.40; *n nom sg* **māre** 5.65, 6.313; *sup* **mǣst** greatest; *f acc sg* **mǣste** 6.175; *n acc sg* **mǣst** 1.39; *and acc sg* 1.2; *sb n nom sg* 6.223. [MICKLE, MO, MOST]
micle (-cc-) *adv* much, very, greatly; 6.50; *comp* **mā** more; 5.46, 6.195*; *sup* **mǣst** most; 1.16. [MICKLE, MO, MOST]

mid (-t) *prep* with, along with, among, by means of; 1.5, 1.62*, 1.85, 1.86, 1.87*, 3.25*, 6.101*, *etc.* [MID]
mihte *see* **magan**.
milde *adj* merciful; *m nom sg* 6.175. [MILD]
mīn *poss adj* my; *m nom sg* 4.24, 6.218, 6.222, 6.224, *etc*; *and m acc sg* **mīn/mīnne** 3.12, 6.248; *m gen sg* **mīnes** 1.96, 6.53; *m dat sg* **mīnum** 1.94, 6.176; *m nom pl* **mīne** 4.10; *f nom sg* **mīn** 6.177; *n instr sg* **mīne** 1.71; *and n acc pl* 6.216. [MY]
mōd *n* spirit, mind, courage; *nom sg* 6.313; *instr pl* **mōdum** 1.106. [MOOD]
mōdig *adj* noble, brave, impetuous; *m nom sg* **mōdi** 6.147; *m nom pl* **mōdige** 6.80; *sup m nom sg* **mōdgast** 1.36. [MOODY]
mōdiglīce (mōde-) *adv* boldly, bravely; 6.200. [MOOD]
mōna *m* moon; *nom sg* 4.7. [MOON]
morgentīd *f* morning; *acc sg* 5.14. [MORN, TIDE]
gemōt *n* meeting, encounter, council; *nom sg* 6.301; *and acc sg* 6.199; *gen sg* **gemōtes** 5.50. [MOOT]
mōtan *ppv* may, be allowed to; *2 sg pres* **mōst** 6.30; *3 sg pres subj* **mōte** 6.95, 6.177; *3 sg pret subj* **mōste** 6.272; *3 pl pres subj* **mōton** 6.180; *3 pl pret* **mōten** 3.62*; *3 pl pret subj* **mōston** 6.83, 6.87, 6.263. [MOTE]
gemunan *ppv* (*w acc/gen*) to remember; *1 sg pres* **gemunu**

6.212; *3 sg pret* **gemunde** 6.225; *3 pl pret* **gemundon** 6.196. [I-MUNE]
murnan *sv* **3** to mourn, worry; 6.259; *imp sg* **murn** 3.24; *3 pl pret* **murnon** 6.96. [MOURN]
mylenscearp *adj* sharpened on a grindstone (*see note*); *m dat pl* **mylenscearpan** 5.24*. [MILL, SHARP]
mynelic *adj* desirable, handsome; *m acc sg* **mynelicne** 1.4. [MIN]

N

nā (ō) *neg adv* not at all, never; 1.37, 6.21, 6.258, 6.268, 6.325. [NE, AY]
nǣfre (ē) *adv* never; 1.108, 4.1, 4.37, 4.39. [NE, EVER]
nægledcnearr *m hapax legomenon* (*see note*) nailed ship; *dat pl* **nægledcnearrum** 5.53*.
nǣnig *indef neg pron* nobody; *m nom sg* 1.40. [NE, ANY]
næs *see* **wesan**.
nalles *see* **nealles**.
nama (o) *m* name; *nom sg* 2.37, 4.24, 6.267. [NAME]
nān *pron adj* no, none; *m nom sg* 4.41; *m dat pl* **nānum** 5.25. [NE, AN]
ne *neg adv* not; 1.108, 1.119, 1.125, 2.8. 2.11, *etc*; *conj* nor; 4.3, 4.4, 4.39, 5.46*, *etc*. [NE]
nēah (ē) *adj* near, nigh, close; *f nom sg* 6.103; *sup* **nīhst** ('last') 1.126. [NIGH, NEAR]
geneahhe (-nehe) *adv* enough, constantly, frequently; 2.25, 2.32, 6.269. [NIGH]

nealles (a) *adv* not at all, by no means; 3.12. [ALL]
nearu *f/n* strait, difficulty, confinement; *n dat pl* **nearwum** 3.40. [NARROW]
genēat *m* (mounted) retainer; *nom sg* 6.310. [NEAT]
nelle *see* **willan**.
nemnan *wv* **1** to name, mention; 1.126. [NEMN]
nēotan *sv* **2** (*w gen*) to use, make use of; 6.308. [*see Holt*]
generian *wv* **1** to save; *3 sg pret* **generede** 5.36. [*see Holt* **nerian** *and* **nesan**]
genesan *sv* **5** to escape, survive, get through safely, bear; *3 pl pret* **genǣson** 4.47. [*see Holt* **nesan**]
nīed (ē) *f* force, necessity, need; *dat sg* **nēde** 5.33; *and acc pl* 2.5. [NEED]
nīhst *see* **nēah**.
geniman *sv* **4** to take, receive; 6.39, 6.252; *3 sg pret* **genam** 3.39; *3 sg pret subj* **genāme** 6.71. [NIM]
nīð *m* strife, affliction, hostility; *acc sg* 4.9; *gen pl* **nīða** 4.21. [NITH]
nolde, noldon *see* **willan**.
norð *adv* north, in the north; 1.138, 5.38. [NORTH]
norðerne *adj* northern; *m nom sg* **norþerna** 5.18*. [NORTHERN]
nū *adv* now, now that, since; 2.39, 3.6, 3.8*, 3.29, 4.7, *etc*. [NOW]
nū gīet *see* **gīet**.

O

of *prep (w dat)* from, out of; 1.8, 1.127, 3.40, 6.7, *etc*. [OF]

ofer *prep (w dat/acc)* over, above, beyond: 1.2, 1.17, 1.37, 3.19, 4.22, *etc*; 6.276 (*in adv phrase* **ofer bæc** 'away'). [OVER]

ofer *m* bank of river; *dat sg* **ofre** 6.28. [OVER]

ofercuman *sv* **4** to overcome; *3 pl pret* **ofercōmon (-an)** 5.72*; *pp m gen sg* **ofercumen** 2.26. [OVERCOME]

ofergān *av* pass away; *3 sg pret* **oferēode** 2.7, 2.13, *etc*. [OVER, GO]

ofermōd *n* excessive spirit, pride, arrogance, over-confidence; *dat sg* **ofermōde** 6.89. [OVER-MOD]

of(o)stlīce *adv* quickly; 6.143. [*see Holt* **ofost**; **-LY** *suffix*]

ofscēotan *sv* **2** to shoot; *3 sg pret* **ofscēat** 6.77. [OF- *prefix*, SHOOT]

oft *adv* often; 1.3, 1.119, 1.127, 2.4, 3.4, 5.8, *etc*. [OFT]

on *prep (w dat/acc)* on, in, into, at, among, about, against; 1.3*, 1.70, 1.91, 1.93, 1.131, 4.29*, *etc*; 5.22, 5.35 (*in phrases* **on lāst legdun** (*see note*), 6.41 **on flot feran**, 6.112 **on gehwæðere hand** 'on either side', 6.27 **on bēot** 'threateningly', 6.211 **on ellen** 'bravely', 6.38 **on hyra sylfra dōm** 'in accordance with', 6.198 **on dæg** 'on that day'). [ON]

oncnāwan *sv* **7** to understand, perceive; 6.9. [ACKNOW]

oncweðan *sv* **5** to answer, respond, echo, protest; *3 sg pres* **oncwyð** 4.7; *3 sg pret* **oncwæð** 6.245. [QUETHE]

ondrǣdan *sv* **7** to fear; *1 sg pret* **ondrēd** 3.19. [ON- *prefix*, ADREAD]

onemn *prep (w acc or dat)* alongside; 6.184. [ANENT]

ōnettan *wv* **1** to hasten; *3 sg pret* **ōnette** 3.42. [*see Holt*]

onfindan *sv* **3** to find out, experience, discover; *1 sg pret* **onfond** 1.131; *and 3 sg pret* 2.4, (**onfunde**) 6.5. [ON- *prefix*, FIND]

onfōn *sv* **7** to receive; *3 sg pret* **onfeng** 6.110. [FANG, ONFANG]

ongēan *adv* back; 6.49, 6.137, 6.156; *and prep w dat* against; 6.100. [AGAIN]

ongietan *sv* **5** to get, realize; *3 pl pret* **ongēaton** 6.84; *pp* **ongieten** 2.10. [ANGET]

onginnan *sv* **3** to begin; attack; *3 pl pres* **ongynnað** 3.55; *3 sg pret* **ongan (o)** 1.9, 3.26, 6.12, 6.17, 6.89, 6.91, 6.228, 6.265; *3 pl pret* **ongunnon** 6.86, 6.261. [ONGIN]

onlūcan *sv* **2** to unlock; *3 sg pret* **onlēac** 1.1. [UNLOUK]

onōrettan *wv* **1** to win, achieve (by fighting); *3 sg pret* **onōrette** 1.41. [*see Holt* **ōret**]

onsendan *wv* **1** to send; (**-on**) 3.37. [SEND]

onwacan *sv* **6** to awake, arise, be born; *3 pl pret* **onwōcon** 1.5. [WAKE]

onwacnian *wv* **2** to awake, arise, spring up; *imp pl* **onwacnigeað** 4.10. [AWAKEN]

ord *m* point, van, beginning, prince; *nom sg* 6.60, 6.69, 6.146, 6.157, 6.253; *and acc sg* 1.48, 6.47, 6.110; *dat sg* **orde** 4.12*, 6.124, 6.226, 6.273. [ORD]

ordwyga *m* van-warrior, champion who fights at the front; *nom sg* 3.6. [ORD, WYE]

oð *conj* until; 4.31, 5.16*. [*see Holt* **oð** *and* **ūð**]

ōðer *pron, adj* one of two, other, second; *pron m nom sg* 6.282; *m acc sg* **ōþerne** 1.97, 6.143, 6.234; *m dat sg* **ōðrum** 3.5, 6.70, 6.133; *and m dat pl* 1.12; *n acc sg* **ōðer** 3.9, 6.207; *n gen sg* **ōðres** 3.38; *n dat sg* **ōðrum** 6.64; *adj m gen sg* **ōðres** 3.21; *f dat pl* **ōðrum** 4.16. [OTHER]

oððæt *conj* until; 1.141, 2.39, 6.278, 6.324*. [*see Holt* **oð**; THAT]

oððe *conj* or, or else: 1.138, 3.10, 3.15, 3.31, 4.48, 6.208, 6.292. [OTHER]

P

plegan *wv* **2** to play, move quickly, exercise; *3 pl pret* **plegodan** 5.52*. [PLAY]

prass *m* array, military force; *dat sg* **prasse** 6.68. [*etymology unknown*]

R

geræcan *wv* **1** to reach, touch; *3 sg pret* **geræhte** 6.142, 6.158, 6.226. [REACH]

(ge)rǣdan *sv* **7** *and wv* **1** to rule, instruct, decide; 1.12; *2 sg pres* **gerǣdest** 6.36; *3 sg pret* **rǣdde** 6.18. [READ, REDE]

(ge)rǣde *n* harness, trappings; *dat pl* **gerǣdum** 6.190. [I-REDE]

rǣdfest (-fæst) *adj* securely-advised, wise, regardful; *m nom sg* 3.58. [REDE, FAST]

rand *m* shield-boss/border, shield; *acc pl* **randan** 6.20. [RAND]

raðe *adv* quickly, soon; 6.30, 6.164, 6.288. [RATHE]

rēaf *m* garment, armour; *nom sg* 3.52; *and acc sg* 6.161. [REAF, REIF]

reccan *wv* **1** (*w gen*) to care for, care about; *3 sg pret subj* **recce** 3.23; *3 pl pret* **rohton** 6.260. [RECK]

recon *adj* prompt; *m nom sg* 3.58. [REKEN]

gerēnod *adj* ornamented, decorated; *n acc sg* 6.161. [*see Holt* **regnian**]

reord *f* voice; *instr sg* **reorde** 1.103. [RERDE]

rīce *n* rule, kingdom; *acc sg* 1.133; *gen sg* **rīces** 1.78, 2.23. [RICHE]

rīce *adj* powerful, noble; *sup m nom sg* **rīcost** 1.15, 6.36. [RICH]

ricene *adv* quickly; 6.93. [*see* REKEN]

rīdan *sv* 1 to ride; 6.291; *3 sg pret* rād 6.18, 6.239. [RIDE]
riht (y) *adj* right, fitting; *n nom sg* 6.190; *sb gen pl* ryhta 3.58. [RIGHT]
rihte *adv* properly, correctly; 6.20. [RIGHT]
rinc *m* man, warrior; *dat pl* rincum 6.18. [RINK]
rohton *see* reccan.
gerȳman *wv* 1 to clear, make room; *pp n nom sg* gerȳmed 6.93. [RIME]

S

sæcc *f* strife; *dat sg* sæcce 5.4*, 5.42*. [*see Holt* sacan]
sæd *adj* sated; *m nom sg* 5.20*. [SAD]
sæl *m/f* joy, pleasure; *dat pl* sælum 2.28. [SELE]
sælida *m* sea-traveller, sailor, Viking; *nom sg* 6.45; *acc sg* sælidan 6.286. [SEA, LITHE]
sæmann (/-n) *m* sea-man, Viking; *nom pl* sæmen 6.29; *dat pl* sæmannum 6.38, 6.278. [SEA, MAN]
sæmest *adj sup* poorest, worst; *m nom pl* sæmestan 1.125. [*see Holt* sæmra]
sæne *adj* sluggish, niggardly; *m nom sg* 1.67. [*see Holt*]
særinc *m* sea-going warrior, Viking; *nom sg* 6.134. [SEA, RINK]
salubrun (sealo-) *adj hapax legomenon* sallow-brown, dusky; *m nom sg* 4.35. [SALLOW, BROWN]
salwigpad (salu-) *adj* having dark plumage, dark-coated; *m acc sg*

saluwigpadan 5.61*. [SALLOW; *see Holt* pad]
samod (o) *adv* also, together; 1.142. [*see Holt*]
sang (o) *m* song, poem, lay; *acc sg* 1.104, 1.108; *gen sg* songes 1.67; *dat sg* songe 1.100. [SONG]
sār *adj* sore, grievous; 2.9. [SORE]
sāwul *f* soul; *nom sg* 6.177. [SOUL]
sceacan (a) *sv* 6 to pass, depart; *3 sg pres* scæceð 1.141. [SHAKE]
sceaft (e) *m* shaft; *nom sg* 6.136; *dat sg* scefte 4.7. [SHAFT]
gesceaft *m/f/n* created thing, creature; *nom sg* 5.16. [SHAFT]
scealc *m* man, warrior; *nom pl* scealcas 6.181. [SHALK]
gesceap *n* fate, destiny; *instr pl* gesceapum 1.135. [SHAPE]
sceard *adj* deprived; *m nom sg* 5.40. [SHARD]
sceatt *m* denarius, penny, money; *gen pl* sceatta 1.92; *dat pl* sceattum 6.40, 6.56. [SCEAT]
scēað (ē) *f* sheath; *dat sg* scēðe 6.162. [SHEATH]
gescēawian *wv* 2 to show; *3 sg pres* gescēawað 2.33. [SHOW]
scēotan *sv* 2 to shoot; *3 sg pret* scēat 6.143, 6.270; *pp m nom sg* scoten 5.19*. [SHOOT]
scield (y/i) *m* shield; *nom sg* 4.7; *acc sg* scild 5.19*; *dat sg* scylde 6.136; *acc pl* scyldas 6.98. [SHIELD]
scieldburh (y) *f* shield-fortification, wall of shields; *nom sg* 6.242. [SHIELD, BOROUGH]

scillingrīm *n* shilling count; *dat sg* **scillingrīme** 1.92. [SHILLING, RIME]
scīnan (ȳ) *sv* 1 to shine, flash, be resplendent; *3 sg pres* **scȳneð** 4.7. [SHINE]
scip (y) *n* ship; *dat sg* **scype** 6.40, 6.56. [SHIP]
scipflota *m* ship-floater, sailor; *nom pl* **scipflotan** 5.11*. [SHIP, FLOTE]
scīr *adj* clear, bright, shining; *f sg instr* **scīran** 1.103; *n acc sg* **scīr** 6.98. [SHIRE]
gescirian (y) *wv* 2 to reckon, count; *past p* **gescyred** 1.92. [*see Holt* **scierian**]
scop *m* poet; *m nom sg* 2.36. [SCOP]
scrīþan *sv* 1 to be on the move, wander; *pp m nom pl* **scrīþende** 1.135. [SCRITHE]
scūfan (ēo) *sv* 2 to shove, thrust; *3 sg pret* **scēaf** 6.136. [SHOVE]
sculan *ppv* shall, ought to, have to, must, be destined; *2 sg pres* **scealt** 3.9, 3.25; *3 sg pres* **sceal** 1.11, 3.29, 6.60, 6.252, 6.312, 6.313; *2 pl pres* **sceole** 6.59; *3 pl pres* **sceolon** 6.54, 6.220; *1 sg pret* **sceolde** 1.100, 1.126; *and 3 sg pret* 4.29, 6.16; *and 3 sg pret subj* 2.12; *3 pl pret* **sceoldon** 1.121, 6.19, 6.105, 6.291, 6.307. [SHALL]
se *dem pron, def art, dem adj* he, she, it, the, that; *m nom sg* 1.2, 3.8, 5.37, *etc*; *m acc sg* **þone** (a) 1.93, 5.61, 5.62*; *m gen sg* **þæs** 6.131, 6.141, 6.160, 6.165; *m dat sg* **þæm** (ā) 1.91, 1.127, 3.13, 3.21, 3.34, 3.59, 5.29*; *m instr sg* **ðȳ** (ī) 3.24, 3.25, 3.38; *f nom sg* **sēo** (īo) 2.16, 5.16*, 6.104, 6.144, 6.284; *f acc sg* **þā** 1.118, 6.74, 6.78, 6.139, 6.163, 6.325; *f gen sg* **þǣre** 6.95; *and f dat sg* 1.131; *n nom sg* **þæt** 1.67, 1.111, 1.125, 2.19, 2.23; *and n acc sg* 1.131, 2.12, 2.14, 2.35, 5.64; *n gen sg* **þæs** 2.7, 2.13, 2.26, *etc*; *n dat sg* **þǣm** (ā) 6.10, 6.35, 6.63, *etc*; *n instr sg* (*before comp*) **þȳ** 5.46; *m nom pl* **þā** 1.107, 1.125, 3.32, 5.57; *and m acc pl* 1.110; *m gen pl* **þāra** (ǣ) 1.14, 1.17, 1.36, 3.3, 4.48, 5.26*; *f acc pl* **ðā** 3.61; *and n dat pl.* **ðām** 3.28. [THE]
se *rel pron* who, that; *m nom sg* 1.77, 1.140, 6.27, 6.75, 6.153, 6.310; *n acc sg* **þæt** 2.41, 6.289; *n gen sg* **þæs** 5.51, 5.68*; *m gen pl* **þǣre** (ā) 5.26. [THE]
sealde *see* **sellan**.
sealobrun *see* **salubrun**.
(ge)sēcan (-ean) *wv* 1 to seek, search for, try to get; 3.27, 3.30, 4.27, 5.55*, 6.222; *1 sg pret* **sōhte** 1.110, *etc*; *2 sg pret* **sōhtest** 3.18, 3.20; *3 sg pret* **gesōhte** 1.7, 6.287; *3 pl pret* **(ge)sōhton** (-un,-an) 5.27*, 5.58*, 5.71*, 6.193. [SEEK]
secg *m* man; *nom sg* 2.24, 3.5*, 5.17, 6.159; *acc pl* **secgas** 6.298; *gen pl* **secga** 5.13*. [SEGGE]
(ge)secgan *wv* 3 to say, tell, explain; 1.54, 1.100, 2.35, 6.30; *imp sg* **sege** 6.50; *3 sg pres* **segeð** 6.45; *3 pl pres* **secgað** 1.137, 5.68; *3 sg pret* **(ge)sǣde** 4.44, 6.120, 6.147. [SAY]

sefa *m* spirit, mind, heart; *dat sg*
  sefan 2.9, 2.29. [*see Holt*]
sēl *adj* good; *comp m acc sg* **sēllan**
  (ȳ)1.108, 2.6; *sup m acc sg* **sēlast**
  1.14; *sup m acc pl* **sēlestan** 1.110.
  [SELE]
sēl *see* **wel**.
self (y) *pron* self; *m nom sg* 4.17,
  4.27; *refl m acc sg* **selfne** 3.22; *m
  dat sg* **selfum** (y) 2.35, 2.29,
  3.37; *m gen pl* (**hyra**) **sylfra** 6.38;
  f gen sg **sylfre** 2.9. [SELF]
(ge)sellan (y) *wv* 1 to give, pay;
  3.57, 6.38, 6.46; *3 sg pres* **syleð**
  1.133; *1 pl pres subj* **syllon** 6.61;
  1 sg pret **(ge)sealde** 1.93; *and 3
  sg pret* 2.41, 6.188, 6.271; *3 pl
  pret* **gesealdon** 6.184. [SELL]
gesēman *wv* 1 to arbitrate between,
  decide terms of peace between;
  6.60. [SEEM, I-SEME]
sendan *wv* 1 to send; 6.30; *3 sg
  pret* **sende** 6.134; *3 pl pret* **sendon** 6.29. [SAND]
seofon *num* seven; *m nom* **seofene**
  5.30. [SEVEN]
gesēon *sv* 5 to see; *1 sg pret subj*
  gesāwe 3.13; *3 pl pret* **gesāwon**
  6.84, 6.203. [SEE]
seonobend *f* sinew-band; *acc pl*
  seonobende 2.6. [SINEW,
  BEND]
setl *n* setting place; *dat sg* **setle**
  5.17*. [SETTLE]
sibb *f* kinship, peace; *gen/instr sg*
  sibbe 1.46. [SIB, I-SIB]
gesierwed (y) *adj* armed; *m nom
  sg* 6.159. [*see Holt* **searo**]
siex *num* six; 1.91. [SIX]
sīgan *sv* 1 to sink; *3 sg pret* **sāh**
  5.17. [*see Holt*]

sige *m* victory; *acc sg* 3.57. [*see
  Holt*]
sigebeorn *m* hapax legomenon
  victory-man/warrior; *gen pl* **sigebeorna** 4.38. [*see* **sige**; BERNE]
sigedryhten *m* victory-lord; *dat sg*
  sigedryhtne 1.104. [*see* **sige**;
  DRIGHTIN]
sim(b)le (y) *adv* always; 1.131,
  1.138, 3.18, 3.57. [*see Holt* **simbel**]
sinc *n* treasure; *acc sg* 3.37, 6.59.
  [*etymology unknown*]
sincfæt (y) *n* treasure-casket; *dat
  pl* **syncfatum** 3.28. [*see* **sinc**,
  FAT]
sincgiefa *m* treasure-giver; *acc sg*
  sincgyfan 6.278. [*see* **sinc**,
  GIVE]
singan *sv* 3 to sing; 1.54; *3 pl pres*
  singað 4.5; *3 sg pret* **sang** 6.284.
  [SING]
sittan *sv* 5 (*weak pres*) to sit; *3 sg
  pres* **siteð** 2.28; *3 sg pret* **sæt**
  2.24. [SIT]
sīþ *m* going, journey, experience;
  dat sg **sīðe** 4.19; *and instr sg* 1.6.
  [SITHE]
gesīþ *m* comrade (in arms); *gen pl*
  gesīþa 1.110, 1.125. [SITHE]
gesið(ð) *n* company; *dat sg*
  gesiþþe 2.3. [*see Holt* **sīð**]
siðian *wv* 2 to travel; 6.177; *1 sg
  pres subj* **siðie** 6.251. [SITHE]
siþþan *adv* afterwards; 1.43.
  [SITHEN]
siþ(þ)an *conj* after, since; 1.47,
  2.5, 5.13, 5.69*. [SITHEN]
sixtig *num* sixty; *acc pl* 4.38.
  [SIXTY]

slǣp *m* sleep (figuratively, 'death'); *acc sg* 2.16. [SLEEP]
geslēan *sv* 6 to strike, win by striking; *3 sg pret* slōh (-g) 1.38, 1.44, 6.163, 6.285; *3 sg pret subj* slōge 6.117; *3 pl pret* geslōgon 5.4*. [SLAY]
smǣte *adj* refined, pure; *n gen sg* smǣtes 1.91. [SMEAT]
snell *adj* keen, bold; *m nom pl* snelle 6.29. [SNELL]
sōfte *adv* easily; 6.59. [SOFT]
sōna *adv* soon, immediately, at once; 4.46. [SOON]
sorg *f* sorrow, pain, grief; *acc sg* sorge 2.3; *dat pl* sorgum 2.24. [SORROW]
sorgcearig *adj* fraught with sorrow, sorrowful; *sb nom sg* 2.28. [SORROW, CHARY]
sorglufu *f* distressing love; *nom sg* 2.16. [SORROW, LOVE]
spēdan *wv* 1 to be prosperous, be wealthy; *2 pl pres* spēdaþ 6.34. [SPEED]
spell *n* tale, story; *acc sg* 1.54, 6.50. [SPELL]
spere *n* spear; *nom sg* 6.137; *acc pl* speru 6.108. [SPEAR]
spillan *wv* 1 to destroy; 6.34. [SPILL]
sprecan *sv* 5 to speak; 1.9; *3 sg pret* sprǣc 6.211, 6.274; *3 pl pres* sprecaþ 1.137; *3 pl pret* sprǣcon (ē)(-an) 1.107, 6.200, 6.212. [SPEAK]
sprengan *wv* 1 to break, shiver; *3 sg pret* sprengde 6.137. [SPRENGE]
springan *sv* 3 to spring (away); *3 sg pret* sprang 6.137. [SPRING]

stæð *n* shore, river-bank; *dat sg* stæðe 6.25. [STAITH]
standan *sv* 6 to stand, lie; 6.19, 6.171*; *3 sg pres* standað 3.50, stynt 6.51; *3 sg pret* stōd 4.35, 6.25, 6.28, 6.145, 6.152, 6.273; *3 pl pret* stōdon 6.63, 6.72, 6.79, 6.100, 6.127, 6.182, 6.301. [STAND]
stānfæt (a) *n* stone-vessel, sheath; *dat sg* stānfate 3.35. [STONE, FAT]
stede *m* place, position; *acc sg* 6.19. [STEAD]
stedefæst (æ) *adj* steadfast, unyielding; *m nom pl* stedefæste 6.249; *sb m nom pl* stædefæste 6.127. [STEAD, FAST]
stefn *m* prow; *dat sg* stefne 5.34. [STEM]
stemnettan *wv* 1 *hapax legomenon (see note)* to stop (talking); *3 pl pret* stemnetton 6.122.
stēoran *wv* 1 to steer, rule, correct; *3 sg pret* stȳrode 4.18. [STEER]
steppan *sv* 6 (*weak pres*) to step, advance; *3 sg pret* stōp 6.8, 6.78, 6.131. [STEP]
stihtan *wv* 1 to direct, command, exhort; *3 sg pret* stihte 6.127. [*see Holt*]
stille *adv* quietly; 3.35. [STILL]
stingan *sv* 3 to stab, pierce; *3 sg pret* stang 6.138. [STING]
stīð *adj* hard, severe; *n nom sg* 6.301. [STITHE]
stīðhycgende (-hic-) *adj* firm of purpose, resolute; *m nom pl* 6.122. [STITHE, HIGH]
stīðlice *adv* sternly, loudly; 6.25. [STITHE, -LY suffix]

strēam *m* current, river; *acc sg* 6.68. [STREAM]
stund *f* time, short while; *acc sg* **stunde** 6.271 (**æfre embe st.** 'repeatedly'). [STOUND]
styrian *wv* 1 to stir up, disturb, exhort; *3 sg pret* **styrode** 4.18. [STIR]
suhtergefæderan *m pl* nephew and uncle; *m nom pl* **suhtorfædran** 1.46. [*see Holt* **sweger**; FATHER]
sum *indef pron* some, someone; *m nom sg* 6.149, 6.164; *m acc sg* **sumne** 1.138; *m dat pl* **sumum** 2.34; *f acc sg* **sume** 6.271; *n acc sg* **sum** 6.285. [SOME]
sunne *f* sun; *nom sg* 5.13. [SUN]
sunu *m* son; *nom sg* 3.11*, 4.33, 6.76, (-a) 6.298; *and acc sg* 5.42. [SON]
sūð *adv* south; 1.138. [SOUTH]
sūþerne *adj* southern, of southern make; *m acc sg* 6.134. [SOUTHERN]
swǣþer *indef pron* whichever (of two); *n acc sg* 4.27. [SO and WHETHER]
swā *adv, conj* so, thus, as, in this manner; 1.131, 1.44, 1.50, 1.135, 2.7, 2.9 (*twice*), 2.13, 3.56, 4.19, 4.41, 5.7, *etc.* [SO]
swān *m* herdsman, young man; *acc pl* **swānas** 4.39*. [SWON]
swancor (o) *adj* supple; *f acc pl* **swoncre** 2.6. [*see Holt*]
swāt *n* blood; *dat sg* **swāte** 5.13*. [SWOTE]
swātfāh (-g) *adj* blood-stained; *m nom sg* 3.5. [SWOTE, FAW]

sweart *adj* swarthy, black, dark; *m nom sg* 4.35; *m acc sg* **sweartan** 5.61. [SWART]
swefan *sv* 5 to sleep, rest, die, perish; 3.31. [SWEVE]
swegl *n* sky, heaven; *dat sg* **swegle** 1.101*. [*see Holt* **swegel**]
sweltan *sv* 3 to die; 6.293. [SWELT]
sweng *m* blow, stroke; *gen sg* **swenges** 6.118. [SWENG]
sweorcan *sv* 3 to become gloomy; *3 sg pres* **sweorceð** 2.29. [SWERK]
sweord (o/u) *n* sword; *nom sg* 6.166; *and acc sg* 6.15, 6.161, 6.237; *gen sg* **sweordes** 5.68*; *dat sg* **swurde** 3.28, 4.13, 6.118; *instr sg* **sweorde** 1.41; *acc pl* **sword** 4.15, 6.47; *gen pl* **sweorda** 5.4*; *dat pl* **sweordum** 5.30; *and instr pl* 1.120. [SWORD]
sweordplega *m* sword-play, fight, fighting; *dat sg* **sweordplegan** 3.13*. [SWORD, PLAY]
sweordlēoma (swurd-) *m hapax legomenon* (*see note*) sword-light, flashing light from a sword; *nom sg* 4.35. [SWORD, LEAM]
sweordwund *adj* sword-wounded; *m nom sg* 3.5. [SWORD, WOUND]
sweostorsunu (u) *m* sister's son; *nom sg* 6.115. [SISTER, SON]
geswīcan *sv* 1 to fail; *3 sg pres* **geswīceð** 3.2. [SWIKE]
swilce (y/e) *adv, conj* likewise, also, as if; 1.70, 5.19*, 5.30*, 5.37*, 5.57. [SUCH]
swinsian *wv* 2 to sing out, make music; *3 sg pret* **swinsade** 1.105.

[*see Holt* **swinn** *and* **swan**]
swīðe *adv* very, fiercely; 6.115, 6.118, 6.282. [**SWITH**]
sȳ *see* **bēon**.
symle *see* **simbel**.

T

tǣcan *wv* **1** to teach, direct, show how; *3 sg pret* **tǣhte** 6.18. [**TEACH**]
tǣsan *wv* **1** to lacerate, tear; *3 sg pret* **tǣsde** 6.270. [**TEASE**]
getēon *sv* **2** to draw, pull, withdraw; *3 pl pret* **getugon** 4.15. [**TEE**]
tīd *f* time; *nom sg* 6.104. [**TIDE**]
til *adj* good; *m acc sg* **tilne** 2.38. [**TILL**]
tīr *m* glory; *nom sg* 6.104; *acc sg* 5.3*. [*see Holt*]
tō *prep* (*w dat*) to, toward, about, for, in; 1.94, 1.134, 1.67, 1.95, 2.3, 3.7, 3.59, 3.60, 4.14, 4.20, 4.27, 5.17, 5.28, 5.34, 6.8, 6.28, 6.29, *etc*. [**TO**]
tō *adv* too; 3.20, 6.55, 6.66, 6.90. 6.150, 6.164. [**TO**]
tōberstan *sv* **3** to break, shatter, burst open; *3 sg pret* **tōbærst** 6.136, 6.144. [**TO-** *prefix*, **BURST**]
tōbrecan *sv* **4** to break open, collapse; *pp f nom sg* **tōbrocen** 6.242. [**TO-** *prefix*, **BREAK**]
tōgædere *adv* together; 6.67. [**TOGETHER**]
getoht *n* battle; *dat sg* **getohte** 6.104*. [*see Holt* **tohte**]
tōtwǣman *wv* **1** to divide, break up; *pp n nom sg* **tōtwǣmed** 6.241. [**TOTWEME**]

trym *m/n* step, pace; *acc sg* 6.247. [*see Holt* **trem**]
trymian *wv* **1** to strengthen, make strong in spirit, encourage; 6.17; *3 pl pret* **trymedon** 6.305; *pp n acc sg* **getrymmed** 6.22. [**TRIM**]
tungol *m/n* heavenly body, star; *nom sg* 5.14. [*see Holt*]
getwǣman *wv* **1** to divide, defer, cause to cease; *3 sg pret* **getwǣmde** 3.48*. [**TWEME**]
twēgen *num* two; *m nom* 6.80; *n gen* **twēga** 3.9, 6.207. [**TWAIN**]

Þ/Ð

þǣr *adv* there; 1.52, *etc* (*6 times*), 3.60, 5.17, 5.32, 5.37, 6.17, 6.64, 6.65, 6.68, *etc*. [**THERE**]
þǣr *conj* where; 6.23, 6.24, 6.28. [**THERE**]
þæs þe *conj* because, for, since; 1.95, 3.26, 3.40. [**THE**]
þæt *conj* that, provided that, in order that, so that, in that; 1.108, 1.132, 2.10, 2.11, 2.16, 3.20, 3.36, 3.47, 4.19, 4.44, 5.8, 5.48, 6.9, 6.20, 6.30, 6.63, 6.105, 6.119, 6.135, 6.137, 6.221, 6.243, 6.251, *etc*. [**THAT**]
þā *adv* then, thereupon; 1.9, 1.97, 4.2, 4.13, 4.14, 4.28, 4.43, 4.46, 5.53, 6.2, 6.12, 6.17, 6.25, *etc*; *correl w* **þā** *conj* 6.7, 6.23, 6.86. [**THE**]
þā *conj* when; 1.94, 6.5, 6.10, 6.16, 6.22, 6.84, 6.121, 6.165, 6.199, *etc*. [**THO**]
þā gīet *see* **gīet**.
þā hwīle þe *see* **hwīle**.

þanc *m* thanks; *acc sg* 6.120, 6.147. [THANK]
geþanc *n* thought, purpose; *acc sg* 6.13. [THANK]
geþancian *wv 2* to thank, give thanks to; *1 sg pres* geþance 6.173. [THANK]
þancword (o) *n* thank-word, thanks; *acc pl* 1.137. [THANK, WORD]
ðanon (ðonan) *adv* thence; 1.109. [THENNE]
þe *adv (w comp adj)* the; 6.146, 6.312 *(twice)*, 6.313. [THE]
þe *rel pron conj* that, which, who, what, on which; 1.2, 1.13, 1.17, 1.107, 1.133, 4.9, 5.26, 5.68, 6.36, 6.52, 6.77, *etc*. [THE]
ðeah *adv* however; 3.57, 6.289. [THOUGH]
þeah þe *conj* although; 1.126, 3.16. [THOUGH, THE]
þearf (æ) *f* want, need; *nom sg* 6.233; *acc sg* þearfe 1.137, 6.175; *and dat sg* 6.201*, 6.232, 6.307. [THARF]
þearle *adv* severely, sorely; 5.23, 6.158. *[see Holt* þearle*]*
þeaw *m* custom, habit; *dat pl* þeawum 1.11. [THEW]
þegn (/-en) *m* thane, servant, retainer, warrior *(see notes at 1.37 and 4.13)*; *nom sg* 4.13; *and acc sg* 6.151; *nom pl* þegenas 6.205, 6.220; *and acc pl* 6.232. [THANE]
þegenlīce *adv* loyally, nobly; 6.294. [THANE, -LY *suffix*]
geþencan *wv 1* to think, imagine, consider, intend; 2.12, 2.31; *1 sg pres* þence 6.319; *3 sg pres*

(ge)ðenceð 3.61, 6.258, 6.316; *3 sg pret* ðōhte 3.36. [THINK]
þenden *conj* while, as long as; 1.134, 3.23. *[see Holt]*
þēod *f* people, nation, region; *acc sg* þēode 1.128; *and dat sg* 6.90, 6.220; *gen pl* þēoda 1.11, 6.173; *dat pl* þēodum 5.22*. [THEDE]
þēoden *m* prince, lord; *nom sg* 6.120, 6.178, 6.232; *and acc sg* 6.158; *dat sg* þēodne 6.294. [THEDE]
þēodenstōl *m* princely-stool, throne; *acc sg* 1.13. [THEDE, STOOL]
geþēon *sv 1/3* to prosper, thrive; 1.13; *3 sg pret* geþāh 1.16. [THEE]
þēs *dem pron* this; *m nom sg* 4.7; *m acc sg* þisne (y) 4.9, 6.32, 6.52; *m instr sg* þīs 6.316; *m acc pl* þās 6.298; *and f acc sg* 2.31; *f gen sg* þisse 4.4; *and f dat sg* 3.30, 6.221; *f acc pl* þās 3.26; *n nom sg* þis 4.3, 6.45; *n gen sg* þisses 2.7, 2.13, *etc*; *n instr sg* þīs 5.66*; *n dat pl* þissum 5.67*. [THIS]
geþicgan *sv 5 (weak pres)* to receive; *1 sg pret* geþah 1.65*; *and 3 sg pret* 1.3, 2.40. [THIG]
ðīn *poss adj* thy, your; *n acc sg* 3.6; *m acc sg* ðīnne 3.17; *n acc sg* þīn 6.178; *f acc pl* þīne 6.37; *f dat pl* ðīnum 6.50. [THINE]
þing *n* thing, case, affair; *acc sg* 2.9. [THING]
geþōht *m* thought; *acc sg* 2.22. [THOUGHT]
(ge)þolian *wv 2* to endure, hold out; 6.6, 6.201, 6.307. [THOLE]

þonne *adv* then; 1.106, 2.31, 3.62. [THEN]
þonne *conj* when, than; 1.100, 1.103*, 1.120, 3.53, 3.55, 4.40, 6.195, 6.213. [THEN]
þrāg *f* time; *acc sg* þrāge 1.88. [THROW]
geþrang *n* throng, crowd; *acc sg* 6.299. [THRING]
þrīe (ēo) *num* three; *m gen* þrēora 6.299. [THREE]
þrīste *adv* boldly, resolutely; 2.12. [THRISTE]
þrītig *num* thirty; 2.18. [THIRTY]
þrymm (/-m) *m* power, force; *acc sg* 1.49. [THRUM]
ðū *2 pers pron* thou, you; *nom sg* 3.9, 3.18, 3.20, 3.24, 3.25, 3.46, 4.27, 6.30, 6.36, *etc*; *acc sg* ðē 3.12, 3.13, 3.22; *gen sg* ðīn 3.23 (*see entry as poss adj*); *dat sg* ðē 3.19, 3.24, 4.26, 6.29, 6.30, 6.173, 6.177, *etc*; *dual dat sg* **incrum** (u) 1.104; *nom pl* gē 3.56, 6.32, 6.34, 6.56, 6.57, 6.59; *acc pl* ēow 6.41; *and dat pl* 6.31, 6.46, 6.48, 6.93. [YOU]
þurfan *ppv* to need, have reason to; *3 sg pret* þorfte 5.39, 5.44; *1 pl pres* þurfe 6.34; *3 pl pres* þurfon 6.249; *3 pl pret* þorftun 5.47*. [THARF]
ðurh *prep* through, by means of; 3.14, 3.42*, 6.71, 6.141, 6.145, 6.151. [THROUGH]
þurhwadan *sv 6* to pass through, pierce; *3 sg pret* þurhwōd 6.296. [THROUGH- *in combination*, WADE]

ðus *adv* thus; 3.49, 6.57. [THUS]
ðȳ *adv* therefore; 3.19. [THY]
ðȳ *conj* that, because; 3.13*. [THY]
þyncan *wv* 1 to seem; *3 sg pres* þinceð 2.29, 6.55; *3 sg pret* þūhte 6.66. [THINK]
ðyrl *adj* pierced, perforated; *m nom sg* 4.45. [THIRL]

U

unbefohten *adj hapax legomenon* (*see note*) unopposed, without a fight; *m nom pl* **unbefohtene** 6.57. [UN- *prefix*, BE- *prefix*, FIGHT]
undearnunga (-inga) *adv* without concealment, openly; 4.22. [UN- *prefix*; *see Holt* **dearnunga**]
under *prep w dat/acc of motion* under, at the lower part of; 1.101, 1.143, 4.8. [UNDER]
unearg *adj* undaunted, not cowardly; *m nom pl* **unearge** 6.206. [UN- *prefix*, ARGH]
unforcūð *adj* noble, of untainted reputation; *m nom sg* 6.51. [UN- *prefix*, FORCOUTH]
unforht *adj* unafraid; *m nom pl* **unforhte** 6.79. [UN- *prefix*; *see Holt* **forht**]
unhneaw *adj w gen/instr* unniggardly, generous, liberal; *m acc sg* **unhneawne** 1.139; *sup f acc sg* **unhneaweste** 1.73. [UN- *prefix*; *see Holt* **hneaw**]
unmǣg *m* evil kinsman (*see note*); *m nom pl* **unmǣgas** 3.55. [UN- *prefix*, MAY]
geunnan *ppv (w gen)* to grant; *2 sg pres subj* **geunne** 6.176.

[UNNE]
unorne *adj hapax legomenon (see note)* simple, humble; *m nom sg* 6.256. **[UNORN]**
unrīm *n* countless number; *nom sg* 5.31. [UN- *prefix*, RIME]
unryht *n* wrong; *dat sg* **unryhte** 3.27. [UN- *prefix*, RIGHT]
unscende *adj* blameless, glorious; 3.52. [UN- *prefix*, SHEND]
unwāclīce *adv* not weakly, bravely; 6.308. [UN- *prefix*, WOKE, -LY *suffix*]
unweaxen *adj* not fully grown; *m nom sg* 6.152. [UN- *prefix*, WAX]
ūp *adv* up, on high; 5.13*, 5.70*, 6.130. [UP]
ūpganga *m* landing, passage to land; *acc sg* **ūpgangan** 6.87. [UPGANG]
ūre *poss adj* our; *m nom sg* 6.232, 6.240, 6.314; *m acc sg* **ūrne** 6.58; *m dat pl* **ūrum** 6.56; *n nom sg* **ūre** 6.313. [OUR]
ūt *adv* out; 3.41, 5.35, 6.72. [OUT]
ūþwita *m* learned man; *nom pl* **ūðitan** 5.69. [UÐWITE]

W

wāc *adj* weak, slender; *m acc sg* **wācne** 6.43. [WOKE]
wācian *wv 2* to weaken, turn coward; 6.10. [WOKE]
(ge)wadan *sv 6* to go, advance, pass, penetrate; 6.140; *3 sg pret* **(ge)wōd** 6.130, 6.157, 6.253; *3 pl pret* **wōdon** 6.96, 6.295. [WADE]

wæl *n* slaughter, dead bodies, hence 'battlefield'; *nom sg* 5.65, 6.126, 6.303; *dat sg* **wæle** 6.279, 6.300. [WAL]
wælfeld *m hapax legomenon* slaughter-field, battlefield; *dat sg* **wælfelda** 5.51. [WAL, FIELD]
wælrest *f* slaughter-bed, death in battle; *acc sg* **wælræste** 6.113. [WAL, REST]
wælsliht *m* slaughter-stroke, deadly blow; *gen pl* **wælslihta** 4.28. [WAL, SLEIGHT]
wælspere *n* slaughter-spear; *acc sg* 6.322. [WAL, SPEAR]
wælstōw *f* slaughter-place, battlefield; *gen sg* **wælstōwe** 6.95; *and dat sg* 5.43, 6.293. [WAL, STOW]
wælwulf *m* slaughter-wolf, murderous adversary; *nom pl* **wælwulfas** 6.96. [WAL, WULF]
wæpen *n* weapon; *nom sg* 6.252; *and acc sg* 6.130, 6.235; *gen sg* **wæpnes** 6.168; *dat sg* **wæpne** 6.228; *gen pl* **wæpna** 6.83, 6.272, 6.308; *dat pl* **wæpnum** 6.10 (tō w. fōn 'take up arms'), 6.126. [WEAPON]
wæpengewrixl *n* weapon-exchange; *gen sg* **wæpengewrixles** 5.51. [WEAPON, WRIXLE]
wærloga *m* oath-breaker, traitor; *dat pl/gen sg* **wærlogan** 1.9. [WARLOCK]
wæter *n* water; *acc sg* 5.55, 6.91, 6.98; *dat sg* **wætere** 6.64, 6.96. [WATER]

wandian *wv* 2 to flinch, draw back; 6.258; *3 sg pret* **wandode** 6.268. [WONDE]
wandrian *wv* 2 to wander, fly round; *3 sg pret* **wandrode** 4.34. [WANDER]
wāðol *adj hapax legomenon* (*see note*); 4.8.
wēa *m* woe, misery, harm; *acc sg* **wēan** 2.4; *and gen sg* 2.25; *gen pl* **wēana** 2.34, 4.25*. [WOE]
wēadǣd *f* woe-deed, evil-deed; *nom pl* **wēadǣda** 4.8. [WOE, DEED]
weald *m* wood, forest; *dat sg* **wealde** 5.65. [WOLD]
geweald *n* (*w gen*) power, authority; *acc sg* 1.77, 3.42*, 6.178. [WIELD]
wealdan *sv* 7 to wield, rule, control; 1.10, 3.63, 6.83, 6.95, 6.168, 6.272; *3 sg pret* **wēold** 1.18, *etc.* (*7 times*); *3 pl pret* **wēoldan** 1.129. [WIELD]
weall (/-l) *m* wall, rampart; *acc sg* 3.15. [WALL]
wealdend (a) *m* ruler, lord; *nom sg* 6.173. [WALDEND]
weg (æ) *m* way, direction, path, journey; *acc sg* 4.43 (*in adv phrase* **on wæg** 'away'). [WAY]
wegan *sv* 5 to carry, bear; *3 pl pret* **wǣgon** 6.98. [WEIGH]
wel *adv* well; 1.107; *comp* **sēl** better; 4.38, 4.39; *sup* **sēlast** 1.101. [WELL, SELE]
wela (io) *m* wealth, riches; *acc pl* **welan** 3.62; *gen pl* **wiolena** 1.78*. [WEAL]
wēn *f* expectation; *dat pl* **wēnan** 2.25. [WEEN]

wēnan *wv* 1 to expect, think; *2 sg pret* **wēndest** 3.46; *3 sg pret* **wēnde** 6.239. [WEEN]
wendan *wv* 1 to wend, turn, go; 6.316; *3 sg pres* **wendeþ** 2.32; *1 sg pres subj* **wende** 6.252; *3 pl pret* **wendon** 6.193, 6.205. [WEND]
weorc (o) *n* work, deed; *nom sg* 3.2. [WORK]
weorðan *sv* 3 to become, come to pass, come about; *3 sg pret* **wearð** (æ) 3.24, 5.32, 5.65, 6.106, 6.113*, 6.114, 6.116*, 6.135, 6.138, 6.202, 6.241, 6.288, 6.295; *3 sg pret subj* **wurde** 6.1; *3 pl pret* **wurdon** (-un) 2.15, 5.48*, 6.186. [WORTH]
weorðian *wv* 2 to honour, adorn; *imp sg* **weorða** 3.22; *pp f nom sg* **geweorðod** 3.51. [WORTH, I-WURTHI]
weorðlīce (u) *adv* worthily, honourably, splendidly; 6.279; *comp* **wurþlīcor** 4.37. [WORTHLY]
wer *m* man; *gen pl* **wera** 4.37; *instr pl* **werum** 1.130. [WERE]
werian (**wergan**) *wv* 1 to defend, guard; 1.121; *3 sg pres* **wereð** 3.53; *3 pl pret* **weredon** 6.82, 6.283. [WERE]
wērig *adj* weary; *m nom sg* 5.20; *m nom pl* **wērige** 6.303. [WEARY]
werod (eo) *n* troop, band, body of men; *nom sg* 6.64, 6.97; *and acc sg* 6.102; *dat sg* **weorode** 6.51; *and instr sg* 5.34. [WERED]
wesan *sv* 5 to be; *imp pl* **wesað** 4.12; *1 sg pret* **wæs** 1.57, *etc* (*18 times*), 2.36, 2.37; *and 3 sg pret*

1.14, 1.34, 1.36, 1.91, 1.111, 2.8, 2.11, 2.19, *etc*; *neg 3 sg pret* **næs** 1.67, 6.325; *3 sg pret subj* **wǣre** 2.26, 6.195, 6.240; *3 pl pret* **wǣran** 1.125. [BE]

west *adv* west; 6.97. [WEST]

wicg *n* horse; *dat sg* **wicge** 6.240. [WIDGE]

wīcing *m* Viking, raider; *acc sg* 6.139; *acc pl* **wīcingas** 6.322; *gen pl* **wīcinga** 6.26, 6.73, 6.97; *dat pl* **wīcingum** 6.116. [VIKING]

wīde *adv* widely, afar, far and wide; 1.53, 2.22, 4.25. [WIDE]

wiernan *wv* 1 to refuse, withhold; *3 sg pret* **wyrnde** 6.118; *3 pl pret* **wyrndon** 5.24. [WARN]

wīf *n* woman; *instr pl* **wīfum** 1.130. [WIFE]

wifle javelin; *instr sg* 3.55*. [*see Holt* **wifel** *and* **wifer**]

wīg *m/n* warfare; *nom sg* 1.119; *and acc sg* 3.15; *gen sg* **wīges** 5.20*, 5.59*, 6.73, 6.130; *dat sg* **wīge** 6.10, 6.128, 6.193, 6.235, 6.252. [*see Holt*]

wiga *m* warrior; *nom sg* 3.43, 6.210; *acc sg* **wigan** 6.75, 6.235; *and nom pl* 6.79, 6.126, 6.302; *gen pl* **wigena** 6.135. [WYE]

wīgend *m* warrior, fighter; *nom pl* 4.10, 4.47, 6.302. [*see Holt* **wīgan**]

wīghaga *m hapax legomenon* (*see note*) battle-wall, wall of shields; *acc sg* **wīhagan** 6.102. [*see* **wīg**; HAW]

wīgheard *adj* hardened in war, fierce in battle; *m acc sg* **wīgheardne** 6.75. [*see* **wīg**; HARD]

wīgplega *m* battle-play, fighting; *dat sg* **wīgplegan** 6.268; *instr sg* 6.316. [*see* **wīg**; PLAY]

wīgrǣden *f* plan of battle; *acc sg* **wīgrǣdenne** 3.22. [*see* **wīg**, READ *and* REDE]

wīgsmiþ *m* warrior; *nom pl* **wīgsmiþas** 5.72. [*see* **wīg**; SMITH]

willa *m* desirable thing; *gen pl* **wilna** 1.78. [WILL]

willan *av* will, be willing, wish; *1 sg pres* **wille (y)** 2.35, 6.216, 6.221, 6.247, 6.317; *2 sg pres* **wille (y)** 4.27; *3 sg pres* **wile** 1.13, 1.140, 6.52; *3 pl pres* **willað** 4.9, 6.35, 6.40, 6.46; *2 sg pres subj* **wylle** 4.27, 6.37; *3 sg pret* **wolde** 4.21, 6.11, 6.129, 6.160; *3 pl pret* **woldon** 6.207; *neg 1 sg pres* **nelle** 6.246; *3 sg pret* **nolde** 6.6, 6.9, 6.275; *3 pl pret* **noldon** 6.81, 6.185, 6.201. [WILL]

wīnburg *f* wine-borough, town of revelry; *gen pl* **wīnburga** 1.77. [WINE, BOROUGH]

windan *sv* 3 to wind, twist, swing, turn; 6.322; *imp pl* **windað** 4.12; *3 sg pret* **wand** 6.43; *3 pl pret* **wundon** 6.106; *pp n instr sg* **wundnan** 1.129. [WIND]

wine *m* friend, lord; *nom sg* 3.12, 3.46, 6.250; *acc pl* **winas** 6.228. [WINE]

winedryhten (i) *m* beloved lord; *acc sg* 6.248, 6.263. [WINE, DRIGHTIN]

winemǣg *m* beloved kinsman; *acc pl* **winemāgas** 6.306. [WINE, MAY]

gewinn *n* battle, strife; *acc sg* 6.214; *dat sg* **gewinne** 6.248, 6.302. [WIN, I-WIN]
gewinnan *sv 3* win, gain; 6.125. [WIN, I-WIN]
winter *m* winter, year; *gen pl* **wintra** 2.18, 2.38; *instr pl* **wintrum** 6.210. [WINTER]
winterceald *adj* wintry-cold; *f acc sg* **wintercealde** 2.4. [WINTER, COLD]
wiolena *see* **wela**.
wīs *adj* wise; *m nom sg* 6.219. [WISE]
wīsian *wv 2* to guide, instruct; *3 sg pret* **wīsode** 6.141. [I-WISSE]
wislic *adj* certain, assured; *m acc sg* **wislicne** 2.34. [WISLY]
witan *ppv* to know, understand; *1 sg pres* **wāt** 3.36, 6.94; *1 sg pret* **wisse** 1.101; *3 sg pret* **wiste** 6.24. [WIT]
gewītan *sv 1* to depart, go, pass away, die; *3 sg pret* **gewāt** 4.43, 5.35, 6.72, 6.150; *3 pl pret* **gewitan** 5.53*. [WITE]
witod *adj* appointed, destined, fated; *n nom sg* 4.26. [WIT]
wit(t)ig *adj* wise, prescient, knowing; *nom sg* 2.32. [WITTY]
wið *prep w dat/acc* towards, against; 1.42, 3.54, 5.9, 5.52, 6.31, 6.35, 6.39, 6.82, 6.103, 6.277, 6.290, 6.298; *w gen* 6.8, 6.131. [WITH]
wiþerlēan *n* requital; *nom sg* 6.116. [WITHER, LEAN]
wlanc (o) *adj* proud; *m acc sg* **wlancne** 6.139; *f acc sg* **wloncan** 1.118; *and n dat sg* 6.240; *m nom pl* **wlance** 1.106, 3.62, 5.72,

6.205. [WLONK]
wlītan *sv 1* to look, gaze; *3 sg pret* **wlāt** 6.172. [*see Holt*]
wolcen *n/m* lump, ball, cloud, sky; *dat pl* **wolcnum** 4.8. [WELKIN]
word *n* word; *acc sg* 6.168; *dat pl* **wordum** 3.12, 3.45; *and instr pl* 1.107, 6.26, 6.43, 6.210, 6.250, (-**on**) 6.306. [WORD]
wordhord *n* word-hoard, vocabulary; *acc sg* 1.1. [WORD, HOARD]
worn *m/n* great number; *acc sg* 1.9. [*see Holt* **wearn**]
woruld *f* world; *acc sg* 2.31; *dat sg* **worulde** 6.174. [WORLD]
woruldgesǣlig *adj hapax legomenon* prosperous in this world; *m nom sg* 6.219. [WORLD, I-SELI]
wrǣc *f/n* misery, persecution; *acc sg* **wrǣce** 2.4; *gen sg* **wrǣces** 2.1. [WRACK]
wræcc(e)a (e) *m* exile, adventurer; *nom sg* **wreccea** 4.25*; *nom pl* **wræccan** 1.129. [WRETCH]
wrāþ *adj* hostile; *gen sg sb* **wrāþes** 1.9. [WROTH]
(ge)wrecan *sv 5* to avenge; 6.208, 6.248, 6.258, 6.263; *3 sg pret* **wrec** 6.279; *3 sg pret subj* **wrēce** 6.257. [WREAK]
wudu *m* wood; *acc sg* 1.121, 6.193. [WOOD]
wulf *m* wolf; *acc sg* 5.65. [WOLF]
wund *adj* wounded, sore; *m nom sg* 4.43, 6.113, 6.144. [WOUND]
wund *f* wound, sore, wounding; *acc sg* **wunde** 6.139, 6.271; *acc*

pl **wunda** 4.47; *dat pl* **wundum (-un)** 5.43*, 6.293, 6.303. [WOUND]

gewundian *wv* 2 to wound; *pp m nom sg* **gewundod** 6.135. [WOUND]

wylfen *adj* wolfish, savage, cruel; *m acc sg* **wylfenne** 2.22. [WOLFEN]

wynn *f* benefit, joy; *gen pl* **wynna** 6.174. [WIN]

(ge)wyrcan *wv* 1 to work, make, form; 6.81, 6.102, 6.264; *infl inf* **wyrcenne** 1.72; *3 sg pres* **gewyrceð** 1.142. [WORK]

wyrm (u) *n* snake, dragon; *dat pl* **wurman** 2.1. [WORM]

wȳscan *wv* 1 to wish; *3 sg pret* **wȳscte** 2.25. [WISH]

Y

yfel *n* misery, ill, evil; *gen sg* **yfles** 1.51, 6.133. [EVIL]

ymbe (e) *prep w acc* about, around, at, upon, near, along; 1.121, 2.12, 4.33, 5.5, 6.214, 6.249, 6.271 (**æfre e. stunde** 'repeatedly'). [EMBE, UMBE]

yrhðo *see* **iergðu**.

GLOSSARY OF PROPER NAMES

A

Ægelmund the first king of the Langobards (*see* Paulus Diaconus, *Historia Langobardum*, I.15); *acc sg* 1.117.

Ælfere, with Maccus, died defending the ford against the Viking host; *nom sg* 6.80.

Ælfhere father of Waldere; *gen sg* Ælfheres 3.11, 3.50*.

Ælfnoð a warrior on the English side who died in battle with his companion Wulfmær; *nom sg* 6.183.

Ælfrīc father of Ælfwine; *gen sg* Ælfrīces 6.209.

Ælfwine son of Ælfric, grandson of Ealhhelm, and a relative of Byrhtnoth; *nom sg* 6.211, 6.231.

Ælfwine the Langobard king Alboin (565-572); *dat sg* 1.70.

Ǣnēnas an unidentified tribe; *dat pl* Ǣnēnum 1.61.

Æscferð son of Ecglaf, one of Byrhtnoth's hostages; *nom sg* 6.267.

Ætla Attila, king of the Huns (433-453); *nom sg* 1.18; *gen sg* Ætlan 1.122, 3.6.

Æþelgār father of the Godric who remained loyal; *gen sg* Æþelgāres 6.320.

Æþelrēd (II) 'the Unready', king of England (978-1016; *see note* 6.53); *gen sg* Æþelrēdes 6.52, 6.151, 6.203.

Æþelstān king of the West-Saxons (924-939); *nom sg* 5.1*.

Æþerīc brother of Sibyrht; *nom sg* 6.280.

Alewih an otherwise unknown Danish king; *nom sg* 1.35.

Alexandreas Alexander the Great (336-323 B.C.); *nom sg* 1.15.

Amoþingas a tribe from the Norwegian island Hindø; *dat pl* Amothingum 1.85.

Ānlāf son of Guthfrith, commander of the Norsemen; *nom sg* 5.46; *gen sg* Ānlāfes 5.31*; *dat sg* Ānlāfe 5.26.

B

Bāningas a tribe from the district Bainaib in middle Germany near the Elbe; *instr pl* Bāningum 1.19.

Beadeca Baduila/Totila, king of the Ostrogoths (541-552 -*a tentative identification*); *acc sg* Beadecan 1.112.

Beadohild daughter of Nithhad and mother of Widia by Welund; *dat sg* Beadohilde 2.8.

Becca king of the Banings; *nom sg* 1.19.

Becca Berchtung of the Wolfdietrich story (*according to Malone, Becca is a hypocoristic form derived from the second element of* Theodberht); *acc sg* Beccan 1.115.

Billing king of the Werns; *nom sg* 1.25.

Breoca king of the Brondings (*see Beowulf* 449-606); *nom sg* 1.25.

Brondingas the Brondings (*the home of this tribe has not been identified for certain*); *instr pl* **Brondingum** 1.25.

Brunanburh *f* (*the site of the battle in Text 5*); *acc sg* 5.5*(*see note*).

Bryten *f* Britain; *acc sg* **Brytene** 5.71.

Burgendan the Burgundians; *gen pl* **Burgenda** 3.46; *dat pl* **Burgendum** 1.19; *and instr pl* 1.65.

Byrhtelm father of Byrhtnoth; *gen sg* **Byrhtelmes** 6.92.

Byrhtnoð alderman of Essex, leader of the English forces; *nom sg* 6.17, 6.42, 6.101, 6.127, 6.162; *and acc sg* 6.257; *gen sg* **Byrhtnoðes** 6.114.

Byrhtwold an old and tried retainer of Byrhtnoth's household; *nom sg* 6.309.

C

Cælic king of the Finns; *nom sg* 1.20.

Casere a generic term for the Roman Emperor; *nom sg* 1.20; *and dat sg* 1.76.

Ceola father of Wulfstan; *gen sg* **Ceolan** 6.76.

Constantinus (**-stontinus**) Constantine, commander of the Scots; *nom sg* 5.38*.

Crēacas the Greeks; *dat pl* **Crēacum** 1.76; *and instr pl* 1.20.

D

Dēan the Daukiones of Ptolemy (*Primer of Geography*, II.11.16); *dat pl* **Dēanum** 1.63.

Dene the Danes; often used for Vikings in general; *dat pl* **Denon** 6.129; *instr pl* **Denum** 1.35.

Dēor poet of the Heodenings, and (perhaps) the narrator of (all of) *Text 2*; *nom sg* 2.37.

Dingesmere m; *acc sg* 5.54*.

Dunnere a humble peasant, one of Byrhtnoth's loyal retainers; *nom sg* 6.255.

Dyflen Dublin; *acc sg* **Difelin** 5.55*.

E

Ēadgils king of the Myrgings; *dat sg* **Ēadgilse** 1.93.

Ēadmund prince and brother of Æthelstan the king; *nom sg* 5.3.

Ēadric a faithful English retainer; *nom sg* 6.11.

Ēadweard (se langa) one of Byrhtnoth's loyal retainers; *nom sg* 6.117, 6.273.

Ēadweard king of the West-Saxons and father of Æthelstan and Eadmund; *gen sg* **Ēadweardes** 5.7*, 5.52.

Ēadwine the Langobard king Audoin (*c.* 546-565); *acc sg* 1.117; *gen sg* **Ēadwines** 1.74.

Ēadwine the father of Ealhhild; *gen sg* **Ēadwines** 1.98.

Ēadwold brother of Oswold and one of Byrhtnoth's loyal retainers; *nom sg* 6.304.

Ēaha a Danish warrior; *nom sg* 4.15.
Ealhelm alderman of central Mercia (940-51), grandfather of Ælfwine; *nom sg* 6.218.
Ealhhild the daughter of Eadwine and the wife of Eormanric (*see note* 1.45-48); *nom sg* 1.97; *dat sg* **Ealhhilde** 1.5.
Ēastgota Ostrogotha, a king of the Ostrogoths (*see* Cassiodorus, *Variae* XI.I *and* Jordanes, *Getica* 89); *acc sg* **Ēastgotan** 1.113.
Ēastseaxe the East-Saxons; *gen pl* **Ēastseaxena** 6.69.
Ēastþyringas the Thuringians; *dat pl* **Ēastþyringum** 1.86.
Eatul Italy; *dat sg* **Eatule** 1.70.
Ebrēas the Hebrews; *dat pl* **Ebrēum** 1.83.
Ecglāf father of Æscferth; *gen sg* **Ecglāfes** 6.267.
Ēgypte the Egyptians; *dat pl* **Ēgyptum** 1.83.
Elsa from the context, probably a king of the Langobards otherwise unknown; *acc sg* **Elsan** 1.117.
Emerca the Gothic hero Erpamara (*fl.* 1st century A.D.; *see* Jordanes, *Getica* 89); *acc sg* **Emercan** 1.113.
Engle (in *Text 1* the continental Angles); *nom pl* 5.70, 1.44; *dat pl* **Englum** 1.61.
Eolum see **Ilwan**
Eormanrīc (Ear-) the Ostrogothic king Eormanric (*fl. c.* 350-75; *see note* 1.7-9 and 2.21); *nom sg* 1.18; *gen sg* **Eormanrīces** 1.8, 1.111, 2.21; *dat sg* **Eormanrīce** 1.88.

Eowan perhaps the inhabitants of the Swedish island Öland; *instr pl* **Eowum** 1.26.
Exsyringas the Assyrians; *dat pl* **Exsyringum** 1.82.

F

Fīfeldor the estuary of the Eider; *dat sg* **Fīfeldore** 1.43.
Finn king of the East Frisians (*see Beowulf* 1069-1159 *and Text 4*); *nom sg* 1.27.
Finnas the Finns; *dat pl* **Finnum** 1.76; *and instr pl* 1.20.
Finnsburuh *f* Finn's fortress; *nom sg* 4.36.
Folcwalding literally 'Son of the Folk-Ruler', patronymic surname of Finn, the Frisian king; *nom sg* 1.27.
Freoþerīc from the context, probably a king of the Heathobards; *acc sg* 1.124.
Frēsan the Frisians; *gen pl* **Frēsna** 1.27; *dat pl* **Frȳsum** 1.68.
Fridla the Gothic king or hero Fridigernus; *acc sg* **Fridlan** 1.113.
Froncan the Franks; *dat pl* **Froncum** 1.68; *and instr pl* 1.24.
Frumtingas a faction of the Suevi in 5th century Spain; *dat pl* **Frumtingum** 1.68.

G

Gadd kinsman of Offa; *gen sg* **Gaddes** 6.287.
Gārulf a Frisian warrior; *nom sg* 4.31; *and acc sg* 4.18.
Geat the husband of Mæthhild (*see note*); *gen sg* **Geates** 2.15.

Gēatas the Geats of *Beowulf*; *dat pl* **Gēatum** 1.58.
Gefflēgan the Aviones of Tacitus (*Germania* 40); *dat pl* **Gefflēgum** 1.60.
Gefþan the Gibids, a Gothic tribe (*see Beowulf* 2494); *dat pl* **Gefþum** 1.60.
Gefwulf king of the Euts, otherwise unknown; *nom sg* 1.26.
Gifica king of the Burgundians; *nom sg* 1.19.
Gīslhere king Gislaharius of the Burgundians; *acc sg* 1.123.
Glomman the Glamms, possibly the Lemovii of Tacitus (*Germania* 43); *dat pl* **Glommum** 1.69; *and instr pl* 1.21.
Godrīc son of Odda, first among the English forces to turn in flight, brother of Godwig and Godwine; *nom sg* 6.187, 6.237, 6.325.
Godrīc son of Æthelgar, remained loyal to Byrhtnoth; *nom sg* 6.321.
Godwīg son of Odda, brother of Godric and Godwine; *nom sg* 6.192.
Godwine son of Odda, brother of Godric and Godwig; *nom sg* 6.192*.
Gotan the Ostrogoths in Anglo-Saxon poetry; *gen pl* **Gotena** 1.89, 1.109, 2.23; *instr pl* **Gotum** 1.18.
Gūðhere (-ere) a Frisian warrior; *nom sg* 4.18.
Gūðhere king of the Burgundians (*c.* 411-437); *nom sg* 1.66; *dat sg* 3.25.

Gūþlāf one of the Danish force; *nom sg* 4.16.
Gūðlāf a Frisian, father of Garulf; *gen sg* **Gūðlāfes** 4.33.

H

Hæleþan a tribe living near the Randers Firth in North Jutland; *dat pl* **Hæleþum** 1.81.
Hælsingas an otherwise unknown tribe; *instr pl* **Hælsingum** 1.22.
Hætwere the Hetware of *Beowulf* (2363 *and* 2916), and the historical Chat(t)varii; *instr pl* **Hætwerum** 1.33.
Hæðnas the inhabitants of Hedemark, Norway; *dat pl* **Hæðnum** 1.81.
Hagen (-a) kinsman of Guthhere; *gen sg* **Hagenan** 3.47*.
Hagena king of the Rugians (Holmryge); *nom sg* 1.21.
Hāma an adventurer (*see note* 1.129); *nom sg* 1.130; *acc sg* **Hāman** 1.124.
Heaðobeardan the Heathobards of *Beowulf* (2032, 2037 *and* 2067); *gen pl* **Heaðobeardna** 1.49.
Heaþorēamas the Heathoræmas of *Beowulf* (519); *dat pl* **Heaþorēamum** 1.63.
Heaþorīc probably the Heiðrekr of the *Hervararsaga*; *acc sg* 1.116.
Hēhca father of Eormanric; *acc sg* **Hēhcan** 1.112*.
Helm king of the Wulfings; *nom sg* 1.29.
Henden king of the Glomman; *nom sg* 1.21.
Hengest a Danish/Jutish leader (*see note*); *nom sg* 4.17.

Heodeningas the Heodenings, a royal family descending from Heoden, or a tribe ruled by a family of this name; *gen pl* **Heodeninga** 2.36.

Heorot the hall of the Danish king Hrothgar where Beowulf battled with Grendel and his mother; *dat sg* **Heorote** 1.49.

Heorrenda the poet who succeeded Deor among the Heodenings; *nom sg* 2.39.

Herefaran an otherwise unknown tribe ruled by a king Hringweald; *gen pl* **Herefarena** 1.34.

Herelingas either the followers of Herela, or more specifically, the Harlung brothers Aki and Egarð; *acc pl* 1.112.

Hlīþe probably Hloðr of the *Hervararsaga*; *acc sg* 1.116.

Hnæf king of the Hocingas, son of Hoc and brother of Hildeburh (*see Text 4 and Beowulf* 1069-1159); *nom sg* 1.29; *dat sg* **Hnæfe** 4.40.

Hōcingas the Hocings, the Half-Danes of *Beowulf* (1069); *instr pl* **Hōcingum** 1.29.

Holen an otherwise unknown king of the Wrosnan; *nom sg* 1.33.

Holmrycgas the Rugians (*see* Jordanes *Getica* 4, 'Hulmerugi'); *instr pl* **Holmrycgum** 1.21*.

Hrǣde the Nest(-Goths); *gen pl* **Hrǣda** 1.120.

Hrēðcyning king of the Hrethgotan, here Eormanric; *gen sg* **Hrēðcyninges** 1.7.

Hrēðgotan the Ostrogoths; *dat pl* **Hrēðgotum** 1.57.

Hringweald literally 'Ring-Ruler', an otherwise unknown king of the Herefaran; *nom sg* 1.34.

Hronan an otherwise unknown tribe; *dat pl* **Hronum** 1.63.

Hrōðgār king of the Danes and sometime ruler of Heorot in *Beowulf* (*fl.* late 5th century; *see note* 1.45-48); *nom sg* 1.45.

Hrōþwulf king of the Danes (*fl.* early 6th century), Hrothgar's nephew in *Beowulf* (1017 *and* 1181; *see note* 1.45-48); *nom sg* 1.45.

Hūn king of the Hætwere; *nom sg* 1.33.

Hūnas the Huns; *dat pl* **Hūnum** 1.57; *and instr pl* 1.18.

Hundingas the Langobards; *dat pl* **Hundingum** 1.81; *and instr pl* 1.23.

Hungār (from ***Hundgār**) a king of the Langobards (Lamissio in Paulus Diaconus, *Historia Langobardorum*); *acc sg* 1.117.

Hwala in West-Saxon genealogies, the grandson of Sceaf; *nom sg* 1.14*.

I

Idumingas probably the Livonian tribe called Ydumaei by Henricus Lettus (Heinrich von Lettland (d. 1259) in the *Chronicon Livoniae*); *dat pl* **Idumingum** 1.87.

Ilwan the Helvecones of Tacitus (*Germania* 43); *dat pl* **Eolum** 1.87.

Incgenþeow see **Ongenþeow**.

Indēas the Hindus of India; *dat pl* **Indēum** 1.83.
Ingeld son of Froda and king of the Heathobards (*Beowulf* 2064; *see note* 1.45-48); *gen sg* **Ingeldes** 1.48.
Īras the Irish; *gen pl* **Īra** 5.56*.
Isrāhēlas the Israelites; *dat pl* **Isrāhēlum** 1.82.
Īste the Ostrogoths; *dat pl* **Īstum** 1.87.

L

Leofsunu a loyal retainer from Sturmer, Essex; *nom sg* 6.244.
Lēonas the Leuoni of Ptolemy (*Primer of Geography*); *dat pl* **Lēonum** 1.80.
Lidingas a Norwegian tribe ; *dat pl* **Lidingum** 1.80*.
Longbeardan the Langobards; *dat pl* **Longbeardum** 1.80; *and instr pl* 1.32.

M

Maccus an Old Irish name, with Ælfhere, he died defending the ford against the Viking host; *nom sg* 6.80.
Mæringas literally 'the borderers', here the Visigoths; *gen pl* **Mæringa** 2.19.
Mæðhild the wife of Geat (*see note*); *dat sg* **Mæðhilde** 2.14.
Meaca king of the Myrgings; *nom sg* 1.23.
Mearchealf an otherwise unknown king of the Hundings; *nom sg* 1.23.
Mimming in Germanic story, a famous sword said to have been forged by Weland; *acc sg* 3.3.
Moide the inhabitants of the Danish island Møn; *dat pl* **Moidum** 1.84.
Myrce the Mercians; *nom pl* 5.24; *dat pl* **Myrcon** 6.217.
Myrgingas Widsith's own tribe; *gen pl* **Myrginga** 1.96; *dat pl* **Myrgingum** 1.4, 1.42, 1.84; *and instr pl* 1.23.

N

Nīðhād Widia's grandfather and father of Beadohild; *nom sg* 2.5; *gen sg* **Nīðhādes** 3.40.
Norðhymbre the Northumbrians; *dat pl* **Norðhymbron** 6.266.
Norþmann the Norseman; *nom pl* **Norþmen** 5.53; *gen pl* **Norðmanna** 5.33.

O

Odda father of Godric, Godwig and Godwine; *gen sg* **Oddan** 6.186, 6.238.
Ōfdingas an Ostrogothic royal house; *dat pl* **Ōfdingum** 1.86.
Offa the king of Angeln, the Offa of *Beowulf* (1949 *and* 1957; *see note* 1.35-39); *nom sg* 1.35, 1.38, 1.44; *dat sg* **Offan** 1.37.
Offa a loyal retainer who died at Maldon; *nom sg* 6.198, 6.230, 6.286, 6.288; *gen sg* **Offan** 6.5.
Ongel Angeln, the pre-migration homeland of the Angles; *dat sg* **Ongle** 1.8; *and instr sg* 1.35.
Ongendmyrgingas a branch of the Myrgings; *dat pl* **Ongendmyrgingum** 1.85.

Ongendþēow (Incgen-) the king of the Swedes who figures in *Beowulf* (1968 *et passim*); *nom sg* 1.31; *and acc sg* 1.116.
Ordlāf a Danish warrior; *nom sg* 4.16.
Ōswine an otherwise unknown king of the Eows; *nom sg* 1.26.
Oswold brother of Eadwold, a loyal retainer of Byrhtnoth; *nom sg* 6.304.

P

Pante the river Blackwater in Essex; *acc sg* **Pantan** 6.68, 6.97.
Peohtas the Picts; *dat pl* **Peohtum** 1.79.
Perse the biblical Persians (or perhaps the Parisii, a British tribe); *dat pl* **Persum** 1.84.

R

Rǣdhere an otherwise unknown hero/king; *acc sg* 1.123.
Rondhere an otherwise unknown hero/king; *acc sg* 1.123.
Rondingas a tribe from Telemark, Norway; *instr pl* **Rondingum** 1.24.
Rugas (Holmrycgas of 1.21) the Rugii; *dat pl* **Rugum** 1.69.
Rūmstān a Burgundian hero; *acc sg* 1.123.
Rūmwalas the Greeks, sometimes used generically for the inhabitants of the Eastern Roman Empire; *dat pl* **Rumwālum** 1.69.

S

Sǣdene the (Sea-)Danes; *instr pl* **Sǣdenum** 1.28.
Sǣferð king of the Sycgan; *nom sg* 1.31.
Sceafa king of the Langobards; *nom sg* 1.32.
Sceafthere an otherwise unknown king of the Ymbran; *nom sg* 1.32.
Scilling either a scop who sang with Widsith or a name for his musical instrument (*see note*); *nom sg* 1.103.
Scottas the Scots, the Irish; *gen pl* **Sceotta** 5.11, 5.32*; *dat pl* **Scottum** 1.79.
Scridefinnas the Lapps; *dat pl* **Scridefinnum** 1.79.
Scyttisc (i) *adj* Scottish; *m nom sg* (*as sb*) 5.19*.
Seafola a (faithless?) retainer; *acc sg* **Seafolan** 1.115.
Seaxe the Saxons; *nom pl* 5.70*; *dat pl* **Seaxum** 1.62.
Secca the Frankish Sigiwald, a kinsman of King Theodric; *acc sg* **Seccan** 1.115.
Secgan (y) a Germanic tribe allied with the Danes; *gen pl* **Secgena** 4.24; *dat pl* **Sycgum** 1.62; *and instr pl* 1.31.
Sercingas probably the Siraci of Tacitus (*Annals* XII.15); *dat pl* **Sercingum** 1.75.
Sēringas the Seres, sometimes used generically to refer to eastern or central Asian tribes; *dat pl* **Sēringum** 1.75.
Sibryht brother of Ætheric, and a loyal retainer of Byrhtnoth's; *gen sg* **Sibryhtes** 6.282.
Sifeca perhaps Eormanric's evil counsellor; *acc sg* **Sifecan** 1.116.

Sigeferþ a Secgan warrior; *nom sg* 4.15, 4.24.

Sigehere king of the Sea-Danes; 1.28.

Sturmere Sturmer, Essex; *acc sg* 6.249.

Sūþdene the South-Danes; *dat pl* **Sūþdenum** 1.58.

Swǣfe the Suebi living north of the Eider River in Western Sleswick; *nom pl* 1.44; *dat pl* **Swǣfum** 1.61; *and instr pl* 1.22.

Swēon the Swedes of Uppland; *dat pl* **Swēom** 1.58; *and instr pl* 1.31.

Sweordwere the Suardones of Tacitus (*Germania* 40); *dat pl* **Sweordwerum** 1.62.

Þ/Ð

Þēodrīc king of the Franks (511-534), the Sigiwald of Gregory of Tours (*Historia Francorum* III.23-24), who later (erroneously) came to be known by this name; *nom sg* 1.24; *acc sg* 1.115.

Ðēodrīc Theodric of Verona (452-526), king of the Ostrogoths, murderer of Odoaker (493), and Arian heretic (*see note* 2.18); *nom sg* 2.18, 3.36.

Þrowend the Þrøndr of Trøndelagen, Norway; *dat pl* **Þrowendum** 1.64.

Þurstan father of Wistan; *gen sg* **Þurstanes** 6.298.

Þyle king of the Rondings; *nom sg* 1.24.

Þyringas the Thoringi of Gregory of Tours (*Historia Francorum* II.9); *dat pl* **Þyringum** 1.64; *and instr pl* 1.30.

U

Unwēn a Gothic prince, son of Eastgota; *gen sg* **Unwēnes** 1.114.

W

Wada king of the Hælsings; *nom sg* 1.22.

Wærne the Varini of Tacitus (*Germania* 40); *dat pl* **Wærnum** 1.59; *instr pl* **Wernum** 1.25.

Walas used generically for the inhabitants of the Roman Empire; *gen pl* **Wala** 1.78 (*see* **Rumwalas** *and* **Casere**).

Wald literally 'Ruler', an otherwise unknown king of the Woings; *nom sg* 1.30.

Waldere Walter or Waldere of Aquitaine; *nom sg* 3.43.

Wealh a Welshman or Briton, or generically for 'foreigners'; *acc pl* **Wēalas** 5.72.

Weland (-und) the smith of Germanic legend; *nom sg* 2.1; *gen sg* **Welandes** 3.2, 3.41.

Wenlas the Wendlas of *Beowulf* (348); *dat pl* **Wenlum** 1.59.

Westseaxe the West-Saxons; *nom pl* **Wesseaxe** 5.20*; *gen pl* **Wesseax- ena** 5.59.

Wicings the Heathobards; *gen pl* **Wicinga** 1.47; *dat pl* **Wicingum** 1.59.

Widia (**Wudga**) a Gothic champion (Vidigoia) mentioned in Jordanes (*Getica* 5 *and* 35; *see note* 1.129, 2.8-12 *and* 3.41); *nom sg* 1.130, 3.41; *acc sg* **Wudgan** 1.124; *dat sg* **Widian** 3.36.

Wīdsīð a poet, the central figure in *Text 1*; *nom sg* 1.1.
Wigelm a warrior related to Wistan; *gen sg* **Wigelmes** 6.300*.
Winedas the Wends, often used generically to describe the Slavs; *dat pl* **Winedum** 1.60.
Wistan *m* son of Thurstan; *nom sg* 6.297.
Wīstle the inhabitants of the area around the Vistula; *gen pl* **Wīstla** 1.121.
Witta king of the Swæfe, and perhaps grandfather of Hengest and Horsa (*see* Bede, *Ecclesiastical History* I.15); *nom sg* 1.22.
Wiþergield an Heathobardish warrior of *Beowulf* (2051); *acc sg* 1.124.
Wiþmyrgingas a tribe living near the With River in Sleswick; *gen pl* **Wiþmyringa** 1.118 (*see* **Myrgingas and Ongendmyrgingas**).
Wōd an otherwise unknown ruler of the Thyringas; *nom sg* 1.30.
Wōingas an otherwise unknown tribe; *instr pl* **Wōingum** 1.30.
Wrosnan a tribe of the Danish islands; *instr pl* **Wrosnum** 1.33.
Wudga see Widia.
Wulfhere a prince of the Hræde; *acc sg* 1.119.
Wulfings the Wylfingas of *Beowulf* (461 *and* 471); *instr pl* **Wulfingum** 1.29.
Wulfmær kinsman of Byrhtnoth; *nom sg* 6.113.
Wulfmær (se geonga) son of Wulfstan, companion of Ælfnoth, who died in battle; *nom sg* 6.155, (**Wulmær**) 6.183.

Wulfstān *m* son of Ceola, father of Wulfmær 'se geonga'; *nom sg* 6.75; *gen sg* **Wulfstānes** 6.155; *dat sg* **Wulfstāne** 6.79.
Wyrmhere the Ormarr of the *Hervararsaga*, the joint leader with Wulfhere of the Hræde in the war with the Huns; *acc sg* 1.119.

Y

Ymbran an unidentified tribe; *instr pl* **Ymbrum** 1.32.
Ȳte the Euts/Jutes (*see Bede, Ecclesiastical History* I.15); *instr pl* **Ȳtum** 1.26.